The Birth of
Modern America

The Birth of
Modern America

By
John McClymer
Assumption College

Brandywine Press • Maplecrest, NY

To Gerd Korman
Friend, Mentor

Contents

Preface

Shortly after I began work on this book, I had the opportunity to talk briefly with the late John Higham, a deservedly revered figure whose *Strangers in the Land: Patterns of American Nativism, 1860–1925* (1954) has influenced generations of scholars. I had a question. Why did millions of ordinary Americans join the new Ku Klux Klan in the 1920s? After all, their primary objectives either had already been achieved or, as in the case of the restriction of immigration from southern and eastern Europe, were about to be. The Klan stood for prohibition, for the supremacy of those of northern European ancestry, for racial segregation. It railed against the growing influence of Catholics and Jews. It championed old-fashioned moral values. Prohibition was the law of the land; so was immigration restriction shortly to be. A series of brutal race riots during and immediately after World War I, in which white mobs destroyed black neighborhoods, had emphasized yet again the second-class status of African Americans. The fate of Al Smith's presidential candidacy in 1928 showed the limits of Catholic acceptance. Why the crusade? It was a very good question, Higham responded. He was going to devote his next book to the Klan, he thought. For me he had a word of advice. "Don't look for a rational explanation."

I have, in putting together this synthesis of the interwar years, kept his advice in mind. People do, from time to time, pursue their best interests across its pages. More often they pursue pleasure, or salvation, or a guarantee of their own privileged position as the real Americans. Sometimes they pursue art, sometimes commerce, often both simultaneously. Most often they quarrel—over jazz music, over wearing one-piece bathing suits without stockings, over the teaching of evolution, over the "fundamentals" of Christian belief, over race, over ethnicity, and, of course, over politics.

A new, modern America came into existence in the 1920s and 1930s. Consumer demand drove a New Era of capitalism. A new consumer ethos, in which pleasure defined the good life, came into direct conflict with traditional religious but also business values. Intersecting with this new ethos was a new popular culture, one largely shaped by black and ethnic Americans. A new federal government, which provided entitlements to old age pensions and unemployment compensation among other benefits and regulated uncounted parts of daily life, emerged out of the economic and social crisis of the Great Depression. Anyone studying the interwar years needs to take Higham's advice to heart.

I have also sought to heed the injunction of another eminent historian of immigration, ethnicity and labor, Gerd Korman. "You need to be able to smell the places you write about." I have necessarily generalized broadly in this book. But I have also looked very closely at local cases whether company-sponsored minstrel shows in Worcester, Massachusetts or the Pentecostal revival at the Azusa Street Church in Los Angeles or the race riot in Tulsa, Oklahoma or bank failures in Chicago. Most of all I have attempted to suggest the ways in which the interwar generation bequeathed to us the America we now live in.

John McClymer
Assumption College

Introduction

By today's standards, Sadie Frowne was a well-behaved young woman. Yet in a magazine article early in the twentieth century, this Jewish immigrant from Poland living independently on her wages discussed her life in a way that makes clear to a reader today what would happen to nineteenth-century Victorianism. She enjoyed herself going to dances or an amusement park, though she confessed that some friends scolded her for spending too much on clothes. The Sadies of the early twentieth century were the customers who kept the dance halls going. In so doing, they did more than the Greenwich Village artists and intellectuals to break through the social conventions of Americans not much older than Sadie's friends.

That fundamentalist Protestants lamented the sins of entertainment is to be expected. Less so is that even in the 1920s the more earnest of the "new women," liberated reformist intellectuals, would lament as well, recoiling from the apparently primitive rhythms of jazz along with the freer contact between male and female youth who mingled at the dance halls. But neither preachers nor progressive intellectuals could stop more well-to-do youth, male and female, from going there out of curiosity, learning the new steps, and in turn introducing their friends to some of the styles and tastes of the working class. Thereby Sadie's cohorts nurtured the flappers, the more affluent and more widely remembered young women of the years following World War I.

The "working girls" as Sadie's contemporaries referred to them were the vanguard of American social and cultural change between the world wars that is the subject of this book. Presented here are some of the people and institutions less credited for that change, or less identified with it. Working girls like Sadie are among them. So are the factories that hired the children hawking both its commodities and a creed of pleasure that made buying things a commandment. The New Era capitalism, so it was called, of the 1920s shaped many of the cultural transformations of the times, including much that would appear to go counter to it. In saving New Era capitalism, the New Deal of the 1930s gave it further shape and definition. So while much of this book is about public culture in the interwar period and mated and reflected the comprehensive chapter on the politics of the New Deal rounds out the story.

Eugenics and the Ku Klux Klan make a strange pair, but they were one mated and reflective of the cultural diversity of the period. On the surface they could not be farther apart. The educated eugenicists who wished to purify the country of what they thought to be its racially inferior stock, by which they meant pretty much anyone who did not come of Nordic, northern European ancestry, thought that they were doing good science. They were doing very bad science, but behind a facade of Darwinism and genetic studies that made them look sophisticated. In this they were buying, and marketing, the facile belief in science that attended a seemingly flawless capitalist, industrialized economy. How could anyone doubt that a system so productive of washing machines and vacuum cleaners drew on a similarly flawless science? Klansmen, to the contrary, no more naïve in their convictions than were eugenicists who embraced the day's scientific fashions, hated the direction of modern science, which threatened their fundamentalist version of Christianity. They should also have hated New Era capitalism for undermining the moral rules of the nation's religious past. But a selective use of Christianity endorsed capitalism, or at the very least condemned immigrant radicals; and the members of the Klan rejoiced at anything in science that justified their claims for the superiority of Nordic peoples.

Eugenics and the Klan were part of a reaction among Americans who thought they must go to the defense of their country and its older ethnic stocks. Stretching far back in American history, the attempt to define what you have to be in order to justify full American citizenship took in the twenties its fullest form. The war had accelerated two reforms of the period, woman suffrage and prohibition, and by the mid-twenties the nation also had an immigration policy that discriminated against peoples of other than northern European stock. Superpatriots thought of this as confirming an essential Americanness. Good Americans did not drink and they did not come from southern Europe, and a virtuous American womanhood would help keep the country's politics safe from saloons and foreigners. Another force driving the Americanization movement was the labor unrest that followed the war. That is among the contradictions of the period. While American industrialism drew waves of immigration and American capitalism turned to preaching an ethos of pleasure, patriots rushed to protect capitalism against immigrant radicals believed to be behind the postwar wave of strikes.

Among the newer ethnicities the Americanizing drives were met by strategies that by analogy call up an American tradition, the effort of some light-skinned African Americans to pass for white. Among the Swedes in the Massachusetts industrial town of Worcester, as an illustration, the attempt of newcomers to establish their American credentials took on tactics that included trashing Irish Catholics and playing to stereotypes of African Americans common among natives of older European ancestry. That they were both northern European and Protestant made their passage relatively easy. But what more distinctively recent ethnic communities throughout the country achieved was not assimilation into traditional American culture but a sufficient modifying of it to accommodate them. Especially in the highly commercialized field of entertainment, new immigrant groups along with black Americans during the twenties and after went further to remake American culture. They did not need to enter it; to a large extent it was now theirs. Still, race made for a barrier harder to break through than ethnicity. Hollywood, in good part a creation of new immigrant Americans, found elaborate ways of marginalizing black and Chinese characters, notably in having white actors take the role.

The New Era capitalism of the postwar decade meanwhile managed to sell the public not only the particular goods of the market but the virtue of pleasure itself. In so doing, advertisers had to overlook an important component of capitalist ideology, the belief that business and technology are successful because they embody thrift, hard work, and the deferring of gratification. Instead, the commercials of the age managed to associate capitalism with leisure and consumption. In inviting Americans to be consumers, capitalism and advertising had invaluable assistance from the timeless force of sex. The musical revues of the twenties, along with abbreviated beachwear and the resultant beauty contests, announced a loosening of Victorian constraints and a release of the urge to buy.

As industrialism together with black and immigrant-stock entertainers and artists were remaking the culture, fundamentalists fought to defend themselves from the forces of modernity. In embracing the concept of an imminent Second Coming of Christ and the Rapture, in which the faithful will be taken into Heaven, American fundamentalism worked out a solution to the question: If we are the true Americans, why are we on the defensive? The fundamentalist answer closed the contradictions. As Protestant, evangelical Christians we are the chosen, and ultimately we will win. Meanwhile, let the forces of modernity enjoy their brief ascendance. They will find out how brief it is. One fundamentalist became extraordinarily skilled at drawing on commercialism itself, which the religious far right had a peculiarly dense inability to see as the enemy to traditional mores. Aimee Semple McPherson began as an earthy fundamentalist preacher. After the war, though, she was both preacher and entertainer. In her radio station KFSG, Kall Four Square Gospel, and in her Temple conveniently close to Hollywood, from which she drew on technicians and actors, Aimee sold Christianity and, with a whiff of sexuality, herself. In the course of her ministry Sister popularized Pentecostalism, speaking in tongues. By a misreading of the Acts of the Apostles, this species of fundamentalist Christianity has remained a startling presence in evangelical Protestantism, even invading the Roman Catholic Church. What could be farther from capitalism and advertisement?

Commercialism is supposed to degrade everything it touches. In the interwar years, however, commerce while cheapening much that fell under its domain nurtured a robust art that may be labeled "modern" in contrast to the self-consciously aloof and elitist style known as Modernism. In the comics, in radio shows, in Hollywood with the aid of producers, artists especially of immigrant background produced a rich and imaginative variety of forms. And they did it to make money. If New Era advertisers had wanted to make a better case for the health of the period than they did, they could have pointed to the popular arts. But that would not have made money. Aside from some remarkable work that included brilliantly illustrated advertisements for industrial and entrepreneurial rather than consumer goods, ads kept to selling soap and other commodities they trivialized.

The Great Depression threatened to bring it all to an end, in the process revealing the weaknesses in the foundations of New Era capitalism. That it did not do so is owing to the New Deal. The Roosevelt administration did not end the Depression. The Second World War did that. Instead, the New Deal made things a bit easier for the poor and the unemployed of the Depression years. It also built into law a number of entitlements, most importantly Social Security, that soften the effects of capitalism, a set of regulations that in restraining Wall Street make it a safer place for investment, and federal backing for banks and savings funds. So capitalism and what right-wingers call socialism coexist in a form that is provisionally satisfactory for the American public. For our benefit or not, we inherit a modified capitalism, a fundamentalist Christianity, and above all a consumer mentality that mocks both Christian morality and the virtues once ascribed to business and industry.

Thomas R. West
The Catholic University of America

The Birth of
Modern America

I

Eugenics and the Ku Klux Klan

Eugenics

This photograph is of the infant selected as the most perfect baby in the Panama Canal Zone by the Eugenics Society of America. Beautiful Baby and Fitter Family contests commanded great interest during the interwar years. At state fairs, for example, the Eugenics Society would set up exhibits at which visitors could answer questionnaires supposedly revealing their family's fitness. Some questions dealt with facts about their ancestors. What was the age at death? Others concerned the health of family members. Did they have any "physical, mental or temperamental defects"? But the emphasis was upon cultural measures, such as education, occupation, and "special talents, gifts, tastes, or superior qualities." In addition to getting a photo in the local newspaper, the winning family won the assurance that its place was among nature's elite. Any family scoring high enough received a medal proclaiming, "Yea, I have a goodly heritage."

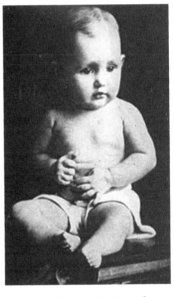

The Eugenics Society exhibits typically used flashing lights to make the movement's central points. Note the proclamation in the display below, "Some People Are Born To Be A Burden On The Rest." A light flashed to mark the $100 in tax money spent every fifteen seconds on the insane, the feeble-minded, criminals, and "other defectives" with bad heredity. Another bulb flashed every sixteen seconds to mark how often a baby was born in the United States. Few of these would be perfect. Every forty-eight seconds another called attention to frequency of births of children who would grow up with the mental age of eight or lower. Every fifty seconds yet another light went on to show the frequency with which Americans went to jail. "Very few *normal* people ever go to jail," the society insisted. At the far right every

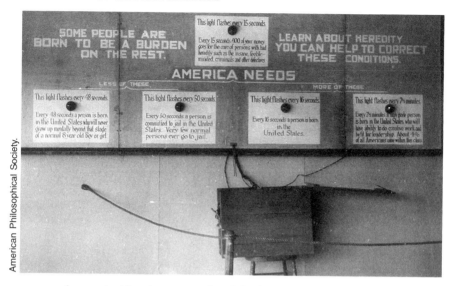

seven and one half minutes a final bulb came on. This marked the birth of a "high grade person who will have the ability to do creative work and be fit for leadership." Only four percent of the American population, the Eugenics Society calculated, fell into this category. Crime, insanity, mental defects, alcoholism, indigence, all resulted from bad heredity. Intelligence, industriousness, moral honesty were outcomes of a "goodly heritage."

A crisis confronted America, eugenics advocates believed. Too many people with bad genes were having too many babies while those with good genes gave birth to too few. In 1916 Madison Grant, one of the most effective leaders of the movement, described the result as *The Passing of the Great Race*; Lothrop Stoddard, for whose bestseller Grant wrote an introduction, noted in 1920 *The Rising Tide of Color Against White Supremacy*. Both books are available online courtesy of white supremacy organizations that still extol Grant and Stoddard as intellectual pioneers. Eugenics activists, as both book titles demonstrate, asserted a paradoxical message. Members of the "great race," people of northern and western European backgrounds (with the noteworthy exception of Irish Catholics), faced the proliferation of peoples, in the words of the University of Wisconsin sociologist E. A. Ross, "whom evolution has left behind."

But how could the least fit possibly endanger the most fit? Wasn't the story of evolution "the survival of the fittest"? No, according to eugenicists. They made two sorts of arguments, both beginning with human interference in the workings of natural selection.

Advanced societies, went one part of the argument, no longer allowed the less fit to die. Instead, charitable organizations and the state intervened to protect people with various disabilities, making it possible for the less fit to reproduce. But this did not explain why the members of the "great race" themselves failed to reproduce. Once again, the answer eugenics gave had to do with human intervention in the natural process of selection. In comparatively primitive societies, including the American colonies, children had been economic assets. The emergence of modern industrial nations turned children into drains on a family's finances. Members of these advanced societies had fewer children. Immigrants, coming from less developed areas, continued to have large families. So did people in Asia, Africa, and Latin America. Hence the "rising tide."

Eugenicists did not call for abandoning the charitable protection of the weak, however much they decried the consequences. They did condemn the low birth rates within what they called the superior races, to which, it seems, leading eugenicists themselves belonged. Recognizing the inevitability of human alterations in the workings of nature, they called for a better management of the process. No longer should we allow nature to select human traits; having already intruded upon the process, we should continue to do so but in a scientific manner. Here is how the Eugenics Record Office at the Cold Spring Harbor Biological Laboratory on Long Island in New York State phrased it in 1927:

[I]f a race is to make progress along the lines of natural abilities, those in control must see to it that there shall be fit matings and many children among those most richly endowed by nature, and that hereditary defectives and degenerates not be permitted to re-

EUGENICS IS THE SELF DIRECTION OF HUMAN EVOLUTION

ANATOMY PHYSIOLOGY BIOLOGY GENETICS PSYCHOLOGY MENTAL TESTING ANTHROPOMETRY HISTORY GEOLOGY ARCHEOLOGY ETHNOLOGY ANTHROPOLOGY GEOGRAPHY STATISTICS LAW POLITICS GENEALOGY BIOGRAPHY ECONOMICS MEDICINE SURGERY PSYCHIATRY SOCIOLOGY EDUCATION RELIGION

LIKE A TREE EUGENICS DRAWS ITS MATERIALS FROM MANY SOURCES AND ORGANIZES THEM INTO AN HARMONIOUS ENTITY.

American Philosophical Society.

produce at all. . . . The State can be expected to take means to bring about these ends only when due pressure is brought to bear by aroused citizens. Thus law, science, individual enlightenment, and personal resolve, each has its part to play in working out the eugenical ideal, that is, in improving the inborn character and talents of succeeding generations.

By the 1920s eugenics was a well-established branch of biology. High school and college textbooks, for example, ordinarily devoted a chapter to it, including that used by John T. Scopes to teach evolution in Dayton, Tennessee. That book's treatment begins with the observation that experience has shown how plants and animals could be improved by proper breeding techniques. Surely, its authors continue, it is reasonable to assume the same would hold for human beings.

Who was "most richly endowed by nature"? Scientists at the Cold Spring Harbor Laboratory, supported by Carnegie and Harriman funding, sought to find out. Or more precisely, they looked for evidence to support what other eugenists had already concluded. An example lies in the 1925 Eastern States Exposition "Fitter Family" contest. Poor eyesight ran in the winning family. So did nervousness. Neither prevented its members from being adjudged fit. Designers of the questionnaires had already determined the meanings of fitness in a way that mirrored almost perfectly an old-stock model of respectability. A clergyman who also lectured on literary subjects headed the winning family. Several of the children had completed college; all had at least graduated from high school. The males held good jobs, as did several of the females. The mother kept house. The family's interests and hobbies ran to mathematics, literature, and music in addition to golf. No member had ever committed a crime, become indigent, or had a child out of wedlock (at least so far as revealed by their answers on the form).

Who were the "hereditary defectives and degenerates?" Again, the state fair exhibits make the answer clear. Criminals, the mentally ill, the developmentally disadvantaged, and the indigent: All had been "born to be a burden." These defectives and degenerates supposedly appeared with disproportionate frequency among certain racial and ethnic groups. An expert noted: "One result recurs persistently wherever American children are tested by nationality of ancestors. American children of Italian parentage show a low average of intelligence. The selection of Italians received into this country has yielded very few gifted children."

Intelligence Tests

In the judgment of many eugenicists, intelligence tests administered to military recruits showed incontrovertibly that on average, Italians and other immigrants possessed low intelligence. That was the opinion of Lewis Terman of Stanford, who helped create the original Stanford Binet IQ tests. Seventy percent of the foreign-born draft sample scored 90 or lower on these IQ tests, compared to forty-six percent among the native-born white draft sample. A score of 100 was normal. Terman claimed that the test measured intelligence and was not biased by the inclusion of cultural clues. Subsequent researchers have found, quite to the contrary, that the tests tilted sharply toward questions that reflected the training, schooling, and cultural surroundings of white, middle-class Americans. Although not quite so crude as to observe that native-born Americans spoke better English than Italian immigrants, the findings tended toward just that kind of revelation.

Who were "those in control" who "must see to it that there shall be fit matings and many children among those most richly endowed by nature, and that hereditary defectives and degenerates not be permitted to reproduce at all"? Eugenicists contemplated—and to a large extent achieved—a government far more powerful and intrusive than that created by the Founding Fathers. Consider just a brief list of the movement's successes in the 1920s: State after state adopted variants of Virginia's Purity law, which outlawed interracial marriage, as well as a model sterilization law drafted by Harry Laughlin of the Eugenics Records office that provided for the involuntary sterilization of criminals, defectives, and degenerates. The Immigration Restriction Act of 1924, which established immigration quotas that would hold until 1965, closely followed the recommendations of Laughlin's testimony. The Virginia Purity law provided a model used by Nazi lawmakers. Hundreds of thousands were sterilized in the United States against their will. Like eugenics itself, restrictive laws drew on prejudices ingrained in American culture. Laughlin's role served to provide a scientific covering for an openly discriminatory policy.

The eugenics movement was not simply ignorance and prejudice prettied up with statistics. Its members worked with what they understood to be scientific method. But their failure to distinguish between genetic and environmental influences on I.Q. and similar tests, and their bias in reflecting popular beliefs that had nothing to do with scientific inquiry, have subsequently discredited most of their work.

Cleanliness

During the interwar years eugenicist opinions fitted well with habits of mind not only of more primitive racists but also of the American educated middle classes. A case in point is the preoccupation with germs and infections, quickened by medical discoveries that appeared to find germs lurking everywhere. Science, according to the eugenicists, could cleanse the genetic stock; science, so declared advertisements for soap, could rid homes and neighborhoods of the potentially

Crowds Breed Contagion

HUMAN beings were meant to live in the open, guarded by the prophylactics of sunshine and pure air.

There is always danger of contagion in crowds—in factories, elevators, street cars, theatres.

Doctors and great health institutes have proved that most disease germs pass from one person to another by actual contact. Things which many people touch are always dangerous—car straps, public telephones, door knobs, books, soiled money, stair rails. Germs are carried by hands to mouth, nose or food.

In every crowd there are almost certainly several "carriers" of disease germs.

A "carrier" is a person who is perfectly well but who formerly had a mild, undiscovered case of diphtheria, influenza, measles, or some other illness. The person soon recovered and became immune to the disease but the germs multiplied by millions, harmless to the "carrier" but of deadly menace to everyone else. "Carriers" move about in every class of society. There are thousands of them.

There is only one protection from this danger—perfect, scientific cleanliness.

If you will purify hands and face frequently with a true health soap, especially after contacts with crowds, there is less likelihood of the germs entering your body through

mouth or nose or passing on to your wife and children.

Lifebuoy Protects

Lifebuoy is a true health soap. Its creamy, copious lather releases a wonderful antiseptic ingredient which goes deep down into every pore, purifying—removing body odors—combating the menace of dirty things.

Soap cannot be made that is more pure, more bland, more beautifying than Lifebuoy. Its rich, nourishing oils of palm fruit and coconut keep the skin soft, free from blemishes—and purified.

You know Lifebuoy is a health soap by its wholesome, pungent odor. The odor vanishes quickly—but the protection remains.

Mothers—you who are "health doctors" to your families—guard those you love by placing a cake of Lifebuoy at every place where there is running water. Lever Bros. Co., Cambridge, Mass.

MORE THAN SOAP—A HEALTH HABIT

deadly microorganisms that in the folklore of the day were thought to grow on any single square inch of unscrubbed surface.

One of a series of advertisements the J. Walter Thompson advertising agency created for Lifebuoy soap in the 1920s appears on the left. Crowds mean danger, the copy proclaims, because "almost certainly" carriers of various dread diseases can be found in every one. "How many 'Typhoid Marys' are there in this crowd?" the copy asks. Such carriers, it explains, can be perfectly healthy people who carry millions of disease germs to which they themselves remain immune. "Typhoid Mary," the Irish cook Mary Mallon, had infected several families who employed her. She was quarantined for three years but released in 1910 on her promise not to take cooking jobs. Mallon broke her word and found a job at a maternity hospital. There she infected another twenty-five people, two of whom died. Assuming various names, but always working as a cook, Mallon avoided arrest until 1919. At the time of the Lifebuoy ad, she had once again been quarantined, where she remained until her death in 1938. The most dangerous carrier, the same ad suggests by placing him in the foreground, is the one working-class figure. Everyone else is visibly clean, but his hat is soiled and he is not clean-shaven.

In the early 1920s, disease held special terrors for people. The great influenza pandemic of 1918 and 1919 had claimed over twenty-one million lives worldwide, more than twice as many as died in the Great War. Over 450,000 lost their lives in the United States, as against 115,000 in combat. Yet one health lesson the influenza outbreak taught was that washing with soap provided no protection against a number of communicable diseases, a lesson the Thompson agency either never learned or deliberately ignored. Instead it played upon common fears and then promised an illusory protection. "Typhoid Mary" had infected so many because she did not wash properly. The people she

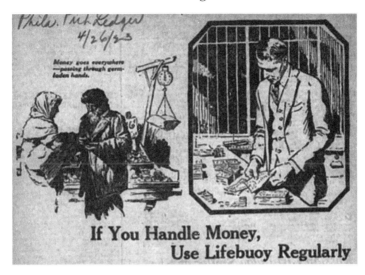

infected could not have protected themselves by washing. The germs lived in their food.

In another ad, the danger of infection arises from tainted money. "A soiled dollar bill under a microscope is an ugly sight." Bank cashiers face special risks, but so does everyone else who handles money. The "germ-laden hands" that contaminated the dollar bill in the ad belong to a peddler, possibly intended to be Jewish, and his immigrant customer. Her shawl, his beard, and the outdoor setting convey their status. Jews stereotypically pushed carts through crowded neighborhoods.

Once again, this ad describes an imaginary public health risk. Paper provides no breeding ground for germs. And once again, the protection Lifebuoy promises is equally fictitious. No soap could keep hands antiseptically pure. Nonetheless the ad warns handlers of money always to wash with Lifebuoy before touching their wives or children.

This is one of several advertisements to single out peddlers as carriers of disease. In doing so, the Thompson agency was borrowing from popular medical ideas heavily influenced by eugenics. Particular peoples, some medical experts contended, were especially prone to carry a particular disease. Jews, they claimed, showed a greater likelihood than gentiles to transmit typhus. As a result, Polish Jews coming to the United States in the immediate postwar period faced almost certain quarantine, while Polish Catholics from the same regions did not.

In "There is no Substitute for Health," the ad campaign again turned to the specter of the carrier of disease. "Doctors have proved that practically all contagions," the wording misleadingly argues, are spread by healthy yet menacing people as are shown in the illustration. Who last touched the trolley car strap grasped by the clean-cut young family man in the straw hat, the copy asks. Later, playing ball with his children, the ad threatens, he may in turn infect them. Or they may infect him. "Children will play with stray animals" that presumably also may carry disease. So it falls to Mother in her role of Health Doctor to protect her family by making sure that they all wash with Lifebuoy. In an ad announcing that "Mothers know it safeguards health and beauty," no visible human source of contagion, no dirty workingman, no immigrants are depicted. Instead a healthy Lifebuoy family beams. Mother as the Health Doctor puts the copy in the first person. Doubtless Lifebuoy aimed to encourage the mothers reading the ad to identify the "I" with themselves even as they align with the hundreds of mothers who express complete faith in the soap.

Inventing an expert such as the Health Doctor became a common ploy among advertisers. Unlike some advertisements, this one did not give the Health Doctor a specific name, but it did give her a face and made her a mother. In the one ad illustrating the Lifebuoy family, the Health Doctor says, "I simply cannot find the words to express the emotions aroused by this lovely picture," adding "I wish it could hang in every American home."

One striking thing about the advertisement below is the size of the family. Here there are four, all under ten years of age. Why so many? This is not an exception. "Lifebuoy families" ads featured lots of small children. Other ads did not. The norm was two, one girl and one boy. The answer lies with the influence of the eugenics movement. Its message was that individuals with the richest genetic inheritance should mate and reproduce while whoever is "born to be a burden to others" ought to be discouraged or prevented from having children. In practice this meant encouraging whites of northern and western European background to have more children and working to reduce to virtually zero the immigration of southern and eastern Europeans, along with Africans, Asians, and Pa-

cific Islanders. The Lifebuoy campaign echoed the eugenics message. It too promoted the healthy, happy family as the finest thing in the world. It too associated that family with northern and western European ancestry. The only times a Lifebuoy ad featured someone lacking Nordic features were to personify the danger of contagion. Even the best of mothers, one ad warned, "can't wash other people's children."

One ad entitled "If They Could Always Be Safe From Dirt" shows a wealthy couple looking in on their sleeping children before stepping out for the evening. Tomorrow, the copy warns, the toddlers will come in contact with a hundred dangerously dirty things, including unclean playmates and the germ-laden fruit of peddlers. This shows an insidious conjoining of familiar stereotypes, the peddler with his cart and the association of dirt with immigrants from southern and eastern Europe. The eugenics advocate Edward A. Ross, author of the best-selling *The Old World in the New* (1912), quoted an unnamed physician in his chapter on "Racial Consequences of Immigration": "The Slavs are immune to certain kinds of dirt. They can stand what would kill a white man."

"What a splendid generation is in the making," exults "Why America wins Olympics," an ad by the J. Walter Thompson agency. "Every schoolyard [is] a training camp," while summer camps and beaches "pour vitality into splendid little bodies." Even more important is that in millions of homes "intelligent mothers are enforcing the first law of health—cleanliness." Winning was a birthright for people belonging to the right sort of homes: "Of Course Your Boy Will Get The Job," one ad affirms. "No businessman could resist those clear eyes, that alert sturdy body. He sees in your boy the qualities of success. . . ." Yet this boy still needs to be protected from the very real dangers that surround him. His mother, the Health Doctor, must continue her active service in "the worldwide fight against dirt as the direct cause of almost all communicable diseases." Mothers "in every civilized country" are turning to Lifebuoy in this never-ending crusade against "dirt germs." "I do not like to deny my children the joy of playing in the dirt," one "intelligent mother" of a Lifebuoy family affirms in an ad insisting that "Mothers Know It Protects." "But when the dirt is in a city park, it might prove dangerous." Why should a city park be more likely to pose a health risk? Presumably for the same reason that public telephones, currency, and trolley car straps threaten. "Other people's children" play in the park, children the Health Doctor cannot wash, children who do not look like the children in the Lifebuoy ads and the Fitter Family photographs. These children do not have golden hair and fair skin. They grow up in crowded tenements, not in the nice homes the Lifebuoy families occupy. Few go to summer camp. Yet they share public spaces. They and their parents hang on those trolley straps, breathe into the public telephones, handle dollar bills.

"Other people's children" represent those young immigrants the eugenics movement helped restrict, whose role in American public life
the postwar Ku Klux Klan sought to reduce or eliminate.

None of this means that the Thompson agency wanted to promote
eugenics or immigration restriction or the Ku Klux Klan. It wanted
to sell soap. In the Lifebuoy campaign, the agency created an imaginary public health menace by preying upon very real fears of contagious disease. No matter that it misrepresented how such diseases
spread and offered an illusory protection against this mythical threat.
In selling soap in this way, the agency needed a bogeyman with which
to frighten. It also needed to associate the menace with dirt. The carrier was dangerous; but if the argument stopped there, anyone could
be threatening; even the Health Doctor might be harmful, for anyone
could be a carrier. So the ad agency needed to link the carrier with
dirt. For this commercial purpose the eugenics movement offered
everything the advertiser needed. The Health Doctor could be a carrier, and the clean young man in one of the ads could infect his children after handling the trolley strap; but the dirty carriers were most
dangerous, and eugenics made clear who they were.

The Ku Klux Klan

We are pleased that modern research is finding scientific backing for these convictions [about the importance of "racial instincts"]. We do not need them ourselves; we know we are right in
the same sense that a good Christian knows that he has been saved
and that Christ lives—a thing which the intellectual can never understand. These convictions are no more to be argued about than
is our love for our children; we are merely willing to state them
for the enlightenment and conversion of others. (Hiram Wesley
Evans, "The Klan's Fight for Americanism," *The North American Review*, March-April-May 1926)

This declaration from Hiram Wesley Evans, Imperial Wizard of the
second Ku Klux Klan, measures both the distance and the intersec-
tion between the KKK and the eugenics movement. Modern secular
science did not fit the mode of the Klan. The world against which the
order had set itself was that of secularism, cosmopolitan intellectuals, the city and the questioning mentality of science. Yet Evans, while
making it clear that his fellow Knights drew their convictions from
deeper springs, allowed that science might have something to say.
"One Klan leader and minister," a historian of the movement writes,
"maintained that 'the methods employed in stock-raising' should be
applied to human reproduction. He envisioned 'elimination of the
unfit' people and races from sexual activity and 'development of the
fit to the highest degree through the process of scientific study.'" Such

statements define the larger culture within which elitist eugenics and backwater racism could meet in uncomprehending alliance. For that culture promoted within much of the population a trust in science as simple as a fundamentalist's trust in a revival preacher, and a misunderstanding of science as large as the fundamentalist's ignorance of the rigors of theology.

The Klan, even while preaching that it was at war with its surroundings, believed that it represented what the nation, at bedrock, really was. So Evans wrote:

Though men and women drop from the ranks they remain with us in purpose, and can be depended on fully in any crisis. Also, there are millions who have never joined, but who think and feel and—when called on—fight with us. This is our real strength, and no one who ignores it can hope to understand America today.

The KKK was a secret organization, and few localities have accurate membership records. Even so, it is clear that the membership was very large. Most historians of the Klan estimate that at least four million men belonged at the height of its popularity in about 1924. Hundreds of thousands joined the female counterpart, the Kamelia. Evans was only slightly off in boasting that no one who hoped to understand America in the 1920s could succeed without first encountering the views—and the feelings—of Klan members and sympathizers. It is not simply a matter of numbers. Whatever appeal the KKK had for people who simply liked to join fraternal organizations, the Klan made it clear that it had purposes beyond good fellowship. Klansmen considered themselves at war with anyone they identified as seeking to take their country away from them.

The modern Klan took much of its initial inspiration from *The Birth of a Nation*, the director D. W. Griffith's artistically brilliant but blatantly white-supremacist film of 1915. It was based on a novel glorifying the KKK of the post-Civil War era. The Klan of that earlier time—many groups, actually, that were labeled collectively by the name of the most prominent of them—had been composed of thugs who dressed in outlandishly ghostlike costumes and bullied freed slaves and white southerners who supported Republican rule. But some southerners chose to remember the Klan as a brave guerrilla band defending southern rights.

The movie was an enormous success, deservedly for its technical innovations, despicably for its racism. President Woodrow Wilson, a Virginian white supremacist, praised it. In its wake came several lynchings in the South. Its more lasting effect, besides its influence on the development of film, lay in inspiring the formation of the twentieth-century Knights of the Invisible Empire, one of several names by which the second Ku Klux Klan has been called. It began in a gathering late in 1915 on Stone Mountain in Georgia. Joining in 1920, Hiram Evans became Imperial Wizard, the head of an organization that gloried in secrecy, ritual, and bizarre titles of rank.

The nineteenth-century Klan had been in revolt against the re-making of the South by the victorious Union. The small Klan that survives in the twenty-first century is an extremist group, appealing to an embittered fringe of society. But the Klan of the 1920s was a more mainstream organization than has previously been supposed. A cross-section of white Protestant America, it differed somewhat only in containing a larger proportion of skilled workers to unskilled, a greater proportionate membership among low-income, white-collar job holders, and a greater ratio of ministers. Most Klansmen were reputable members of their communities. The Klan's causes—anti-Catholicism, immigration restriction, prohibition—were widely accepted, as was segregation. The reasons for the popularity and influence of the KKK in the twenties are critical for understanding the culture wars of the era. Why did millions think that they needed more than the two-party system could provide? Why did millions join an organization that championed policies either already triumphant or advocated by the Republicans and a wing of the Democratic Party? Imperial Wizard Evans provides some clues in his *North American Review* essay.

Klan leaders disdained ideas and had little interest in debating opponents. *The North American Review*'s readership, moreover, was likely to be skeptical of anything Evans might write. It was one of the oldest journals of opinion in the country. Its readers were highly educated and concerned with ideas. For contributions to the subsequent issue, the editors of the *Review* had invited several noted critics of the KKK, among them W. E. B. Du Bois, a leading African American intellectual. The Imperial Wizard apparently anticipated what these critics might say. For example, he admitted that in its early days Klan leaders "began to 'sell hate at $10 a package'"—the cost to join. Hate and the "invisible government ideas," a reference to the Klan's vigilante activities, "were what gave the Klan its first great growth, enlisted some 100,000 members, provided wealth for a few leaders, and brought down upon it a reputation from which it has not yet recovered." Evans would have hardly made such an admission in an official Klan publication. None of this inspires confidence in the essay as a guide to what the KKK was actually about.

But then Evans turned to addressing a number of issues with stunning candor. "The Klan's Fight for Americanism" makes no apologies for the organization's efforts to impose on national policy its views of civil libertarians, immigrants, Catholics, Jews, and peoples of color. Instead it makes a strong claim for the Klan's "progressive conservatism," which remains undefined, and celebrates its influence in American public life.

The essay shows Evans at his most careful in presenting the Klan to the public. He made it clear that the movement began not in a process of reasoning—perhaps no movement does—but in a set of feelings, some tentative, others passionate.

There appeared first confusion in thought and opinion, a groping and hesitancy about national affairs and private life alike, in sharp contrast to the clear, straightforward purposes of our earlier years. There was futility in religion, too, which was in many ways even more distressing. Presently we began to find that we were dealing with strange ideas; policies that always sounded well, but somehow always made us still more uncomfortable.

Finally came the moral breakdown that has been going on for two decades. One by one all our traditional moral standards went by the boards, or were so disregarded that they ceased to be binding. The sacredness of our Sabbath, of our homes, of chastity, and finally even of our right to teach our own children in our own schools fundamental facts and truths were torn away from us. Those who maintained the old standards did so only in the face of constant ridicule.

So Imperial Wizard Evans claimed "to speak for the great mass of Americans of old pioneer stock." Their ancestors, "hardy, adventurous and strong men and women," had won a continent and created the American nation. Their "remarkable race character," passed on to their descendants, "made the inheritance of the old-stock Americans the richest ever given to a generation of men." In spite of this, "these Nordic Americans for the last generation have found themselves increasingly uncomfortable, and finally deeply distressed."

To the spiritual disintegration Evans added crises in economics and politics. "We found our great cities and the control of much of our industry and commerce taken over by strangers, who stacked the cards of success and prosperity against us." "We" could no longer guarantee our children's futures. Hence the declining birth rate of Nordic Americans. Coupled with this claim came the belief that an alien "they" controlled American politics. Under the bloc system of voting, every "kind of inhabitant except the Americans gathered in groups that operated as units in politics, under the orders of corrupt, self-seeking and un-American leaders, who both by purchase and threat enforced their demands on politicians."

As a consequence of these usurpations, "the Nordic American today is a stranger in large parts of the land his father gave him." As a simple statement of fact, this was wildly incorrect. But it was true, as

Klan recruiters kept reminding potential members, that Irish Catholics and others who did not fit the KKK's concept of real Americans controlled city government in Boston, New York, and other major urban centers. Irish Catholic women dominated the ranks of schoolteachers, their brothers the ranks of the police. All this Klan spokesmen might point to in explaining why Catholics had enjoyed such success keeping Bible reading out of the schools or why bootleggers openly flouted the Volstead Act.

Who were "they"? Who had stolen the patrimony of the Nordic Americans?

Most worrisome among them were Catholics. The "Roman Church" is "fundamentally and irredeemably, in its leadership, in politics, in thought, and largely in membership, actually and actively alien, un-American and usually anti-American. Old stock Americans . . . see in the Roman Church today . . . the most dangerous alien power with a foothold inside our boundaries," Evans wrote. This, like the Klan's appropriation of eugenics, sounded a theme broadly heard in American public life.

Among the "them" who were not Catholic were the Jews. Evans avoided some anti-Semitic stereotypes. Warning of "The Menace of Modern Immigration," he conceded at the Texas State Fair on Klan Day of 1923 that Jews were a talented people who obeyed "eugenic" laws. They could not become real Americans, however, for centuries of persecution had engrained in them a congenital inability to feel patriotism. No Jew, no matter whether his ancestry in the United States had stretched back a thousand years, could experience the sentiments of love for his country of birth an immigrant from Britain might feel within a year. By 1926, in his *North American Review* essay, Evans conceded that some Jews might indeed become true Americans: "The Jew's abilities are great, he contributes much to any country where he lives. This is particularly true of the Western Jew, those of the stocks we have known so long. Their separation from us is more religious than racial. When freed from persecution these Jews have shown a tendency to disintegrate and amalgamate."

"They" were, in sum, anyone whose background and views did not accord with the "racial instincts" of the Nordic American. Truth, Evans was convinced, lay in the intuitions within the Nordic psyche. What Nordic Americans felt, however inarticulately, was confirmed in their feeling it. There was a kind of eugenics of ideas. Nordic Americans have learned, Evans wrote of what he called "alien ideas," that they

are just as dangerous to us as the aliens themselves, no matter how plausible such ideas may sound. With most of the plain people this conclusion is simply based on the fact that the alien ideas do not work well for them. Others went deeper and [have] come to understand that the differences in racial background, in breeding, instinct, character and emotional point of view are more important than logic. So ideas which may be perfectly healthy for an alien may also be poisonous for Americans.

Americanism is "a thing of the spirit, a purpose and a point of view, that can only come through instinctive racial understanding." Most "aliens" do not "understand those principles, even when they use our words in talking about them."

So the KKK was a brotherhood, and its female auxiliary the Kamelia a sisterhood, of feeling, of intuition. In the United States at the time, fraternal orders thrived. The oldest was the Masons. Catholics had the Knights of Columbus. There were Moose and Elk lodges and any number of others, their members pledged to uphold the principles of the group and to treat one another as a family. Here is how one KKK pamphlet phrased it:

> When we voluntarily entered Klandom, we came into a Realm of special relations and special duties. Fraternal love became the bond of union. Klansmen committed themselves to the practice of "Klannishness toward fellow-Klansmen." . . .Wherever there is need for loving service, a Klansman must go speedily to help that distressed Klansman. . . . One Klansman is weak; it is a privilege to strengthen him. Another Klansman has fallen; it is a privilege to restore him. A Klansman is in danger; it is a privilege to safeguard him. A Klansman is jeopardized; it is a privilege to protect him. A Klansman is seeking to rise; it is a privilege to assist him. *A Fundamental Klan Doctrine* (1924)

In the Klan as in other orders, meetings stressed ceremony. There were formal titles that members were expected to use; there were processions into and out of meetings with the order of march carefully fixed. Members used the analogy of religious services to describe and elaborate these rituals. Another common element was the wealth of offices, their number usually far in excess of practical needs. The men's scheme of organization provided the model. The proliferation of ranks, degrees, and offices meant that many members could anticipate holding one or another exalted position. Hiram Wesley Evans provides the ultimate example. He was a Texas dentist who became Emperor and Imperial Wizard. Respected magazines like *Forum* and the *North American Review* asked him to write articles. By 1924 millions heeded his words. Politicians feared his influence. The Klan gave thousands of others similar, if smaller, opportunities to wield power. People who were otherwise entirely undistinguished headed realms or, if they were not that exalted, kounties or klaverns.

Every fraternal order offers these satisfactions; the Klan offered another peculiar to itself: the heady sense of being on the frontlines of a great cultural war. There was prohibition to be upheld; the liberated young flapper and her boyfriends were flaunting old sexual standards; there were aliens and alien ideas; churches were turning away from the old-time religion. The Klan was at war, sharing the excitement that a few years earlier the war in Europe had awakened. War, wrote a pacifist Viennese who observed the early days of World War I, gratifies what Freud identified as the "revulsion against culture," those "subconscious primitive instincts of the human animal." You did not actually have to serve in the military to satiate those instincts. Whoever at home joined the Loyalty Leagues and Defense Societies during the World War and used that position to bully immigrants or censure liberal ministers or get rid of teachers or ban books or movies got to gratify aggressive instincts. The KKK promised to release "the free, splendid beast of prey," as Hitler phrased the power that he wanted to awaken. The Klan aimed to create an Order before which non-Nordics would tremble. None of this contradicted a message of love and fraternity. "It is always possible," Freud argued in *Civilization and its Discontents* (1930), "to bind together a considerable number of people in love, so long as there are other people left over to receive the manifestations of aggressiveness."

This new war had the advantage that you were very unlikely to get killed. Yet violence there was, not only by Klansmen but against them. Events in and near Worcester, Massachusetts, a center for both Klan and anti-Klan activity in the mid-1920s, demonstrate the allure intimidation and aggression held for both members and opponents of the Invisible Empire.

On September 28, 1923, when the KKK launched a major recruiting drive with a rally at Mechanics Hall, the Maine Realm's King Kleagle Eugene Farnsworth was the principal speaker. Klan publicity described him as the "most loved and most feared man in New England." He told a packed Mechanics Hall that real Americans were losing control of their own country. "Sixty-two percent of all our political positions, elected or appointed, are occupied by Roman Catholics." Catholics also dominated the police. "In all our towns and cities of 10,000 people or more, 90 percent of the police forces are Catholics." Catholics also dominated the public schools. "Not a single one of them believes in our public schools." The message made sense to many Worcester Protestants. Each year, for the past several, two Irish Americans had squared off in the election for mayor. A majority of the police and of the public school teachers was Catholic. Another Klan speaker, J. E. Strout, promised that all this was about to change: "When Worcester folks see 20,000 or 30,000 Klansmen in uniform parading the streets of Worcester, and this time isn't far off, so fast is the organization gaining strength in Worcester, then we will definitely be ready for action. . . ."

They would take Worcester back with the ballot, Strout immediately added, "for Klansmen are not violent." That statement was largely true for the Worcester Klan. It was not true of its opponents. On July 2, 1924 warriors against the Klan threw rocks at an initiation ceremony in Stow, Massachusetts. Local police had to summon assistance from state police barracks in Concord and Framingham. On July 11, opponents stole signs leading to a Klan rally in Westboro, a town ten miles east of Worcester. On the twenty-ninth of that month, there was a confrontation in Lancaster, Massachusetts. That same night in Spencer, about ten miles from Worcester, two hundred stoned automobiles carrying Klansmen away from a Klonvocation.

The Klan's answer to this violence against it was to hold in Worcester the first Klonvocation of the Eastern Realm, which attracted fifteen thousand Klansmen from throughout New England. On October 17, 1924, the day before the rally, a kavalkade of twenty-four cars, almost all with Maine license plates, drove into the Agricultural Fairgrounds in the Greendale section of the city. They carried the first contingent of the estimated four hundred husky guards, as the *Worcester Evening Post* described them, who were to patrol the fairgrounds while the big initiation went on. Each entrance to the grounds would have ten Klansmen in full regalia guarding it. Only people giving the secret password would be admitted. The highlight of the day was to be a biplane, its wings lined with red lights so as to resemble a fiery cross, flying over the fairgrounds at dusk. On its trip into the city, however, the pilot had to make a crash landing. Bullet holes in the fuselage lent credence to the rumor sweeping the fairgrounds that the K of Cs, as the Catholic Knights of Columbus were called, had shot it down. Whatever actually brought the plane down—the pilot claimed the bullet holes had been made earlier—it was quickly repaired. According to the Worcester *Sunday Telegram*, a paper that consistently backed the Klan, it glowed "like a red ruby in the sky" and "thrilled the great crowd more than the speeches or even the constant display of fireworks had done." This was the high water mark of the Klan in Worcester. It was short-lived.

As the great rally broke up just before midnight, the thousands of Klansmen and their families passed beyond the areas secured by guards and out into the streets of the city. According to newspaper reports, they encountered a crowd of about eight hundred young men gathered across from City Hall who stoned the cars, jumped on the running boards, pulled the occupants out, and beat them. For hours roving bands attacked "every automobile passing through the center of the city that gave the least suspicion of containing Klansmen," reported the *Telegram*. The police "did their best," the paper conceded, but the attackers were so numerous and so "unruly that it was impossible to keep [them] in check and the occupants of automobiles were punched and thumped severely." Some of the automobiles were "nearly dismantled," others burned or overturned. The fairgrounds also came under attack. Benches were torn apart; Klan symbols were defaced or destroyed. The Rev. U. M. Layton, pastor of the Trowbridge Memorial [Methodist] Church and a supporter of the Klan, claimed that a thousand new members would join "for every rock thrown at Klansmen." Instead the anti-Klan's campaign of violence and intimidation succeeded. After the first Klonvocation of the Eastern Realm there were no further public Klan gatherings in Worcester.

An American Fascism

Is it appropriate to label the Klan of the 1920s fascist? Surely that is one of the most overused, and misused, terms in today's discourse. But as one scholar concludes: "Not only in its world view, but also in its dynamics as a social movement, the [second] Klan had much in common with German National Socialism and Italian Fascism." Klan leaders of the 1920s and 1930s acknowledged this kinship, she points out. Exploring some of these parallels will reveal much about the KKK and its appeal.

Evans and other Klan leaders exploited the "mobilizing passions" that a student of fascism has identified as characteristic of that ideology: passions that function in fascist movements to recruit followers and in fascist regimes to "weld" the fascist "tribe to its leader." A controlling passion is for "the primacy of the group." Allegiance to a group, in this case self-styled real Americans of Nordic stock, comes before all other loyalties; it comes before mere personal ambition. Another conviction is "that one's group is a victim." Other nationalities, less worthy, had gained power, so believed Klansmen. "Dread of the group's decadence under the corrosive effect of individualistic and cosmopolitan liberalism" is another characteristic of fascism. It holds as well of the KKK. To protect the group its members must form "a brotherhood (fascio) whose unity and purity are forged by common conviction, if possible, or by exclusionary violence, if necessary." Belonging to the group provides its members with a sense of importance. That too the Klan provided. As a member, you were a Knight, and possibly a Kleagle, and conceivably Imperial Wizard. Finally comes "the beauty of violence and of will, when they are devoted to the group's success."

Evans saw as his principal task the articulation of emotions that conform closely to welding passions. He wrote in his 1926 *North American Review* essay:

We in the lead found ourselves with a following inspired in many ways beyond our understanding, with beliefs and purposes that they themselves only vaguely understood and could not express, but for the fulfillment of which they depended on us. We found ourselves, too, at the head of an army with an unguessable influence to produce results for which the responsibility would rest on us — the leaders—but which we had not foreseen and for which we were not prepared. As the solemn responsibility to give right leadership to these millions, and to make right use of this influence, was brought home to us, we were compelled to analyze, put into definite words, and give purpose to these half conscious impulses

Evans and his colleagues clearly succeeded in putting "these half conscious impulses" into "definite words." The measure of their success is that they built the largest fascist movement of the 1920s, Italy's alone excepted. But failure quickly followed.

Some historians suggest that fascist movements thrive where established conservative political parties are weak, as was the case in Italy, Germany, and Spain. It is not entirely accurate to label as conservative the Republican Party of the 1920s, but it and a great number of Democrats, most of them southern, did successfully fulfill much of an agenda that, with whatever help from the Klan, made the organization ultimately superfluous. An impressive case is immigration restriction. The Republicans delivered with the Johnson-Reed Act of 1924; it targeted nationalities the Klan labeled dangerous, southern and eastern Europeans, most of whom were Catholics or Jews. The Klan vociferously opposed the role of Catholics in public life. Since Catholic officeholders and office seekers clustered in the Democratic Party, it was usually the Republicans who provided the candidates to oppose them. The Klan supported prohibition, a measure that President Hoover called "noble in purpose." The Klan, then, mobilized for causes that did not need it.

As an additional reason for the Klan's failure to translate its influence into long-term political power, historians point to the scandals within the leadership of the KKK, ranging from instances of fraud to

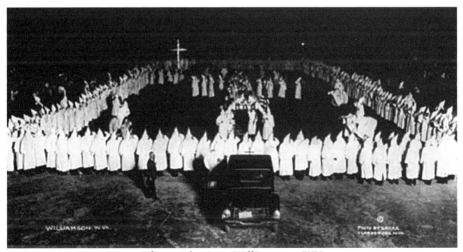

Klan gathering, Williamson, WV

the trial of D. C. Stephenson, leader of the order in Indiana, for kidnapping across interstate borders and rape. However sincere the convictions of millions of members, Klan leaders had much of the character of confidence artists and opportunists generally. Their inability to keep all this hidden from the membership undoubtedly weakened the KKK.

As it was, the Klan exerted significant influence. This was true in many localities where Klan members effectively policed their communities. They might object to a theater showing risqué pictures or warn an alleged wife beater to desist or pressure a school committee to crack down on an outspokenly liberal teacher or to ban a particular book. Klan influence, easily identified with Protestantism or patriotism, was felt in many political races where a reputed Klan vote put one or another candidate in office. Here the secrecy of the Klan could work to enhance or to diminish its role. Unlike the vote other blocs could promise, that of the Klan was not readily measurable. A more modest conclusion would be that the Klan and the impulses it articulated did much to give form and ritual to the spirit of the twenties.

II

Who is an American?

The War and the Meaning of Americanism

World War I strained to the breaking point the founders' notion of nationality as defined essentially by a political contract pretty much open to anyone, at least anyone white. You were an American if you chose to come here, or stay here, and fulfilled the daily responsibilities that came with that decision. Once President Woodrow Wilson's administration entered World War I, it acted upon a different idea. It commandeered the foreign-language press, created its own ethnic organizations, and organized patriotic festivities. It sent out all over the country volunteers with prepared speeches, banned newspapers and other publications it deemed un-American, arrested critics of the draft, and did all it could to bring patriotism to a "white-hot" level. That is how George Creel, the Director of the Committee on Public Information, described his agency's mission. In communities everywhere hundreds of thousands of men and women set out to enforce patriotism and to define in practice the meaning of Americanism. They were organized as Four Minute Men in the case of speakers delivering crafted talks or as members of state Councils of Defense that organized Americanization programs and Liberty Loan drives. As volunteers with the Committee on Protective Work for Girls, Americans policed encounters between soldiers and young women lest either yield to the passion of the moment. As agents for the National Security League, they received Justice Department sanction to hunt out disloyalty wherever it might be lurking.

All of this activism at the state and local level meant that the new Americanism sanctioned by the government rose concurrently with vigilante groups. These targeted immigrants, many of whom contributed to wartime Liberty Loan campaigns under duress, along with schoolteachers and ministers who leaned towards pacifism or expressed any criticism of the fervent patriotism of the day. Activists also closed red light districts and gambling dens. The administration's handling of the war on the home front created an unprecedented opportunity for private citizens to band together against any local deviations from their own moral standards. Such advocates of Hundred Percent Americanism repudiated the nation's republican heritage even as they called for a heightened national loyalty. Being an American required being an American of a certain type, and they had that type closely in mind. They wanted a government that censored and manipulated what the public had a right to know, that jailed its critics and suppressed dissent, that policed sexual morality. There had been plenty of Americans throughout the nation's history who had at least a minimal idea of an American type: assuming, for example, that it included Protestant Christianity and the use of English. Now such notions took on the force of an imperative. The justification given was at first the war, then the postwar turmoil at home and abroad.

Federally orchestrated Americanism occurred simultaneously with several other important social changes during and just after the conflict. The Eighteenth Amendment imposed prohibition on the whole country; the Nineteenth guaranteed women the vote. In the immediate aftermath of the Armistice, labor militancy flared as employers cut back on wages. The war itself, putting men into the military at the same time that it cut off usual sources of unskilled labor from Europe, had drawn northward hundreds of thousands of African Americans who filled jobs in Chicago's stockyards, Detroit's assembly lines, Pittsburgh's steel mills, and New York's garment factories. The war also brought an abrupt end to housing construction. Black migrants sought living quarters where they could find them, often in neighborhoods formerly the preserve of working-class whites. Shifts in racial patterns were now added to the ethnic and cultural diversities that had changed the demographic and social composition of the country.

Race War Takes to the Streets

White resentment at having to share housing and public space and jobs with African Americans flamed into riots in East St. Louis in 1917, Washington, D.C. and Chicago in 1919. These riots were a grotesque parallel to Wilson administration policies that had introduced segregation in government offices. Racial violence reached a climax in Tulsa, Oklahoma in 1921.

As in Washington, D.C., the accusation by a white woman that a black man had attempted to assault her triggered the riot. Tulsa police arrested the man. A white crowd—a lynch mob in the estimation of Tulsa's large black community—gathered outside the city jail. Several months before, a similar mob had lynched a white suspect. What chance, blacks wondered, would a young black man have? To stave off a lynching, armed African Americans drove to the jail and volunteered to help guard it. The authorities turned them down. The blacks went back to their section of the city. Shortly afterward rumors of an impending attack on the jail impelled them to reassemble. Again the police rejected their help. But some whites at the scene demanded that they disarm. They refused. One white moved to take a black man's

rifle. A shot sounded; a white man fell dead. Blacks retreated to their cars. Whites ran home to get weapons and, in largely uncoordinated bands, headed off "to run the Negro out of Tulsa," as the caption on the photograph above phrased it. All through the night of June 1 and into the following morning thousands of white Tulsans invaded the black section of the city as smaller bands of blacks, some of them World War I veterans, fought to defend houses, businesses, and churches. By the time the governor ordered in the National Guard, the shooting had ended. The entire black community was a smoldering ruin. Hundreds had been killed, chiefly African Americans. Thousands had fled the city. The Guard took hundreds of blacks into protective custody.

Throughout the nation, newspapers condemned the violence and lawlessness. The failure of city and state authorities not only to bring criminal charges against anyone but even to mount any sort of investigation conveyed a different message. Tulsa was a major center of Klan influence in the 1920s. There is no evidence of direct KKK involvement in the riot. No one in the crowd outside the jail wore its regalia. Nor did anyone once the shooting started. The riot expressed spontaneous hate. Instead of inciting or organizing the violence, the Klan simply benefited in its aftermath when untold numbers of white participants joined and supported the Invisible Empire.

Labor Unrest and the Palmer Raids

Labor militancy in the postwar years added to social unrest and upheaval. During the war the Wilson administration had imposed peace by way of arbitration. Samuel Gompers, president of the American Federation of Labor, was appointed to the Council of National Defense, which set wages and established working conditions. Union membership grew. Workers were determined to seek substantial pay hikes once wartime restrictions lifted, and unions were determined to hang on to their gains in membership and influence. Employers were just as resolved to return to a largely unregulated market. The speed with which the Wilson administration dismantled wartime controls and institutions made this situation far worse. The government's cut in war orders threw many out of work. Next Washington rapidly demobilized the military. That poured millions into the job market, though its effects were not fully visible until the deep depression extending from 1920 to 1922. Government arbitration ended in 1919. This abandoned labor and management to their own resources in a series of showdowns.

One of the first, in Seattle, began when shipyard workers struck for higher wages. Management had no choice but to refuse, for Charles Piez, the representative of the federal Shipbuilding Labor Adjustment Board, threatened that he would cut off the industry's supply of steel if it offered amounts above previously established wage levels. His interference infuriated the 35,000 striking metal workers and most of the rest of organized labor in the region. The metal workers asked members of the Seattle Central Labor Federation to stage a sympathy strike, and the Federation agreed. On February 6, 1919, sixty thousand workers joined in. This was only the second general strike in American history, and it encouraged fears of a Bolshevik uprising across the country. The concerted action shut down almost the entire city. The strikers permitted electrical workers to provide power to hospitals and other critical facilities; they granted similar exemptions to sanitation workers to protect the public health. But for several days, nothing moved in or out of Seattle without the approval of a strike committee with a name, the Central Committee, that rang of Bolshevik rhetoric. Anna Louise Strong, a member of the committee and later principal author of its history of the strike, dismissed the idea that the strike was revolutionary in intent. But as a good radical, she also pointed to its revolutionary potential. Strong and her union comrades on the committee refused to accept the popular verdict that the strike had failed. No such doubt remained for the leaders of the steel strike of 1919. It had failed completely and unequivocally. So did a strike by the police in Boston and the vast majority of other tests of the strength of labor.

During the war and immediate postwar period the narrow and intolerant notion of Americanism imposed by the Wilson administration combined with fears of labor radicalism and class war to bring one of the worst periods of governmental repression in the nation's history. In sweeps through the country, the Justice Department under Attorney General A. Mitchell Palmer arrested thousands of suspected revolutionaries. The second wave, on January 1 and 2, 1920, history texts label the Palmer Raids. In sentiment if not in action, some of the detainees undoubtedly espoused revolution; others were guilty of no more than being radicals and foreign-born.

For the moment, Palmer succeeded in alarming many Americans into believing that a Bolshevik uprising was imminent. In this he had considerable help. Newspapers reported whispers as fact and editorialized against Reds and anarchists. The agrarian Nonpartisan League, which had opposed American entry into the war, came under harassment. Then came a reaction against the raids. Even George Creel, who had coordinated Americanism during the war, now deplored "the mad rumors that swept the country," the persecution of the Nonpartisan League, and the actions of the more zealous state Councils of Defense. Yet Creel's, and Wilson's, goal had been "no mere surface unity, but a passionate belief in the United States [welded] into one white-hot mass instinct with fraternity, devotion, courage, and deathless determination." This meant, as Creel was unwilling to admit, appealing to hatred and fear. It meant, as he acknowledged, excesses, empowering local vigilantes to dictate conditions in their communities.

Labor militancy directly challenged the government's wartime definition of Americanism. Steel workers organized immigrants from southern and eastern Europe. William Z. Foster, soon to run for president as the candidate of the American Communist Party, led the steel workers' long and unsuccessful strike. Seattle workers comforted themselves with the dream that although they had not gained any material concessions from the general strike, they now knew "the steps by which an industrial revolution occurs." Even so labor's losses, the Palmer Raids, the continued crackdown at both the state and the national level on left-wing political organizations, all spelled triumph for One Hundred Percent Americanism.

The Eighteenth and Nineteenth Amendments: Writing Americanism into the Constitution

Like the activities of the volunteers of the Wartime Training Camp Commission, who chaperoned dances and patrolled the grounds outside and successfully pressured local authorities to shut down red light districts, prohibition was morality on the march. Progressive reformers concerned over matters of welfare and morality defined alcohol, accurately enough, as a major source of domestic violence, crime, and poverty. Religious moralists condemned drinking as a sin. Saloons, reformers observed, bred political corruption in the nation's cities. Tammany and other machine politicians traded drinks for votes, or so the Anti-Saloon League maintained. To preserve grain, Congress authorized a wartime prohibition on the manufacture of beer and spirits. This provided activists with the final boost they needed to gain ratification of the Eighteenth Amendment. The Amendment and the Volstead Act that gave force to it did not forbid the act of drinking. That would be a more obnoxious intrusion of federal power into people's private lives than the lawmakers were ready to undertake. The law banned more public actions: the manufacture, sale, transportation, import, and export of alcohol. Prohibition brought an abrupt end not only to saloons but also to endless local wrangling over the sale of alcohol. In the South the argument for prohibition included warnings of the supposed menace that drunken black males posed to the honor of white women. The amendment meant that the views of the Drys were to prevail even in areas where the Wets constituted a majority. This would create a law enforcement nightmare, New York Governor Al Smith correctly predicted.

Woman's suffrage also rode to victory on the wave of wartime Americanism. The connections between the two reform movements are numerous and profound. The brutality visited upon women and children by drunken men made the case both for empowering women and for keeping alcohol from men. Since the 1880s, the Woman's Christian Temperance Union had been an important force in the suffrage movement. Its founder Frances Willard, a labor activist as well as an opponent of alcohol, trafficked like other reformers in racism when she argued that the best way to protect white women from black rapists would be to prohibit the sale of liquor. The black anti-lynching crusader Ida B.Wells pleaded to no avail with Willard, telling her she was reinforcing racism and lynching. And by the 1890s both prohibition activists and woman's suffrage proponents had discovered the so-called immigrant menace. Both painted the same picture: a corrupt boss with headquarters in a saloon manipulating immigrant voters. To put an end to the saloon by adopting prohibition and to reduce the relative power of the immigrant voter by enfranchising women were allied solutions. Both movements might have succeeded without riding the wave of wartime Hundred Percent Americanism. But both did ride it. There was little reason for them not to do so. Militant Americanism complemented their standard arguments.

The Sacco-Vanzetti Case

Ben Shahn created the poster below to protest the execution of Bartolomeo Vanzetti and Nicolo Sacco, both electrocuted in 1927. He chose as the text a statement Vanzetti had made to a reporter shortly before their deaths.

The Sacco-Vanzetti Case became the legal cause célèbre of the 1920s. *Only Yesterday* (1931), Frederick Lewis Allen's classic account of the decade, notes that the case initially awakened little interest:

In April, 1920 there had taken place at South Braintree, Massachusetts, a crime so unimportant that it was not even mentioned in the *New York Times* of the following day or, for that matter, of the whole following year. It was the sort of crime that was taking place constantly all over the country. A paymaster and his guard, carrying two boxes containing the pay roll of a shoe factory, were killed by two men with pistols, who thereupon leaped into an automobile that drew up at the kerb [curb], and drove away across the railroad tracks. Two weeks later a couple of Italian radicals were arrested as the murderers, and a year later the Italians were tried before Judge Webster Thayer and a jury and found guilty.

But by 1927 everyone knew about Sacco and Vanzetti. That was partly because Walter Lippmann, a well-known journalist, had asked his friend Felix Frankfurter, a professor at Harvard Law School and later a member of the Supreme Court, to take on the case. Frankfurter did, but not by becoming attorney to the two defendants. Instead he worked to publicize their case. He wrote first an article in the *Atlantic Monthly* and then a book castigating the presiding judge, Webster Thayer, as biased and the trial as unfair. Thayer had allegedly referred to the defendants as "those Italian bastards." Prominent writers and artists in the United States and abroad organized petition campaigns demanding justice for the two.

Technically the controversy involved questions common to all criminal trials: Were the accused guilty? Did they receive a fair trial? Historians continue to debate the first. Most argue that ballistics evidence, developed decades after the trial with new technology, shows that Sacco's pistol had been the murder weapon. Almost all agree that there is no solid evidence that Vanzettti was involved in the robbery or the murders. Almost all agree that whatever the facts, the trial was completely slanted toward conviction. Neither defendant received a fair trial. Liberals succeeded in making the case front-page news. They persuaded the governor of Massachusetts to appoint a special commission, chaired by Harvard University president A. Lawrence Lowell, to review the fairness of the trial and appeals process. The commission lined up behind Judge Thayer.

Ben Shahn, Untitled Poster, ca. 1931

"COME UNTO ME, YE OPPREST!"

–Alley in the Memphis *Commercial Appeal*

Both defendants had alibis, but at least one defense witness admitted lying; and both defendants had been armed when arrested. But eyewitness testimony putting Sacco and Vanzetti at the scene of the crime was questionable. In place of evidence the district attorney centered his case on the evils of anarchism: the belief that the state should be abolished in favor of workers' collectives that would control economic policy and distribute wealth according to need. And he attributed to anarchism the wave of bombings that had shaken the country. Aliens and anarchists of the breed of Sacco and Vanzetti, the prosecution held, have no loyalty to their adopted country. If the jury found the defendants not guilty, they would surely turn their freedom to the nation's harm.

The jury convicted the two. Judge Webster Thayer sentenced them to the electric chair. During their appeal before the same judge, someone bombed his house. He was unharmed and denied the appeal. To conservatives, the executions in 1927 constituted a triumph for Americanism. Commentators who believed that the defendants had been railroaded possessed another idea of what the country meant. Saving Sacco and Vanzetti became, for them, a way of saving the inclusive republic of the founders.

In "Justice Denied in Massachusetts," the Pulitzer Prize winning poet Edna St. Vincent Millay wrote of the executions as a betrayal of America's revolutionary heritage:

> What from the splendid dead
> We have inherited—
> Furrows sweet to the grain, and the weed subdued—
> See now the slug and the mildew plunder.
> Evil does not overwhelm
> The larkspur and the corn;
> We have seen them go under.
>
> Let us sit here, sit still,
> Here in the sitting-room until we die;
> At the step of Death on the walk, rise and go;

Leaving to our children's children this beautiful doorway,
And this elm,
And a blighted earth to till
With a broken hoe.

Upton Sinclair, whose *The Jungle* had alerted readers to conditions in the Chicago stockyards, wrote what he termed a "documentary novel" about the case, entitling it *Boston.* In addition to the poster shown above, Ben Shahn painted "The Passion of Sacco and Vanzetti," which shows the two in their coffins as figures prominent in their conviction and execution stand by, clad in top hats and formal dress or, in the case of Harvard's president Lowell, in academic robes. Fifty years later, Katherine Anne Porter wrote of the Sacco-Vanzetti case as "The Never-Ending Wrong." As a young woman she had taken an active part in the protests against the executions. Nor has interest in the trial lessened. Numerous books, a film, an opera, and countless websites are devoted to the case.

The 1928 Presidential Election

The grueling battle in 1924 for the Democratic nomination between Al Smith and William Gibbs McAdoo lasted 98 ballots until Smith finally withdrew, and only on the 103rd ballot did the nomination go to John W. Davis, a lawyer originally from Lost Creek, West Virginia. Thereafter, nobody gave the Democrats a chance. The La Follette candidacy of that year, despite its remarkable popular showing for a third party, won only a handful of electoral votes.

Over 36 million people voted in 1928, 13 million more than in 1924. Despite the landslide for the highly respected engineer and administrator Herbert Hoover in an era of prosperity, Smith captured almost as many votes as had Coolidge in 1924. Big cities voted Democratic—New York, Boston, Cleveland, St. Louis, and San Francisco. This accelerated a trend that had begun in the 1922 congressional elections. On the other hand, a number of southern states, motivated probably by anti-Catholicism, cast their lot with Herbert Hoover, the first time they had not voted Democratic since the end of Reconstruction.

Why four years after the wreckage in the convention of 1924 did

Candidate	Party	Popular Vote (% of Total)	Electoral College Total
Herbert C. Hoover	Republican	21,391393 (58.2%)	444
Alfred E. Smith	Democrat	15,016,169 (40.85%)	87

Smith partisans turn out in record numbers even though their candidate's defeat was a sure thing?

The short answer is that this race produced a passion rare in American politics. It came from the candidacy of Smith. This is not to say that Hoover lacked popular appeal. A self-made man who had put himself through Stanford, Hoover built a worldwide reputation in engineering, and oversaw refugee assistance programs during and after World War I that efficiently and effectively assisted millions of displaced persons. He served as secretary of commerce in the Harding and Coolidge administrations and properly received, as the most effective member of the administration, much of the credit for the long period of economic growth. There is no mystery as to why Hoover won in 1928. He could not have lost. But though Hoover generated enthusiasm, Smith excited passion in both opponents and followers, including recently enfranchised immigrant women.

Besides Klansmen, whose views were predictable, many Protestant ministers openly opposed Smith simply and explicitly because they believed his Catholicism would make the United States subservient to the Vatican in Rome. Some warned that he would declare all Protestant babies illegitimate and all Protestant marriages invalid. Rumors also circulated that the Pope was building a tunnel under the Atlantic Ocean so the Vatican could set up headquarters in some less crowded area in Florida. Others, less hysterical, still feared that he would accept direction from the Pope on matters ranging from foreign relations to aid to parochial schools. Still less shrill were voters who simply thought northeastern urban Catholicism to be, in thought and custom, foreign to American culture.

Intertwined with the Catholic issue was prohibition. Smith had been an early and vocal critic of the Eighteenth Amendment, which he decried as a "foolish"attempt to legislate morality. It would prove

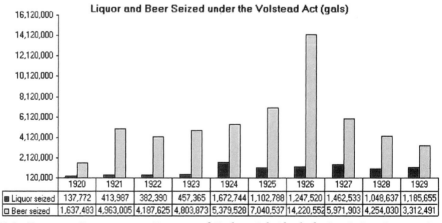

Liquor and Beer Seized under the Volstead Act (gals)

	1920	1921	1922	1923	1924	1925	1926	1927	1928	1929
■ Liquor seized	137,772	413,987	382,390	457,365	1,672,744	1,102,788	1,247,520	1,462,533	1,048,637	1,185,655
☐ Beer seized	1,637,483	4,963,005	4,187,625	4,803,873	5,379,528	7,040,537	14,220,552	5,971,903	4,254,030	3,312,491

U.S. Treasury Department, Bureau of Industrial Alcohol; Statistics Concerning Intoxicating Liquors, December, 1930

Arrests Under the Volstead Act

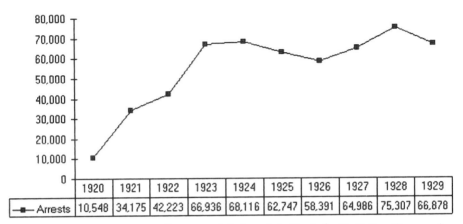

	1920	1921	1922	1923	1924	1925	1926	1927	1928	1929
Arrests	10,548	34,175	42,223	66,936	68,116	62,747	58,391	64,986	75,307	66,878

U.S. Treasury Department, Bureau of Industrial Alcohol; Statistics Concerning Intoxicating Liquors, December, 1930

impossible to enforce, he correctly foresaw. This led supporters of prohibition to refer to Smith as "Al-coholic" Smith. Evangelical Protestants swelled the ranks of both the most zealous supporters of prohibition and the most fearful opponents of Catholics in public office.

As the graph above shows, arrests under the Volstead Act reached their highest point in 1928. The previous peak, 1924, had also been an election year. But as the number of arrests increased, the amount of illegal liquor seized continued to decline. Federal agents along with state and local police arrested 10,321 or 16 percent more people in 1928; yet they seized 413,896 fewer gallons of liquor (or 28 percent less) and 1,717,873 less gallons of beer (again, 28 percent less). One possible explanation is that the government was winning its battle. If the large dealers had been shut down, and the government turned its attention to mopping up the small producers, the data would make sense. This, however, had not happened. Instead the government had less and less success shutting down large operations. Al Capone's enterprise in Chicago was merely the most notorious of the large-scale criminal rings that defied prohibition, often with the assistance of local police and prosecutors. Why then had arrests shot upward? It could be simply that the Coolidge administration in this electoral year was seeking to show its ongoing commitment to prohibition.

Added to the inability of the state, local, and federal authorities to enforce prohibition was the increasing disdain for abstinence expressed by the young and the Smart Set. Wets went from being the tools or dupes of the liquor interests, as educated opinion had held in the immediate prewar years, to being sophisticates who frequented speakeasies and knew how to mix the latest cocktails. Drys went from being enlightened reformers to being Puritans, as H. L. Mencken notably called them. Mencken's *American Mercury* magazine published an essay in 1926 by Senator James A. Reed of Missouri excoriating prohibition advocates as fanatics. He expressed the scorn their reform had engendered by the mid-1920s:

> The reformer cried aloud: "Amend the Constitution, pass the Volstead statute and in the twinkling of an eye evil will vanish! Close the saloons and the jails will empty themselves; cries of poverty will be turned to songs of joy; childish wailings to melodious laughter; drunken blows to fond caresses; and hatred be transmuted into tenderest love. Highwaymen will give up their bludgeons and become ministers of justice. Thieves will no longer 'break through and steal'!" and so on, ad infinitum, ad nauseam.
>
> The legal revolution occurred, but the moral miracle did not come off according to schedule. Men still go philandering, and sometimes maidens listen to their amorous wooings. The fashionable swain, bottle on hip, is received in polite society. He presses his flask to the lips of a girl whose pre-Volstead mother would have scorned a boy with liquor-tainted breath. The fires were put out in the furnaces of the distilleries and breweries, but were lighted under ten thousand illicit stills. Moonshining became a profitable trade, bootlegging a dignified profession, rum-running a romantic calling.

During the prohibition years, drinking did decline, and not only among people of self-control and responsibility who had previously been careful in their use of alcohol. Overindulgence and alcoholism also decreased. Nonetheless, by 1928 opposition to the Eighteenth Amendment was growing. A Voluntary Lawyers' Committee that year persuaded the American Bar Association to adopt a resolution calling for repeal on the grounds that prohibition promoted disrespect for the law and contempt for the Constitution. It was one thing for Flaming Youth to flaunt their parents' morals by frequenting speakeasies or carrying hip flasks. It was another for the ABA to declare prohibition a danger to the rule of law. Smith's open opposition to prohibition—usually a moderate drinker himself, he often served cocktails at day's end to reporters covering his campaign—led its millions of supporters, by no means willing to admit defeat, to rally to the polls to make sure he lost.

Embodying much of what his opponents feared would ruin their America, Smith was the child of immigrants; he had grown up on the Lower East Side of Manhattan, far from the Iowa farm country where Hoover spent his boyhood years. When his father died, Smith went to work to support his mother and siblings. He got a job at age twelve working twelve hours a day at the Fulton Fish Market. Tammany Hall, the notorious Democratic political machine, gave Smith his chance to escape the drudgery of the fish market. He became a process server.

Later, the Hall's leaders chose him for the New York State Assembly. "Don't worry," he was instructed, "just vote the way you are told." Smith did. He also devoted his nights to the study of all of the bills coming before the Assembly. After years of hard work he became the most knowledgeable legislator in the state. Still, he voted as he was told. This led a number of progressive civic groups to name him the worst legislator in the state. He stood out among Assembly members in blocking reform measures.

The turning point in Smith's career came in the wake of the Triangle Shirtwaist Factory Fire of 1911, in which 146 woman garment workers were killed. The state legislature created a Factory Investigating Commission that Smith, as speaker of the Assembly, co-chaired with another Tammany Hall politician, State Senate president Robert Wagner. Progressives despaired, but the Commission turned out to be highly effective. It recommended scores of measures to protect the health and safety of workers, and Smith and Wagner efficiently pushed them through the legislature. This historical juncture marked the birth of urban liberalism, in the sense that the word "liberalism" has since attained. Smith went on to become governor. As chief executive of what was then the largest state, he automatically became a potential presidential candidate, the first Catholic ever to hold such a status in a major party.

Smith remained true to his origins. Not just a Catholic, he was a daily communicant. Not merely a product of Tammany Hall, he was the de facto boss of the machine. He continued to speak with a New York City accent. He smoked cigars and wore a brown derby, then the height of fashion on the Lower East Side but not in the rest of the country. His closest advisor, a Jewish woman, said that women were not the equals of men. The same qualities that horrified Smith's opponents made him a hero to his supporters. Prohibition targeted the urban working class by attacking the ethnic saloon, not the upper-class country club. And the struggle over the ratification of the Eighteenth Amendment had pitted immigrants and Catholics against Protestants and self-proclaimed Hundred Percent Americans. Immigration restriction went after the same groups as prohibition. Smith and Tammany had opposed it. Smith and Tammany also led the campaign against the Red Scare. In 1920 Smith, as governor, vetoed the so-called Lusk Laws that outlawed various radical groups and censored motion pictures. Narrowly defeated in the Harding landslide of 1920, Smith made the repeal of the laws (his Republican successor had signed the measures) the cornerstone of his 1922 gubernatorial campaign. He then took on the KKK at the 1924 Convention. In blocking McAdoo, leader of the rural and small-town forces among the Democrats, Smith reconfirmed his party's hold on urban working-class and ethnic voters. Smith's whole career, including his 1928 campaign, carried the message that they were as good as anybody whose an-

An enthusiastic Smith supporter, n.d.

cestors had come over on the May-flower or fought in the Revolution. The passion Smith's candidacy provoked fueled a pre-election riot in Worcester, Massachusetts, where the 1928 campaign reopened the wounds of the earlier battles over the Klan. An estimated 10,000 Democrats attacked a Hoover parade of some 8,000. Workers from the Norton Company led the parade in company trucks, many of them Swedes and some of them former Klansmen. The route called for the Hoover partisans to file down Main Street and on to Shrewsbury Street and into the heart of the city's blue-collar ethnic neighborhoods. This was an openly provocative act, an invasion of Democratic turf. The destination was to be East Park, where the faithful would be treated to a fireworks display. The Hoover voters never got to the park. As they started down Shrewsbury Street, Smith partisans began hurling bricks, paving stones, and other dangerous objects from rooftops. Joining them were other Democrats who had gathered at six nearby Smith rallies. The two sides went at each other for the next several hours. No one was killed, but several people were hospitalized, including a woman in the Hoover parade who had a car horn stuffed down her throat. The *Worcester Telegram* detailed other injuries, some requiring medical attention. Most involved cuts and abrasions. Several people were knocked unconscious. The violence spilled over to Election Day as Democrats attacked Republicans in Swedish neighborhoods on their way to the polls.

One of the victims went home and drafted a poem, "This is the Morn of Election Day, " that he mimeographed and distributed in Republican wards. It reads in part:

> Last night in a column ten thousand strong,
> We gathered for Hoover and marched along,
> Down Salisbury Street, then to City Hall,
> We paraded and received the cheers of all.
>
> Then to a depot and on to the park,
> Most men and women there carried a mark
> Home on their back from things there thrown,

From rotten eggs to fish and stones.
All because they would leave their homes
To defy Al Smith and the puppets of Rome.

A vote for Al is a vote for rum,
A vote to empower America's scum.
A vote for intolerance and bigotry,
In a land of tolerance and of the free.
We welcomed them in, these foreign gangs,
And now we feel their poisoned fangs,
Our symbols of liberty they cannot see,
They are loyal to a potentate across the sea. . . .

Let Historians write, "Smith also ran"
Now it's time to support the Ku Klux Klan.

The poem captured the simultaneous sense of being entitled—Protestants were the real Americans—and of being endangered. Eugenics expressed the same duality, as did the Klan. So did conservative versions of evangelical Protestantism. All fed off the restrictive notion of national identity the war and the Red Scare had fostered. Klansmen, aggrieved Protestants, advocates of eugenics—all received the benefits of federally sanctioned vigilantism and of Wilson's endorsement of D. W. Griffith's glorification of the first Klan as "history written by lightning." They also prompted and benefited from the rise of anti-Semitism and the growing frustration with the failure to enforce prohibition. Imperial Wizard Hiram Wesley Evans spoke the simple truth when he claimed to speak for millions. The Klan said, to frantic applause, that Americanism was a matter of blood and creed. Americans were members of Madison Grant's Great Race. Very unhappy members.

III

Minstrelsy and Acculturation

Minstrel shows, in which white entertainers smeared themselves in burnt cork and sang so-called plantation songs and told corny jokes in fake African American dialect, had toured the United States since the 1840s. After that they lost some of their audience to vaudeville and then to the movies but remained popular as amateur productions. Church groups, fraternal organizations: All put them on. Elements of minstrelsy also lived on in vaudeville and films. *The Jazz Singer*, the first "talking picture," starred Al Jolson, then America's most popular singer, who recreated several of his most celebrated numbers in blackface. The poster reproduced to the right shows him at the movie's climax singing "Mammy" to his immigrant Jewish mother.

Poster, 1927, private collection of John McClymer

The use of supposed African American appearance, language, and gestures by white performers remained common through World War I and beyond. It was part of a much broader cultural phenomenon that can tell a great deal about the shifting meanings of ethnicity and Americanism and about the relatively unchanging meaning of race in the interwar years. Exploring how first generation ethnics like Jolson who was born in Lithuania and their American-born kin used minstrelsy requires seeing it in context. Various ethnic groups adapted the conventions of the minstrel show to their own purposes. White Americans, both ethnic and old stock, routinely adopted Asian or black identities in the movies and on the radio. Related are the strategies by which white ethnics, especially Jews, adopted identities meant to be mistaken for Nordic.

Minstrels Are We

In 1917, just on the eve of the American entry into the war, the Norton Company of Worcester, Massachusetts, the word's largest man-

36

ufacturer of grinding wheels and other abrasives, put on its annual minstrel show, a part of its Americanization campaign. Much of the workforce was Swedish by birth or ancestry. An advocate of an energetic welfare capitalism program designed to attract and retain good workers, Norton sponsored baseball, basketball, and other teams; it organized garden shows, an annual Folk Festival, employee picnics and outings; it provided facilities for a camera club and a pig club; and it published a company newspaper, *The Norton Spirit*. It pioneered in safety measures and industrial medicine, such as the studies of the effect of workplace toxins and dust on worker health. And it staged an annual minstrel show that involved scores of Norton workers participating as singers, dancers, and comedians. Others constructed sets and made costumes, sold tickets, or publicized the event.

"Passing from Light into Dark," read the caption of a cartoon in a special issue of the *Spirit* promoting the show. The word passing at the time stood for a common theme in American culture: people of mixed blood who sought to live as whites.

PASSING FROM LIGHT INTO DARK

A memo by George N. Jeppson, who started Norton's efforts, explains what the minstrel show had to do with Americanization. "Some within the company," he wrote, "criticized the time and money devoted to these programs." They believed "that a fellow ought to work and choose his own recreation after work." That might be fine for "the Average American who is born here" but not for the "many young men who come here as immigrants and are away from a home or church influence." They needed the assistance of their American-born fellow employees so that they could feel at home in their company and their adopted land. Then, but only then, would they be ready for formal instruction in English and civics in organizations like the YMCA.

Acquiring a cultural and social identity authentic by popular standards was clearly part of what coming to feel at home meant in practice for Norton's immigrant employees. It also included gaining a working knowledge of the racial stereotypes the American majority had embraced. Would Swedes have learned to call a black child a "pickaninny" without company assistance? No doubt in time, but the special issue of the *Spirit* provided a primer in American prejudice. A cartoon shows one of the prospective minstrels in need of fresh material asking an acquaintance whether he knew any new "coon" jokes ("coon" was once an especially ugly slang word for African American). Pat, the minstrel's friend, only knew Irish jokes. This was a Norton in-joke: There were virtually no Irish employees in the company.

And as everyone knew, hostility in Worcester between Swedes and Irish made it extremely unlikely an Irishman would tell a Swede an Irish joke. But alter the brogue to a drawl and change Pat or Mike to Rastus or Rufus and you would have all the new material needed. Irish jokes, unaltered, were common in Norton Company minstrel shows. In 1924, for example, Norton used Saint Patrick's Day as the theme. The fusion of cork make-up and shamrocks suggests much about how immigrants came to feel at home during the interwar years and how they continued to proclaim their ethnic identities.

Immigrant workers learned that you could "black up," that is, pass from light into dark, in a spirit of wholesome fun that the entire family would find amusing because white Americans insisted that African American speech and appearance were intrinsically comic, and because agreeing with that notion showed how American the immigrant had become. The Irish jokes, told in the same makeup, demonstrate that learning how to "blacken" the reputation of some ethnicity becomes another routine part of the acculturation process. The Irish learned this as well. They too put on minstrel shows, most of them parish productions, in which they routinely made sport of other ethnic groups. The front page of the Worcester's Catholic *Messenger* for March 2, 1906, for example, told of the great success of the St. Anne's show featuring "The German School" segment preceding the "Rufus Rastus Johnson Brown" and "Holy Cross 'Choo-choo'" numbers. The following year the boys of St. John's Lyceum put on, according to the *Messenger*, "probably the best amateur minstrel show chorus seen in Worcester in recent years." One of the highlights was a rendition of an Indian song, "Big Chief Battle Ax."

Acculturation, as contemporaries understood it, meant the ongoing adaptation of immigrants and their children to "American" ways. Led by Theodore Roosevelt, who campaigned for the 1916 Republican presidential nomination on a platform calling for military preparedness and the complete obliteration of any trace of ethnicity, those who questioned the patriotism of "hyphenated" Americans assumed that loyal Americans were, as Roosevelt put it, "pro-America, first, last, and all the time, and not pro-anything else at all." Such "One Hundred Percent Americanism" made identity a zero-sum issue. An Italian American, for example, was only fifty-percent American. Acculturation would reduce the fifty percent that was Italian to zero. It assumed that any adoption of American ways meant a corresponding loss of ethnicity. Henry Ford adopted this approach for his immigrant workers. Ford expressed his idea of the melting pot in the *Ford Times* of 1916.

The "Melting Pot" exercises were dramatic in the extreme: A deckhand came down the gang plank of the ocean liner, represented in canvas facsimile. "What cargo?" was the hail he received. "About 230 hunkies," he called back. "Send 'em along and we'll see what

Image from Peter C. Marzio, ed., *A Nation of Nations: The People Who Came to America as Seen Through Objects, Prints, and Photographs at the Smithsonian Institution* (New York, 1976), 373.

the melting pot will do for them," said the other and from the ship came a line of immigrants, in the poor garments of their native lands. Into the gaping pot they went. Then six instructors of the Ford school, with long ladles, started stirring. "Stir! Stir!" urged the superintendent of the school. The six bent to greater efforts. From the pot fluttered a flag, held high, then the first of the finished product of the pot appeared, waving his hat. The crowd cheered as he mounted the edge and came down the steps on the side. Many others followed him, gathering in two groups on each side of the cauldron. In contrast to the shabby rags they wore when they were unloaded from the ship, all wore neat suits. They were American in looks. And ask anyone of them what nationality he is, and the reply will come quickly, "American!" "Polish-American?" you might ask. "No, American," would be the answer. For they are taught in the Ford school that the hyphen is a minus sign.

Ford's was certainly not the way taken by the Norton Company of Worcester, Massachusetts. George N. Jeppson, whose family owned ten percent of the company stock, was very proud that both of his parents were born in Sweden, and the Norton Company under his leadership held an annual folk festival whose centerpiece featured a parade of festooned wagons and cars representing the various nationality groups that made up the work force. Jeppson headed the Swedish Republican Association of Massachusetts, by far the largest ethnic political organization in the state. He promoted Swedish folk culture, especially song, and in 1920 he brought to Worcester the nation's first postwar national convention of Swedish singing societies. But while openly extolling ethnicity, the company did not regard every group as equally valuable. Here, for example, are the lyrics from a comic song written for a company dinner, circa 1908, to be sung to "Tramp, Tramp, Tramp, The Boys Are Marching," and printed on the menu:

> In our Norton Foremen's corps,
> There are Yanks and Swedes galore,
> But hardly an Hungarian, Italian, or Pole . . .

The song ended with a Swedish American toast to Jeppson, sung by Swedes and Yankees (Jepson did not employ Hungarians, Italians, or Poles):

> A skoal for our leader, George N. J.,
> Hip, Hurra,
> He is the man that sets the pace,
> He is the man that steers us straight.

Acculturation and ethnicity could reinforce each other in complex ways. They could also cause conflict, as when American-born children of immigrants rejected their parents' old-country ways. An equally complex interplay can be discerned between the emerging national popular culture, articulated through vaudeville, popular songs, and movies, and local cultural expressions, such as shows sponsored by Norton or a Catholic parish. The Norton skits present simple fusions

Image, c. 1917, from Norton Archives, Worcester Historical Museum.

of ethnicity with some presumably standard and essential American culture. Far more complex was much of the effort to accommodate the two.

An early instance of that effort was the remarkable movie *The Jazz Singer*.

A Jewish American View of Acculturation

The first talkie, though sound appears in only part of the film, *The Jazz Singer* (1927—updated in 1932) is based on "The Day of Atonement," a short story by Samson Raphaelson, who drew upon the life of the famous singer Al Jolson for the movie's dramatic focus: Could Americanism and ethnicity combine? In the movie Jolson, an immigrant who had grown up in Washington, DC, played the title role, giving the piece an autobiographical flavor.

Jolson plays Jakie Rabinowitz, the only child of a cantor in a synagogue on the Lower East Side of New York City. Cantor Rabinowitz expects his boy to take his place some day. But Jakie wants to sing American music. On the evening of Yom Kippur, when Jakie at thirteen is supposed to sing the "Kol Nidre," the song that promises forgiveness to all Jews on the Day of Atonement, a neighbor brings the unwelcome news that the boy Jakie instead is singing "raggy time" songs at a saloon. Cantor Rabinowitz, outraged, finds Jakie performing "Waitin' for the Robert E. Lee," a song identified with Jolson. He drags his son off the stage and administers a thorough whipping (off screen). Jakie runs away, taking only a picture of his mother.

"Years later—and three thousand miles from home," a title reads, "Jakie Rabinowitz had become Jack Robin—the Cantor's son, a jazz singer. But fame was still an uncaptured bubble. . . ." Jack now auditions in a San Francisco cabaret. In the audience sits a beautiful woman, a dancer, who befriends him and gets him a job on her vaudeville circuit. Jack falls in love. He has not, however, forgotten his first love, his mother. He writes her regularly. A title reads:

Dear Mama: I'm getting along great, making $250.00 a week. A wonderful girl, Mary Dale, got me my big chance. Write me c/o State Theater in Chicago. Last time you forgot and addressed me Jakie Rabinowitz. Jack Robin is my name now. Your loving son, Jakie

Signing the letter Jakie in which he reminds his mother of his new name emphasizes the competing claims on his identity. Is he really Jack Robin or still Jakie Rabinowitz?

Soon after, Jakie gets an even bigger break, an offer to star in a new show on Broadway, *April Follies*. The titles read: "NEW YORK! BROADWAY! HOME! MOTHER!" Jack, or Jakie, arrives in New York on his father's sixtieth birthday and rushes to their tenement apart-

Movie Poster, private collection of John McClymer

ment. He has a joyful reunion with his mother. He gives her a diamond necklace, promises that if the show proves a hit, he will move his parents up to the Bronx, and sits at the piano and sings for her. It is an Irving Berlin tune, "Blue Skies." As he finishes the song, his father enters. They renew their old quarrel.

A few weeks later a neighbor seeks out Jack at rehearsal. "Tomorrow, the Day of Atonement—they want you should sing in the synagogue, Jakie . . . your father—he is very sick—since the day you were there." Jakie replies: "Our show opens tomorrow night—it's the chance I've dreamed of for years!" To the neighbor's plea, "Would you be the first Rabinowitz in five generations to fail your God?" Jakie responds, "We in the show business have our religion, too—on every day—the show must go on!" Will he be Jakie Rabinowitz, the cantor's son, or Jack Robin, the jazz singer?

Then comes the visit backstage of Jakie's mother telling him his dying father's last wish—that he sing the "Kol Nidre." But his girlfriend Mary Dale reminds him of his commitment to his career. Jakie tells his mother he must seize this chance to become a star. He goes off to rehearse his big number, and his mother leaves. When he goes after her a bit later, he sees his father, who tells him: "My son—I love you." Mary and the show's producer turn up. Will Jakie sing in the synagogue? The producer tells him that if he does, his career will end. The film cuts to the theatre. It is opening night. "Ladies and Gentlemen, there will be no performance this evening—" The scene then cuts to the synagogue showing Jakie leading the service. His father's last words are "Mamma, we have our son again." The following night the show opens, and Jack Robin scores an enormous triumph. The movie closes as, in blackface, he sings "Mammy" to his mother in the audience. All of the oppositions dissolve. The Yom Kippur service and the Broadway show both go on. Cantor Rabinowitz's son fulfills the family tradition and realizes his ambition to live his own life. He can please his Jewish mother and his gentile girlfriend.

The exchange between Jakie and his father on Cantor Rabinowitz's birthday is especially telling in view of the way the movie ends:

> Cantor Rabinowitz: "You dare to bring your jazz songs into my house! I taught you to sing the songs of Israel—to take my place in the synagogue!"

Jack: "You're of the old world! If you were born here, you'd feel the same as I do—tradition is all right, but this is another day! I'll live my life as I see fit!"

Jakie wants to sing American songs. Who wrote this American music? Irving Berlin, for one: a Jewish immigrant from Russia.

Purists have been quick to point out inconsistencies. Jolson was not a jazz singer and neither "Waitin' for the Robert E. Lee" nor "Blue Skies" was a jazz song. Louie Armstrong, Duke Ellington, Fats Waller, James P. Johnson, and others wrote jazz. Irving Berlin did not. Yet the movie takes the time to indicate exactly what a jazz singer was. Jakie gives his mother a demonstration. He sings the Berlin song straight and then jazzes it up by picking up the tempo.

Another meaning to the term jazz is given in the film. A few years earlier Henry Ford, as part of his crusade to eliminate the Jewish influence in American life, had singled out Berlin and jazz music as especially pernicious threats. Jews, led by Berlin, now controlled the music publishing houses, he charged in the pages of his *Dearborn Independent* and then in *The International Jew: The World's Foremost Problem*. He accused Jews of using this power to drive out genuine American music and to substitute the "mush" and "slush" of jazz that appealed only to the "basest" tastes and instincts. Jakie's outburst about being born in America and therefore wanting to sing American music gives the lie to the Klan's conviction that Jews could not feel patriotism. The film's choice of a title and Berlin's song to exemplify American music overturns Ford's notions about the alien character of jazz, and of Berlin's music, which Ford identified with jazz. Jerome Kern, himself a Jew and the composer of *Show Boat*, put the matter succinctly. Asked to comment on Irving Berlin's place in American music, he responded. "Irving Berlin doesn't have a 'place' in American music. Irving Berlin is American music."

The Jazz Singer, the Norton Swedes, Worcester's Irish Catholics: All saw the assertion of ethnicity as a declaration of their Americanness. In that endeavor Worcester communities and their minstrel shows adopted an American stereotype of blackness. And that also reveals, whatever their intention, the real obstacle to full acceptance in the American community: race, of course. That the black race had been American for hundreds of years and the Swedes, in large numbers, for less than a century was irrelevant.

Eddie Cantor and Whoopee!

Based upon Owen Davis' play *The Nervous Wreck* and produced by Florenz Ziegfeld, the creator of the most famous American *Follies*, the musical comedy *Whoopee!* was a hit on Broadway in 1928. Starring Cantor, it was filmed in 1930, with Ziegfeld and Samuel Goldwyn as co-producers and virtually the entire original Broadway cast recreating their stage roles. Cantor played Henry Williams, a millionaire who heads for a dude ranch in Arizona along with his nurse, Mary Custer, in search of quiet. In a parallel plot Wanenis, apparently the son of an Indian chief, loves the white heiress Sally Morgan, whose father has forbidden their marriage. Henry stands accused of running off with Sally when her attempt to elope with Wanenis fails. Sally has another suitor, the local sheriff, so Henry seeks refuge on the reservation where, disguised as an Indian, he bargains over the price of a rug with a tourist. How can he stay in disguise, for as soon as he opens his mouth, he will reveal himself as a white man? Henry hits upon a solution that made the scene the most celebrated of the film's many comic bits. He speaks Yiddish! All ends happily with the revelation that Wanenis is not really an Indian but was merely raised as one. Since race, and not the culture you were raised in, is what counts, he and Sally can now marry. Henry finally realizes that his nurse loves him, and they too marry. Marriage solemnizes racial purity, a dramatic device Hollywood used over and over.

Cantor, unlike Jolson, was not an immigrant himself but the son of Jewish newcomers and grew up on the Lower East Side of Manhattan before going into vaudeville. Born Edward Israel Iskowitz, Cantor changed his name. The show business name he chose linked together his ethnic background and his ambition to be a singer. While Jolson specialized in big sentimental ballads like "Mammy" or "Sonny Boy" and up-tempo tunes like "Toot, Toot, Tootsie, Good-bye," Cantor's strength lay in comedy, occasionally slightly risqué. In *Whoopee!* for example, his nurse has followed him to a nearby settlement. Henry, thanks to a comic accident with a stove, is disguised in blackface. She too is in disguise, as a cowboy complete with mustache. Immediately recognizing Henry, she accuses him of loving Sally. Henry, who does not recognize her, protests. Relieved and overjoyed, Mary offers to kiss him. "Hey, what sort of cowboy are you anyway?" is Henry's startled reply.

A Jew playing an Anglo American pretending to be an Indian and speaking a combination of broken English and Yiddish wowed the audience. Fanny Brice, another Jewish American vaudeville star, who like Cantor often headlined in Ziegfeld's *Follies* on Broadway, was almost as well known for her "Look at Me, I'm an Indian," sung in a thick Jewish accent, as for "Second-Hand Rose." Giving the bit a further spin, Cantor's Henry Williams talks like a Jewish immigrant peddler as he bargains over the price of a rug. Had a gentile played Williams, the scene would have offended Jews in the audience. But everyone knew Cantor was passing as a gentile. To make certain, the show incorporates several jokes that point to Cantor's background rather than his character's. In one, Wanenis laments that despite all of his attempts to adopt the white man's ways, Sally's father will not accept him. "I even went to your schools," he says. "You went to Hebrew School?" an astonished Henry responds.

"I'm the Kuhn, of Kuhn, Loeb and Co."

Following the stock market crash, Cantor collaborated with the artist Sid Hydeman on *Caught Short: A Saga of Wailing Wall Street*, a set of comic sketches about buying stock on margin during the great bull market and then watching the investments turn to dust. Cantor described himself on the title page as "comedian, author, statistician, and victim." The subtitle makes a pun on the Wailing Wall in Jerusalem, a place sacred to Jews. The cartoon on the facing page features another pun, a "coon" joke that also pokes fun at a well-known Jewish investment bank, Kuhn, Loeb and Co. It was the sort of fresh material the minstrel in the *Norton Spirit* cartoon of 1917 had been seeking.

This appropriation of stereotypes is what makes so daring Cantor's use of Yiddish while portraying a White Anglo Saxon Protestant pretending to be Indian. In playing with them he was playing with danger. Riskier still were the Kuhn/Coon joke and the pun on wailing Wall Street. Not only Jews but all the other national and ethnic groups had to come to terms with stereotypes, often highly insulting, about themselves. Supposedly Jews worshipped money and controlled international finance, if Henry Ford could be believed. So Cantor, self-described victim of the crash, wore his ethnicity on his sleeve.

Cantor moved into radio with a long-running comedy program the year after he made the film *Whoopee!* A few years later another second-generation Jewish American comedian, Jack Benny, scored an even greater success in the new medium. Like Cantor in *Whoopee!* Benny played a gentile with a character trait, that of a miser, negatively associated with Jews. Benny got the longest laugh in radio history with this gag:

> Stick-up man: "Your money or your life!"
> Benny: [a long silence]

Stick-up man: "I said 'Your money or your life!'"
Benny [peevishly]: "I'm thinking! I'm thinking!"

Unlike Jolson and Cantor, Benny did not appear in blackface. Instead he cast Eddie Anderson as his black valet, Rochester. Over the decades, Rochester became less and less a stereotype. But Benny's miserliness became more pronounced each season as his writers looked for new ways to tell the same joke. The jokes worked because the audience was complicit, knowing Benny was Jewish. Through fan magazine and newspaper stories they also knew the truth: He was exceptionally generous. In passing as a gentile, he turned his blue eyes—used in Nazi propaganda as a sign of Aryan origin—into a standing joke. Benny affected distinctive vocal rhythms along with matching gestures, facial expressions, and walk. These too involved the audience as accomplices, for all were stereotypes associated with gay men. The fictional Benny employs them in his character's endless efforts to seduce women, and he never understands why women always turn him down. This too stood passing on its head.

Historians have largely failed to appreciate these complexities. It is true enough that blackface could provide a way for Jewish immigrants from Europe and their American-born children to claim membership in American nationality. Yet their appropriation of minstrelsy forms part of a much wider phenomenon, as the examples of the shows put on by Norton Company and by Irish Catholic parishes suggest. Nor did blackface solely or even primarily allow ethnic groups to assert their own place in American public life, even though it certainly could fulfill that function. The longest-running and most successful use of minstrelsy and blackface in the twentieth century was "Amos 'n Andy." Starting in March 1928 Freeman Gosden and Charles Correll, who as young men had appeared in minstrel shows, launched a daily fifteen-minute radio series detailing the misadventures of the sensible, happily married Amos and the would-be Don Juan Andy. They continuously added characters, such as the slow-moving janitor Nick O. Demus (also called "Lightning"), the shyster lawyer Algonquin J. Calhoun, the fast-talking Kingfish and his sharp-tongued wife Sapphire, members of the Mystic Knights of the Sea Lodge, and their friends, relatives, and neighbors. Within months, "Amos 'n Andy" became the first radio program to have a national hookup. And for decades its faithful audience tuned in by the millions. What was the reason for its success? Their show, the two actors wrote in 1942, upheld traditional values; they noted they had always kept the material "clean." "Radio and the world may have undergone some changes—but people and human values haven't." Among those values, perhaps to the mistaken satisfaction of the audience, might have been counted a secure racial hierarchy.

Most discussions of *The Jazz Singer* and the use of minstrelsy inexplicably overlook "Amos 'n Andy." Reading them leaves the impression that Jews monopolized the use of blackface. Not only is this incorrect. It also makes it impossible to understand the ways in which ethnicity, acculturation, and race intersected.

Show Boat: a Serious Exploration of Passing

In 1927 a play opened on Broadway that contemplated in a starkly serious way the problem of race and the phenomenon of passing.

Central to the plot of *Show Boat* is the attempt of Julie, the greatest leading lady on a Misissippi river boat, to "pass." As the curtain rises, she is successful, happily married to a white man who knows her racial origins, and best friends with Magnolia, daughter of the show boat's owner, Cap'n Andy. But a member of the crew learns her secret and threatens to reveal it unless she sleeps with him. She refuses, and he seeks out the local sheriff in a Mississippi town where the boat has docked. Her husband Bill finds a way of warding off charges of miscegenation; he pricks Julie's finger, then his own, and they press their fingers together. "I got nigger blood in me," Bill tells the sheriff. "One drop of nigger blood makes you a nigger in Mississippi," the sheriff observes, and he orders Cap'n Andy not to put on any shows with a racially mixed cast. Julie and Bill leave the show boat. Magnolia, distraught at what has happened, tries to go with them. "Julie was my best friend" before the revelation of her African American ancestry, Magnolia cries, "and she hasn't changed." Cap'n Andy agrees. Of course she hasn't.

Show Boat challenged all of the settled beliefs of white Americans about race. It persuaded audiences to empathize with Julie, to echo Magnolia's cry that Julie is still the same person she has always been, and to applaud Cap'n Andy's view that in her distress Magnolia has proved herself to be "a damn fine girl." It made audiences wince at the use of "nigger," a word even many educated whites still used casually. Yet Julie's story ends unhappily. Alone, alcoholic, and in despair, she sees Magnolia years later but keeps her presence hidden. But Julie does Magnolia one last good turn by sacrificing her own chance to return to singing. Passing from dark into light ends in tragedy, in popular culture if not in life.

Werner Oland, the Yellow Peril, and "an amiable Chinese"

Far different from the treatment of black Americans, from the crudest minstrelsy to the tragic sympathy of *Show Boat*, was the portrayal of the Inscrutable Oriental in plays, films, and novels in the first half of the twentieth century. That definition of Asians made it impossible to portray them either as cheap clowns or as victims. Inscrutability might hide a wily character, or a courteous and ironic decency. Werner Oland, a Swedish immigrant who played Cantor Rabinowitz in *The*

Jazz Singer, made a movie career of portraying both evil and amiable Asians.

Oland, a Swedish immigrant, had just finished co-starring as the villainous Chris Buckwell in *Old San Francisco* when he acted in *The Jazz Singer*. Buckwell, a Chinese vice lord and the boss of a criminal network, passes himself off as white when he is outside Chinatown. Within it he remains a "depraved heathen," as a title describes him. He covets the beautiful Dolores Vasquez as well as her *rancho*, but he makes the mistake of telling her of his Oriental blood and she then recoils from his advances. In any event, her heart belongs to the handsome Irish American Terrence O'Shaughnessy. But her grandfather refuses any suitor lacking pure Spanish descent. Frustrated by his inability to gain either Dolores or the Vasquez land, Buckwell kidnaps her and turns her over to a prostitution ring run by his Chinese henchmen. Her grandfather dies trying to defend her. Just as the unimaginable is about to happen, the great earthquake of 1906 occurs. Amid the chaos and destruction, O'Shaughnessy rescues Dolores and Buckwell's evil imposture is exposed. Marriage marks the beginning of a new San Francisco. Uniting Chinese and white blood would have been so great a catastrophe that its prevention justified, in poetic license, the carnage of the earthquake. Here, as in *Whoopee!* and numerous other films, marriage certifies racial purity.

In *Old San Francisco* a Swede plays a Chinese pretending to be white. The character, thoroughly acculturated, speaks English without a trace of a Chinese accent. He conforms outwardly in every way, even attending Christian religious services. But he remains inwardly Chinese, the Yellow Peril. He traffics in opium, gambling, and white slavery. He lusts after Dolores. The movie reprises many of the themes of *The Birth of a Nation*. In both films the villain seeks wealth, social acceptance, power, and the hand of the daughter of a prominent family, despite being barred from all of these by his race. In both the villain masters all of the outward forms of white society but inwardly conforms to his racial origins. In both a stalwart young white hero thwarts his diabolical schemes and then marries the heroine. This signals the start of a new era based upon racial purity. This is why in both the unsuccessful attempt to rape the heroine and her subsequent rescue form the dramatic climax. Her honor saved, society can renew itself. And in each the villain is played by a white actor.

The Klansmen of the 1920s could scarcely have endorsed *Old San Francisco*, which heralds the marriage of Dolores Vasquez and Terrance O'Shaughnessy as the beginning of an era. For them true Americans were Protestants of northern European stock. This makes the similarities between *Old San Francisco* and *The Birth of a Nation* in theme and plot devices all the more revealing of the complexities of passing. In both the hero and heroine are kept apart, in one case by ethnic and the other by sectional animosity. These are shown to be less essential than race. White northerners and southerners can reunite, Irish and Hispanic Americans can unite because race endures while sectional and ethnic antagonisms do not.

Oland's success in *Old San Francisco* led to his role as the mysterious Dr. Fu Manchu. Fu's creator, the Irish-born novelist Sax Rohmer, put this description in the mouth of Fu's antagonist, Nayland Smith:

Imagine a person, tall, lean and feline, high-shouldered, with a brow like Shakespeare and a face like Satan, a close-shaven skull, and long, magnetic eyes of the true cat-green. Invest him with all the cruel cunning of an entire Eastern race, accumulated in one giant intellect, with all the resources of science past and present, with all the resources, if you will, of a wealthy government—which, however, already has denied all knowledge of his existence. Imagine that awful being, and you have a mental picture of Dr. Fu-Manchu, the yellow peril incarnate in one man—Nayland Smith to Dr. Petrie, *The Insidious Dr. Fu-Manchu: Being a Somewhat Detailed Account of the Amazing Adventures of Nayland Smith in His Trailing of the Sinister Chinaman* (New York, 1913)

Starting with *The Mysterious Dr. Fu Manchu* in 1929, Oland made three Fu Manchu films. In each his evil scheme is foiled by the Nordic and therefore morally elevated Nayland Smith, described as a nephew of Sherlock Holmes, and Smith's doctor friend, Jack Petrie. Then Oland found a new Asian character to play, Charlie Chan. According to an Associated Press report on the seventy-fifth anniversary of the first Chan mystery:

In 1924, Earl Derr Biggers, a Boston playwright and author, was contemplating a mystery set in tropical Honolulu, where he had vacationed four years earlier. Leafing through a stack of Honolulu newspapers to refresh his memory, the writer came across a small story about Apana [a real Chinese detective] and an opium arrest. Immediately, Biggers hit on the idea of a good-guy Chinese character for his mystery.

"Sinister and wicked Chinese were old stuff in mystery stories, but an amiable Chinese acting on the side of law and order had never been used up to that time," Biggers recounted in a 1931 Honolulu newspaper article.

Like Fu, Chan is highly intelligent. But while faithful to Chinese traditions, he is not an enemy of western values. Earl Derr Bigger went on to write several more stories featuring Chan. By the time of his death the formula was so well established that Twentieth-Century Fox could continue to commission staff writers to turn out three Chan screenplays a year. The character personifies the Wisdom of the East, though his son is totally Americanized. He uses modern forensics, such as fingerprints, yet sets little store by them. Instead he exercises his intuitive understanding of human nature. The Chinese mind, Chan explains, can be likened to a camera with highly sensitive film: He merely observes carefully and waits for the "click." The wisdom of the East abounds in an endless supply of Wise Man say . . . aphorisms on the order of:

Eggs should not dance with stones.
Theory like balloon—easy to blow up, quick to explode.
When tasting soup of crime, use a long spoon.
Insignificant molehill sometimes more important than conspicuous mountain.

Oland's Chris Buckwell had so outraged Chinese Americans that in San Francisco a riot greeted the premiere. Later, Chinese students at Columbia University boycotted an appearance by Sax Rohmer in protest against his stereotyping of the Yellow Peril. But in 1935, Oland made a triumphal tour of China, where he was surrounded by thousands of fans of Charlie Chan. Many refused to believe that Oland was not Chinese. When he died in 1938 just before the shooting of what was to have been his seventeenth Chan film, Twentieth-Century Fox turned it into *Mr. Moto's Gamble* with another European actor, Peter Lorre, as Chan's Japanese counterpart.

Oland's Chan projects a subtle note of intellectual superiority. The Chan of the films, but not of the novels, knows that he is smarter than the white police he helps and the criminals he captures. This knowledge he disguises with elaborate politeness. He can get away with this, so far as audiences are concerned, because they know that Werner Oland is a white pretending to be Chinese. The same holds for Peter Lorre, an immigrant from Germany, who portrayed Mr. Moto much like Oland's Chan.

Hollywood routinely used whites for Chinese and Japanese characters. Boris Karloff, most famous for portraying Frankenstein's monster, replaced Werner Oland in the *The Mask of Fu Manchu*. Not Anna May Wong but Myna Loy, today remembered for playing Nora Charles opposite William Powell in the "Thin Man" series, won the role of Fu's daughter. Wong lost so many parts to Loy that she left Hollywood for several years and pursued her career in Europe. The Japanese American actor Sessue Hayakawa fared little better. More notable, perhaps, was the casting of the 1937 production of Pearl Buck's best-selling novel about the resiliency of Chinese peasants, *The Good Earth*. Paul Muni, an Austrian Jew who got his acting start on New York's Yiddish stage, starred as Wang Lung and the Austrian-born Louise Rainer portrayed O-Lan, a role for which she won an Oscar.

Passing, so long as it meant going from light into dark, was a commonplace of American popular culture. It was more. It was virtually a requirement in movies that gave prominence to Asian or black characters. With the exception of Anna May Wong and Sessue Hayakawa, who did win some supporting parts, Asians were not cast. Whether the scripts called for villains or good guys, dragon ladies or faithful wives, whites got the parts. A few blacks also broke into movies made by the major studios. Noble Johnson, who created his own production company in the early 1920s to make films for African American audiences, played supporting roles in *The Ten Commandments* and other silent films. He continued his career in the sound era. He was the native chief in *King Kong* (1932) and far more remarkably, the Tartan Ivan in *The Most Dangerous Game*, which was shot in the same year with the same crew. This is the first instance, so far as this author has been able to determine, of any black actor's playing a white in a movie. For the most part African Americans got movie work only in crowd scenes or playing servants.

Gus

Blackface permitted characters to act in ways forbidden to whites, Asians, and African Americans alike. One way to appreciate this is to turn again to Jolson's use of minstrelsy. Three of his most successful stage shows featured Gus, a blackface character Jolson first created in his minstrel show days. In *Sinbad*, staged in 1920, Gus is a porter who finds himself in several historic events. In *Bombo*, a production put on the next year, Gus sails with Christopher Columbus. Opening in 1924, *Big Boy* cast Gus as a jockey, the faithful retainer of an old white Kentucky family. The Broadway runs were followed by national tours. The most successful was *Big Boy*, in which Jolson toured for three years. In 1930, Warner Brothers followed up *The Jazz Singer*, the still more successful *The Singing Fool*, and the box office disappointment *Mammy* with the film version of *Big Boy*.

In *Big Boy* Gus's family has worked for the Bedfords for generations. Back in 1870 his grandfather rescued John Bedford's fiancée from the evil John Bagby, dragging Bagby back to justice at the end of a rope. This means, Mrs. Bedford reminds her children, that Gus will ride their prize racehorse Big Boy in the Derby: "We Bedfords must never forget what our darkies remember." Nonetheless, her son contrives to have Gus fired so that another jockey can ride Big Boy and throw the Derby. Gus discovers and stops this wicked scheme. He then rides Big Boy to victory.

What made acceptable to a white audience a black man's subduing the white Bagby is that the actor cast as Gus was himself white. Playing Gus also allowed Jolson to do a type of humor otherwise out of bounds. When Gus learns that Mrs. Bedford's son is being blackmailed over a bad check he had written, he immediately determines to retrieve it. Just then he sees Dolly Graham, one of the gang of blackmailers, slip it down her dress. Gus arranges to have the lights turned off in the restaurant where he is now working. There is much shrieking and clamor during the darkness. Dolly calls out: "Coley [another blackmailer], somebody is after the check!" Later, Gus's friend Joe asks:

"Did you get the check, Gus?"
"Did I get the check? Say, I'm an ol' check getter. When I set out to get me a check I . . . I . . . Oooooh, Mr. Joe, what must that woman think of me?"

Gus holds up her bra instead of the check. No black character could put his hand down a white woman's dress. No white character could either. But Gus could.

The bawdiness of that incident conforms to a tradition of rude humor in minstrel shows. A comic song from the 1850s has Dinah Crow, the sister of the clownish figure Jim Crow, trying to set "de Broadway gals" a good example by only showing "de ankle, insted ob de calf." But the Broadway gals wear "de frock up to de moon," exposing "too much . . . unto de naked eye." New York, Dina laments, is "a wicked place . . . for de gals wear false things, and tink it be no sin." They use "white paint and red, and salve for de lip" and then they promenade all day. In the minstrel shows before the Civil War Dinah was a white man, in blackface and a dress, who would accompany himself on the banjo and offer comic observations on daily life. The blackface meant the performer could speak directly of things that no white woman would be portrayed saying. If fashionable Broadway belles offend Dinah's sensibilities, then their behavior must truly be outrageous.

In minstrelsy, and in *Big Boy*, performers and audiences were accomplices. Performers pretended to be black—this holds for African American minstrels as well who had to use cork makeup and conform to the stereotypes established by whites—and the audiences pretended to believe they were black. Mutual pretense created an imaginary space in which blacks were simultaneously stupid and intelligent, crude and tender, ignorant and sharp-eyed observers of the white world. It was permissible for Dinah to criticize white gals who "wear der petticoats so high, that too much is exposed unto de naked eye," provided she did so in a comic dialect and provided she was in fact white and male. Gus could paw the white Dolly. In the 1924 Norton

Company minstrel show saluting St. Patrick's Day, use of blackface permitted Swedish Americans, Yankees, and other Norton employees to insult Worcester's Irish with unbridled enthusiasm. It was the white skin beneath the cork that permitted such uppity behavior.

Show Boat offers a fascinating variation. Helen Morgan, a white singer and actress, played the mulatto Julie without the use of cork makeup. This was acceptable because Julie is passing. She has to look white. The only hint the audience is given of her racial origins is that she teaches Magnolia a song, "Can't Help Lovin' That Man Of Mine," that black characters in the play indicate only African Americans knew. But while asking white audiences to identify with Julie and to affirm her love for Bill, in doing so rejecting American racial boundaries, the show itself carefully observed them. Today, the estate of Oscar Hammerstein II refuses to permit performances of *Show Boat* in which whites portray black characters. Not so in the original, nor in the first film version in which Morgan recreated her role, nor in the remake in the 1950s.

The Birth of a Nation provides another example. Here too performers and audiences were complicit. The villainous Silas Lynch lusts after the virginal Elsie Stoneman, who faints terrified in his arms when he announces his intention to force her to marry him. It was essential to the whole mythology of the Ku Klux Klan that the film celebrated that he almost succeeds in forcing himself upon her. Ben Cameron, the founder of the Klan in the movie, must save her, and white womanhood, from the most outrageous danger. For the same reason Lynch must menace her because he has black blood. But only George Siegmann, the white actor playing Lynch, could hold and caress Lillian Gish, who played Elsie, without violating racial taboos. So too Werner Oland in *Old San Francisco* and *The Mysterious Dr. Fu Manchu*. In both films the villain has a beautiful white woman in his clutches. Oland's capacity for evil derives from his Oriental blood. So do Fu Manchu's daughter's sadistic impulses in *The Mask of Fu Manchu*:

> Not only was I supposed to have a pet python, but I had my father's male victims turned over to me for torture, stripped; I then whipped them myself, uttering sadistic gleeful cries.

But it was the white Myrna Loy before whom her white victims groveled.

A Final Strategy: The Marx Brothers

Acculturation entailed complex strategies. And as they applied to ethnic groups of European origin they were in flux. The Marx brothers were expert at illuminating the resulting incongruities. Like Cantor and Fanny Brice, they were children of Jewish immigrants and grew up in New York City. Unlike Jolson and Brice, they never portrayed Jews. Groucho's characters are Anglo Americans with names like Otis B. Driftwood; brother Chico takes on Italian characters with such names as Fiorello. Harpo has no ethnic identity. He is pure id, appetite unregulated by conscience. He neither uses nor needs language. He simply grabs whatever he wants, usually sex or food. Groucho and Chico, in contrast, are masters of language that they twist to suit their own purposes. In *A Night at the Opera* they negotiate a contract for a promising tenor. They take turns objecting to each clause. They resolve these disputes by tearing off strips of the contract until each is left holding only a small fragment of paper. What is this last clause, Chico demands to know. Oh, Groucho responds, that is just the sanity clause. There is one in every contract. Chico shoots him a look that says "You can't put that over on me" and declares: "Everybody knows there ain't no Santy Claus." Together the brothers turn to shambles every established WASP institution and practice, from the opera to horse racing to big game hunting to college life to diplomacy. But their Jewish identity, like that of Cantor in *Whoopee!*, is always on display, and passing is the theme. In *Animal Crackers*, for example, they form a barbershop quartet, "from the House of David," to sing "Old Folks at Home." They wear the long beards of Orthodox Jews. Yet Groucho's character is Captain Spaulding, "the African explorer." And Chico plays an Italian musician.

Ethnic Cultures and Mass Culture

A cultural war in the 1920s and thirties centered on issues of race, ethnicity, and religion. Advertising promoted and reflected notions of Anglo conformity. Advertisements for skin creams that claimed to enable women to stay young and ads for automobiles that promised mothers they would no longer be "Marooned!" at home with young children featured white faces with western European features. There were no Roman noses or olive skin. When ads used names, they were Anglo American names. In what the historian Henry May has called the "citadels of culture," such as faculty positions at elite universities and editorships of prestigious journals and publishing houses, members of eastern and southern European ethnic groups made only limited headway. While second-generation immigrants did go to college in greater numbers, the great majority of faculty and administrators, especially in elite institutions, was WASP. So too were editors and publishers. More second-generation immigrants were writing novels, short stories, poetry, and non-fiction in English. But few gained a wide readership. The shelves of libraries and bookstores were filled with WASP names. Someone going in to buy sheet music in the 1920s, on the other hand, would see on the covers the faces of Al Jolson, the black comic singer Burt Williams, and Fanny Brice. Continuing down Main Street past the new movie palace, the window shopper would pass posters advertising current and future shows. Pictures of Rudolph Valentino in *Son of the Sheik* or Ramon Novarro in *Ben-Hur* went with everyday experience. Go home and turn on the radio, and Eddie Cantor or Jack Benny might be on.

What European ethnics used their access to the mass culture to say was often flippant, often funny, often mawkish. It was not trivial. They proclaimed that Catholics and Jews and "Hunkies" and others from southern and eastern Europe were the equals of self-styled real Americans. Ethnic communities eagerly embraced important elements of mass culture and used them for their own ends. They were engaged in battling one another quite as much as resisting discrimination at the hands of old-stock Americans.

European ethnics made their claims for equality within a racial hierarchy in which African and Asian Americans were firmly put, and held, in their places. Americans of white immigrant stock thereby became collaborators in America's centuries-old history of racial exploitation. Even when they took a stand against racism, as in *Show Boat*, they still observed its protocols. Or they unreflectively made use of racial stereotypes, such as in the original lyrics of Irving Berlin's "Puttin' On The Ritz," which poked fun at African American "Lulu Belles and their swell beaux . . . spending their last two bits, puttin' on the Ritz." To his credit, Berlin changed the lyrics when he realized how offensive blacks found them. And his "Supper Time" is a powerful song against lynching. Few followed his lead. Acculturation is about fitting in, finding a niche. Immigrants and their children lived in a society in which endorsing racial and ethnic stereotypes, innocently or disparagingly, aided in defining your own acceptable niche. The temptation was irresistible to seize their opportunities to further the standing of their own kind without overmuch concern with what they were saying of others.

IV

What Sadie Knew:
The Immigrant Working Girl
and the Emergence of the
Modern Young Woman

"Sadie" is Sadie Frowne, a sixteen-year-old New York City garment worker whose autobiography appeared in *The Independent* shortly after the turn of the century as part of a series of "Life Stories of Undistinguished Americans." Hers is one of the few voices of the working girls, as they were then called, we can hear not filtered through the moral comment of a middle-class progressive reformer. Sadie's view of the good life goes counter to the beliefs of several reformers, most notably Jane Addams, and that of the most important evangelical preacher of the era, Billy Sunday. Historians have nearly always heeded Addams' views but never Sunday's. Sadie Frowne did not listen to either of them. Instead she did a lot of thinking for herself and she talked things over with her peers. And she spoke most loudly not in the pages of *The Independent* but through her actions. She and her peers pioneered a cultural ethos that prized pleasure, and a set of mores—dating, treating, going steady—that would come to characterize the "modern young woman" of the 1920s and thereafter.

Two Views of the Permissible
An article in *The Ladies' Home Journal* of August 1921 by Anne Shaw Faulkner, head of the Music Department of the General Federation of Women's Clubs, asks in its title, "Does Jazz Put the Sin in Syncopation?" Her answer was an emphatic *YES*:

Jazz originally was the accompaniment of the voodoo dancer, stimulating the half-crazed barbarian to the vilest deeds. The weird chant, accompanied by the syncopated rhythm of the voodoo invokers, has also been employed by other barbaric people to stimulate brutality and sensuality. That it has a demoralizing effect upon the human brain has been demonstrated by many scientists. . . .
Dancing to Mozart minuets, Strauss waltzes and Sousa two-steps

certainly never led to the corset-check room, which now holds sway in hotels, clubs and dance halls. Never would one of the biggest fraternities of a great college then have thought it necessary to print on the cards of invitation to the "Junior Prom" that "a corset check room will be provided." Nor would the girl who wore corsets in those days have been dubbed "old ironsides" and left a disconsolate wallflower in a corner of the ballroom. Now boys and girls of good families brazenly frequent the lowest dives in order to learn new dance steps. Now many jazz dances have words accompanying them which would then never have been allowed to go through the mail. Such music has become an influence for evil.

Eight years later came an ad campaign for Modess sanitary napkins that measures the distance popular culture had traveled from the old rules Anne Faulkner would want restored. The J. Walter Thompson advertising agency gave the campaign a name, "Modernizing Mother." It heralded the triumph of the "modern young woman" in a series of cultural battles that roiled the 1920s.

Episode one sets the theme. "Millions of daughters," the copy begins, "are teasing mothers back to youth—slamming doors on the quaint ways of the nineties. One by one the foolish old drudgeries and discomforts pass." Life, under the leadership of these daughters, is becoming "easier, more pleasant—sensibly modern." In episode two, the "modern daughter" coaxes her mother up onto the ski slopes. The daughter, confident, fearless, happy, "sane of outlook, wholesome," leads the way. Not just mother but "the world" is having a "hard time" keeping up. The daughter "will not tolerate the traditions . . . [that] . . . kept her mother in bondage." Each episode follows the same format. The "modern" daughter liberates her mother from the constraints of the past by teaching her the latest dance steps, replacing her cotton nightgown with silk pajamas, or taking her for a jaunt in a plane. Mother looks a bit frightened in several scenes but gamely goes along. She is, she recognizes, a product of those "old-fashioned ways" which "cannot withstand the merry onslaught of the modern girl," as episode nine puts it. The daughter's victory, according to the same ad, is complete:

Her enthusiasm is so sane and contagious, she is so everlastingly right in refusing the drudgeries and repressions of

"STEP ON IT, MOTHER▸ THIS ISN'T THE POLKA"

Photoplay (1929)

her mother's girlhood that the whole world is approving her gay philosophy which demands the best and nothing but the best.

The changes that the ads advocated were not primarily intellectual and owed little or nothing to the popularization of Freudian psychoanalysis. The changes were behavioral and reflected a new ethos and a new set of expectations.

The short skirts, the bobbed hair, the rolled stockings, the smoking: All went with jazz to frighten, tantalize, or delight the public. The flappers created by John Held, Jr., such as that reproduced here, became one of the visual icons of the twenties. By the end of the decade, the flapper had gone from iconoclast to trendsetter. Millions of women wore skirts whose hemlines ended at the knee, wore their hair cut short, and smoked. Petting had become acceptable behavior. Chaperones went the way of the corset. All of this was, by decade's end, "sensible" as well as "gay." And the heroine of the hour was the modern young woman.

SHE LEFT
HOME UNDER
A CLOUD

The Working Girl Leads the Way

A few historians have looked at the cultural world of the immigrant working girl, but to find the predecessors of the modern young woman, scholars go primarily to the cultural radicals of the 1910s such as Crystal Eastman, an attorney and women's rights activist. Their behavior did indeed anticipate much that would characterize the modern young woman of the twenties and thirties. These cultural radicals smoked, drank, explored their sexuality, and disparaged Victorianism. Studies of them have clarified much about the rise of the modern young woman. Much, however, remains obscure. How did the kinds of behavior embraced by Eastman and her associates become diffused throughout the larger society? Clustered in Greenwich Village, they formed a narrow circle. Eastman's brother Max edited *The Masses* but the magazine's name reflected its left-wing politics, not its readership. It is not that the radicals were unknown as a group. Lots of people had heard of Greenwich Village and knew, in a vague sort of way, that people there flouted conventional rules of behavior. Walter Lippmann, a member of their set, popularized some of their ideas in *The New Republic*. But it was the Sadie Frownes who shaped the larger culture beyond the salons of the Village.

A typical urban working girl of the early twentieth century might be an immigrant or the daughter of newcomers. She probably worked for a very small wage, but exercised a degree of independence neither her female ancestors in the Old World nor the American daughters of well-born families enjoyed. She seems an unlikely cultural pioneer, for the usual portrayals of the flapper, whether in F. Scott Fitzgerald's *This Side of Paradise* or in movies like *Our Dancing Daughters*, invariably show her to be from so-called old-stock families. Much of the discussion of the flapper fixes on college students, the majority of whom came from northern European backgrounds. The process whereby customs originating in ethnic and racial communities became an invisible presence in the portrayal of first the flapper and then the modern young woman is a startling phenomenon of popular culture in the first half of the twentieth century.

The Return from Toil

Above is John Sloan's "The Return from Toil." He described a "bevy of boisterous girls with plenty of energy left after a hard day's work." One such might have been Sadie Frowne. Sadie was born in Poland to Jewish parents. Her father died when she was ten, and when she was thirteen her mother decided to emigrate. Both worked and earned about fifteen dollars a week, enough to afford a decent tenement apartment. But then the mother contracted tuberculosis and died. "I had saved a little money," Sadie wrote in *The Independent*, "but mother's sickness and funeral swept it all away and now I had to begin all over again." She and a friend roomed together, paid $1.50 a week rent and spent $3.92 per week on food.

It cost me $2 a week to live, and I had a dollar a week to spend on clothing and pleasure, and saved the other dollar. . . .

Some of the women blame me very much because I spend so much money on clothes. They say that instead of a dollar a week I ought not to spend more than twenty-five cents a week on clothes and that I should save the rest. But a girl must have clothes if she is to go into high society at Ulmer Park or Coney Island or the theater. Those who blame me are the old country people who have old-fashioned notions, but the people who have been here a long time know better. A girl who does not dress well is stuck in a corner, even if she is pretty, and Aunt Fanny says that I do just right to put on plenty of style.

However exploited on the job, working girls frequently made their own choices about pleasure. Sadie worked long hours, went to night school several evenings a week, and did her own cooking, cleaning, and laundry.

[A]t the end of the day one feels so weak that there is a great temptation to lie right down and sleep. But you must go out and get some air, and have some pleasure. So instead of lying down I go out, generally with Henry [her boyfriend]. Sometimes we go to Coney Island, where there are good dancing places, and sometimes we go to Ulmer Park to picnics. I am very fond of dancing, and, in fact, of all sorts of pleasure. I go to the theater quite often, and like those plays that make you cry a good deal.

Sadie and her coworkers occasioned as much concern and consternation as the flapper would later, and for much the same reason. Many working girls lived outside of a family setting. Many who did live at home were the primary breadwinners. In the wake of the Triangle Shirtwaist Factory fire of 1911, which claimed the lives of 146 young workers like Sadie, the American Red Cross in coordinating relief efforts for the families of the victims found that almost a third of the Italian and Jewish women who had died were the main or sole support of their families. Another third lived alone or with roommates and subsisted entirely upon their own earnings. Their wages, however meager, allowed them some modicum of discretionary spending. Sadie spent a dollar a week on clothes and pleasure and saved another dollar. Some criticized her. She paid them no mind.

Complementing this autonomy was the emergence of new urban institutions that catered to the working woman and man. Working-class women in New York, Chicago, and other urban centers could not receive suitors in their parlors. They lived in crowded tenements or apartment blocks with no space for entertaining. Like Sadie Frowne, they had no family member to act as chaperone. But now there were dance halls, nickelodeons, and amusement parks. These encouraged encounters between young men and women that served and reinforced their social freedom. Such places offered occasions for sexual play. And the immigrant working woman, and man, pioneered there a new set of social norms. They created ways of behaving—dating, going steady, treating; they took their standards of proper behavior from their peer group; and they paid little attention to the traditional upholders of cultural standards. Such women and men chose their own romantic interests, their own friends, their own pleasure, as Sadie put it. In all of this they flouted convention. Yet they were inventing conventions that in time would reach the whole of society.

To the right is John Sloan's 1907 painting, "Movies, five cents." It captures the diversity of the viewers and the titillation of the entertainment. Sadie Frowne loved melodramas, especially sad ones that made you cry. Many early silent films catered to her tastes. Others, like the one Sloan pictures, emphasized romance and featured what was, for the time, daring behavior. Anyone with a nickel could go to "the pictures"

and forget the troubles of the day. You could also go to meet a potential romantic partner. Young men and women looked each other over in the waiting line and decided whether they would go in together. Once in the darkened theater, they negotiated the degree to which they would emulate the couple on the screen.

Sadie had a steady beau who took her to dances and other amusements. Many young women did not. Since they also did not have much money and since, like Sadie, they believed that "you must go out and get some air, and have some pleasure," they and their male counterparts and local entrepreneurs—many of them immigrants striving to get out of the working class and in need of working-class customers—together developed the system of treating.

There were some four hundred moving picture theaters in New York City. Young women would wait on line for a young man to offer to treat them to the show. In dance halls, owners would let women in for free or for a smaller charge than the men. At the dance hall, the treat often was a drink from the bar. As for the dances themselves: In Jewish neighborhoods dancing was called "spieling," spinning. The woman put her arms around the male's neck, he put his around her waist, and the couple spun in a tight circle to the tempo of the music.

Amusement parks also invited customers to engage in sexual play. Some of the pleasures they offered were innocent enough. You could have yourself photographed as a mermaid or King Neptune by sticking your head through a cardboard cutout. Others openly appealed to more robust wishes. Customers who ventured to Luna Park or Dreamland at Brooklyn's Coney Island encountered a fantastic world of spectacles such as "The Fall of Port Arthur" at Luna Park in 1905. They encountered as well a set of rides designed to appeal to working-class young men and women such as the "Helter Skelter." It was a ride for couples. You took an escalator to the top of a huge chute. There were two separate paths to the bottom. The couple slid down through various curves, initially side-by-side, then separated, and then together again, and landed on a mattress in front of a crowd. Perhaps most riders were onlookers first. Part of the thrill was seeing the clothing of the female riders in disarray as they slid down.

The Defenders of Propriety:
Fundamentalist and Progressive

The new ways were taking shape at a time when evangelical Protestantism, a major buttress of Victorian propriety, had lost much of its credibility. Billy Sunday, the best-known revivalist of his time, was enormously popular. He also was a cheerful, self-identified reactionary. "To Hell with the twentieth century!" he proclaimed. For him the goal of the revival was individual salvation, pure and simple. "I believe that a long step toward public morality will have been taken when sins are called by their right names." Hence Sunday's much repeated Booze sermon. "Whiskey is all right in its place," goes one famous line, "but its place is hell." Prohibition was the only reform Sunday supported. For the rest he professed indifference. "You can't raise the standard of women's morals by raising their pay envelope. It lies deeper than that" was a typically dismissive remark. Dancing was a graver threat to a woman's morals than low wages.

> Sure it is harmful, especially for girls. Young men can drink and gamble and frequent houses of ill fame, but the only way a girl can get recreation is in a narrow gauge buggy ride on a moonlight night or at a dance.
>
> If you can't see any harm in this kind of thing, why I guess the Lord will let you out as an idiot. . . .
>
> The dance is simply a hugging match set to music. The dance is a sexual love feast. . . .
>
> Where do you find the accomplished dancers? In the brothels. Why? They were taught in dancing schools. Listen to me, girls. I have never yet, and never will, flatly contradict the man or the woman who tells me that he or she dances and never knew of premature incitement of passion. I say that I will never contradict them, but I will say then: "Thank God; and get out of it right now, for next time you may."

Yet despite the appeal that what Sunday called "Old Time Religion" held for vast numbers, his message did not work any social transformation. No one was more eager to point this out than Sunday himself.

Sadie Frowne probably heard of Billy Sunday but she certainly did not listen to him. Nor did he attempt to get his message across to her. Sunday's revivals were carefully planned. An advance team would arrive weeks before to organize publicity. All of the posters and hand-bills were in English. No effort was made to canvass immigrant neighborhoods. Sadie existed for Sunday only as a cliché. She was one of the multitude he thought likely to fall into a life of degradation through the dance. That evangelical Protestantism had little, if any, influence over immigrant working men and women is as important as it is obvious. Evangelicals would shape the emerging ethos only from the outside via efforts at prohibition of various sorts.

Sunday did not even try to reach the immigrant working woman and man, but other upholders of Victorian propriety did. Especially important are the "New Women" of the late nineteenth and early twentieth centuries who went into settlement work and then into a host of new professions. The worldly, in some cases politically radical, Jane Addamses seem at poles from Sunday. Yet their recoil from the emergent manners of their time was less colorful but almost as severe.

Here is a comment of a sort common among progressive reformers. Entitled "DIVERTING A PASTIME: How Are We To Protect the City's Youth and Yet Provide for the Natural Demand for Entertainment?" it appeared in *Leslie's Weekly* in 1911. Belle Lindner Israels, a former settlement worker at the Educational Alliance and a regular contributor to *The Survey*, a leading reform weekly, told the story, supposedly typical, of a young immigrant named Frieda:

When Frieda went out to do errands she noticed that there were streets with places other than stores. There were brightly lighted halls, from whose open windows strains of music floated and across which forms flitted in rhythmic motion. One evening she drifted in. She found that she did not need to know English to be welcome. At once she found the things that she missed at home—life, joy, laughter and young people. It was easy here. She was pretty, and as girls are always in demand at dances she soon was being shown the dance by a youth whose evident business it was to give her some return for the twenty-five cents she had paid for a "lesson." Quickly she learned the value of knowing how to dance—and still more quickly did her popularity grow with the boys who came to the hall. From that hall she learned to go to others—others where she was taught that to be really popular it was also essential to learn to drink "stylish drinks" and that dancing without drinking was "slow." Then, one night, when her head was whirling from excitement and dazed with drink, the man who had been playing with her for weeks in order to gain that end took her not home, but to a place where she offered on the altar of her "good time" the sacred gift of her girlhood—all she had to lose. She never turned again from the path that began in the kitchen of the tenement, longing for the birthright of her youth. She followed it through the mazes of wretched slavery to men and walked to its end five years later in a reformatory to which she had been committed and where her nameless baby was born. It was the price paid.

While Sunday condemned the quest for pleasure as sinful, New Women who came of age at the end of the nineteenth century accepted the desire for entertainment among the working poor. Yet their view of the sorts of pleasure the poor indulged in differed little from Sunday's idea of the matter. Addams wrote:

As these overworked girls stream along the street, the rest of us see only the self-conscious walk, the giggling speech, the preposterous clothing. And yet through the huge hat, with its wilderness of bedraggled feathers, the girl announces to the world that she is here. She demands attention to the fact of her existence, she states that she is ready to live, to take her place in the world.

But there were no wholesome outlets for the working girl's desire for pleasure:

In every city arise so-called "places"—"gin-palaces," they are called in fiction; in Chicago we euphemistically say merely "places,"—in which alcohol is dispensed, not to allay thirst, but, ostensibly to stimulate gaiety, it is sold really in order to empty pockets. Huge dance halls are opened to which hundreds of young people are attracted, many of whom stand wistfully outside a roped circle, for it requires five cents to procure within it for five minutes the sense of allurement and intoxication which is sold in lieu of innocent pleasure. . . . We see thousands of girls walking up and down the streets on a pleasant evening with no chance to catch a sight of pleasure even through a lighted window, save as these lurid places provide it. Apparently the modern city sees in these girls only two possibilities, both of them commercial: first, a chance to utilize by day their new and tender labor power in its factories and shops, and then another chance in the evening to extract from them their petty wages by pandering to their love of pleasure.

Reform literature contains many stories like Israels' account of Freida. Working girls who went to dance halls learned that the young men who treated might assume the right to some sexual favor in return. If they did not oblige, they could expect no treat the next time. Doubtless there was the woman who "offered on the altar of her 'good time' the sacred gift of her girlhood." But unless the police records of the time are remarkably incomplete, most did not follow "the mazes of wretched slavery to men." There were Sadie Frownes as well as Freidas among the working girls.

Sadie was no moral lightweight. She worked sixty or more hours a week during the busy seasons. She did not earn much money. Of that little she not only supported herself but also put more than $200 in the bank. She intended to save more before deciding whether or not to marry Henry, who was only nineteen. She was a loyal member of her union. She attended night school.

> Plenty of my friends go there. Some of the women in my class are more than forty years of age. Like me, they did not have a chance to learn anything in the old country. It is good to have an education; it makes you feel higher. Ignorant people are all low. People say now that I am clever and fine in conversation.

Sadie was resilient and resourceful. She and her friends wanted to make something of themselves, to feel "higher." So in seeking pleasure she was by no means a libertine. Pleasure was simply an element of an essentially serious and well-regulated life. That gives to the Sadies of the early twentieth century an influence that a mere pleasure seeker would not have possessed.

Sadie Frowne's sense of entitlement to pleasure and to self-esteem marks a critical difference between the modern woman of the 1920s and the New Woman of the late nineteenth and the early twentieth century. The New Woman was the first to attend college. She longed, as Addams put it in *Twenty Years at Hull House*, for an outlet for her active faculties. Addams herself burned to find something to do, some way of playing an active part in the life around her. She tried medicine, rejected Christian missionary work, and then discovered the settlement house while on a grand tour of Europe. Back in Illinois she and a college friend opened Hull House. Addams, Florence Kelley, founder of the National Consumers' League, Alice Hamilton, who pioneered public health as a medical specialty, and hundreds of others who followed Addams' example discovered myriad ways of inserting themselves into the life about them. These New Women justified their new roles by the ideal of service to others. They could be, and were, as aggressive and ambitious as the men they dealt with. But their aggression and ambition were not for themselves.

Yet the New Woman had only somewhat more success reaching the working girl than Billy Sunday had. Many joined settlement houses. In *I Came a Stranger: The Story of a Hull-House Girl* (1989) Hilda Satt, like Sadie a Jewish immigrant from Poland, described the many ways in which Hull House deepened and shaped her life:

> This oasis in a desert of boredom and monotony became the university, the opera house, the theater, the concert and lecture hall, the gymnasium, the library, the clubhouse of the neighborhood. It was a place where one could become rejuvenated after a day of hard work in the factory.

Thousands benefited from Hull House; hundreds of thousands benefited from the hundreds of other settlements. But this had little effect on the pursuit of pleasure. Wholesome alternatives did not avail any more than did condemnations of dance halls or amusement parks. Evangelical and reform efforts to protect had almost no impact on the emerging popular culture.

The Affluent Discover Working-Class Ways

Dance halls, nickelodeons, and amusement parks started with clear class markers but quickly lost them. The initial clientele of nickelodeons consisted largely of immigrants and their children, as noted in the caption to the *Outlook* illustration (on the right). Dance halls also sought the patronage of the working girl and her male counterpart. Many dance halls were located above saloons. Amusement parks too, starting with Luna Park and its imitators, lured the masses with promises of spectacles, all for a small admission price. Soon, however, the

"The line at the ticket office" drawn by Wladyslaw T. Benda for *Outlook* magazine, June 24, 1911. Going to the pictures would become a frequently indulged pleasure.

working girl and her boyfriend shared these spaces with middle-class and upper-class pleasure-seekers. These new urban settings became crucial areas of cultural diffusion, as Mrs. Shaw Faulkner bemoaned. "Now boys and girls of good families brazenly frequent the lowest dives in order to learn new dance steps." The phrase "good families" had both a class and an ethnic or racial meaning. Children of affluence, children whose ancestors had helped found the colonies, were frequenting these "dives." There were dives in working-class neighborhoods or, worse yet, in Harlem or other African-American communities. Dance halls provided instructors who, for a quarter, would give a private lesson. But most newcomers probably stood and watched and then went out on the floor and tried the steps themselves. Something quite similar took place at Luna Park and other amusement parks. If a middle-class couple left Luna Park or Dreamland for one of the dance halls frequented by Sadie and Henry, they heard ragtime music, perhaps for the first time, and saw people doing the new "animal dances" and other species of rough dancing. They might declare their disapproval and leave. Many did not. They stayed, learned the steps, and enjoyed themselves. At dance halls, at Coney Island, at the movie houses, young men and women of the more affluent ranks of society were the pupils, not the condescending moral instructors, of the youth of the laboring classes.

Many of the rides had spaces where prospective patrons could watch others as they shrieked and clutched at their companions for balance. This too was instruction. Such informal but powerful learning went on at the movie houses as well.

In part, then, this diffusion of working girl behavior was owing to Addams' "most evil-minded" and "most unscrupulous" providers of commercialized pleasure. But commercialization will explain only so much. Consider the popularity of dances that would strike Addams and her colleagues, as well as Billy Sunday, as coarse and illicit. In addition to the cakewalk and the two-step were the Bunny Hug, the Chicken Scratch, the Grizzly Bear, the Snake, the Drab Step, and the Fox Trot. Later came the One Step and the Texas Tommy. As the lyric of one novelty dance tune put it: "Everybody's doin' it./Doin' what?/ Turkey trot." The Turkey Trot, the Bunny Hug, and the other dance crazes swept the nation because people enjoyed doing them, not because wily entrepreneurs enticed them into "lurid places."

James Reese Europe's Society Orchestra accompanied the white Irene and Vernon Castle. Their dance act topped the bill at the Palace and other vaudeville theaters, and they popularized many of the dances. Most were African American in origin. The Castles insisted on Reese's Society Orchestra because, they argued, only black musicians could play the music properly. Yet they offered toned-down, almost decorous versions. This is part of the explanation of how diffusion of cultural practices and values took place. The Castles removed class, ethnic, and racial associations that had served to stigmatize both the music and the dances in the judgment of middle- and upper-class Americans of northern European backgrounds. They did not seek to disguise the origins of the dances. Indeed, by insisting upon Europe's Society Orchestra, they emphasized where the steps had begun. What they offered were elegant, graceful performances of "animal" dances. It was every working girl's dream to dance like Irene Castle. And many a working boy wished he were Vernon Castle. These were the dreams of many of the more affluent as well. But they could not learn to dance like the Castles by taking lessons at the dance academies that did not teach the new steps. The Castles published in 1914 a manual, *Modern Dancing,* but following a diagram in a book was no substitute for having an experienced teacher or watching others. Hence Faulkner Shaw's lament that "boys and girls of good families brazenly frequent the lowest dives in order to learn new dance steps." An added reason, of course, was the attraction of the forbidden.

White musicians, like the Original Dixieland Jass Band, soon began to play versions of the new music. In 1917 the band recorded "Darktown Strutters Ball" for Victor. It was one of the most popular songs of the day. The sheet music displayed black couples, viciously stereotyped, in formal dress, doing the latest dance. It would not take long, however, for black musicians to begin to attract white listeners.

Phonograph records originally marketed only to African Americans were selling more broadly by the mid-1920s.

Working-Class Arbiters of the Permissible

Meanwhile, the immigrant Catholic Church, alongside synagogues and the black American churches, had been reaching the people that neither the evangelicals nor the New Woman could. Just as the new ethos of pleasure came out of the ethnic working class, so did the new inhibitions that reined it in. This dialogue within the ethnic communities was vital to shaping the popular attitudes and behavior of the twentieth century.

The churches' relative success in resisting, restraining, and yet giving some place and decorum to the new ethos is not easy to document. The American Catholic Church did not act on a national basis until World War I. Instead each diocese and, in many cases, each parish operated autonomously. In some instances there are relatively full records of their programs. In others there are not. This makes generalizations hazardous. With this in mind, there are well-documented case studies that suggest the ways in which churches came to terms with new practices like dating.

Chicago's Poles, for example, created dense institutional networks with local parishes as the centers of community life. Parishes sponsored organizations for all kinds of social activities. There were choirs, bands, drama societies, athletic teams. The city's Poles put on plays and dances and concerts. They published newsletters. In each parish a small professional class of doctors, lawyers, and undertakers joined with a small entrepreneurial class of saloonkeepers and contractors to provide leadership. Many of them along with their wives led societies that visited the sick or distributed alms to the needy. Swedish Lutherans, Orthodox Jews, and A.M.E. Zion and other African American churchgoers maintained comparably dense communities.

The closeness of community life meant that canons of respectable behavior were reinforced at every point. School children wore uniforms. Dances did not feature the new jazz or the latest steps. And there were chaperones. Drama societies offered wholesome plays. The example of the Irish schoolteacher or the Polish physician or lawyer modeled behavior. Not everyone within these communities agreed with Victorian values. But such proprieties served numerous functions. One is that they expressed deeply held moral beliefs, especially regarding sexuality. Another is that they provided a means of gaining respectability to people who could not expect to receive it from the larger society. The woman who became president of the Ladies' Sodality or the man who chaired the youth baseball council attained a real measure of status. And given the very large number of parish organizations and the very large number of offices in each, this sort of respectability was within the reach of anyone willing to take the time and trouble to gain it. Status afforded its own pleasures.

From World War I on, as Catholics began to form national organizations, the church's commitment to propriety became more definable. Particularly well documented is its role in movie censorship. Protestant and Jewish groups protested the amount of sexuality, violence, and lawlessness in movies at least as outspokenly as did Catholics. But it was the Catholic Church that could muster millions of members, organized in the Legion of Decency and committed to boycotting any film that the Legion declared objectionable. The new Motion Picture Production Code of 1934, a compendium of Victorian standards broadened to accommodate a degree of the new social freedoms, reflected a Catholic presence. The code then served as a template for radio and television networks. Movies and broadcast media followed Catholic rules throughout the middle third of the century.

Density of parish life made the black and ethnic churches and the synagogues uniquely powerful socializing agencies. Members of highly articulated parish communities found their friends inside the community, socialized at events sponsored by the parish, played in church leagues. Sadie and her friends were much less integrated into the social networks of their ethnic communities. Sadie was a Jew but made no mention of the place of any Jewish organization in her description of her daily life. In this she had any number of nominally Catholic, Greek or Russian Orthodox, Jewish, and Protestant counterparts. Every American city had its population of young people living on their own. Some of their fellow workers did belong to family, church, and ethnic communities. But the unattached had a certain glamour, "plenty of style," as Sadie would put it. Many had nicer clothes because they did not turn their pay envelopes over to their mothers. They went to exciting places. They had sweethearts they could see whenever they wanted. They knew the newest dance steps. So while the immigrant and black churches had far more success in reaching the working girl than did either the evangelical Protestant churches or the New Woman, the new ethos Sadie Frowne expressed so naively continued to gain ground.

Standard-Setters: Peers and the Ethos of Consumption

As it did so, it established a new moral authority, the peer group, to challenge that of the churches and synagogues. If a young woman accepted a treat at a dance hall, just what should she do in return? Churches could hardly attempt to answer. Doing everything would be immoral. But if doing everything was immoral, yet the girl had to do something, how was she to decide? She talked with her friends. They decided collectively what was appropriate. So too in dancing. How high could a young woman lift her skirt in doing the cakewalk? So too with alcohol and a host of other matters. Friends helped decide, and then decisions set limits at the same time that they widened the choices.

The dance halls and amusement parks the New Woman reformers so loathed were early signs of a profound shift in the workings of the

"Can we get those blues from Memphis?" *"Easy! Just turn the dials to 64, Mary, and we'll have 'em right away."*

American economy. By 1920, for the first time in human history, consumer demand would provide the principal impetus to economic growth. The radio provided a new, and extremely powerful, medium of cultural diffusion. Respectable, middle-class whites could now hear the blues in their own living rooms. As consumer choice determined the rides at Luna Park, it dictated what programs would air. There would be relatively decorous programs featuring Rudy Vallee or Fred Waring and His Pennsylvanians. And there would be stations aiming programming at black or Jewish or Polish listeners. In the nature of the medium, anyone could listen to anything, provided the signal was accessible. Recognizing this as a vital selling point, advertisers stressed their product's unique ability to bring in distant programs.

In promoting the range of choices offered by New Era capitalism, advertisers were acting on the same principle as the department store merchants of the prewar years. Department stores were palaces of consumption. Their display windows tempted passersby with visions of luxury and glamour. The message the displays sent was the one Sadie Frowne articulated so emphatically: If a girl wanted to be popular, she needed to put on plenty of style. The message had innumerable variants. John Wanamaker, the Philadelphia and New York department store pioneer, was a devout Presbyterian. But his stores preached the gospel of consumption. Restraint, abstinence, deferred gratification, those cornerstones of Victorian propriety had no place in the successful marketing of the thousands of different products Wanamaker sold. In addition to the great stores were many more modest enterprises for consumers like Sadie Frowne, who could not afford the goods at Wanamaker's. In "Picturesque America," printed in 1909, Harry Grant Dart made fun of the proliferation of stores and their slogans and signs.

The ethos of consumption strikingly reinforced the views expressed by Sadie and her friends. More is better. Pleasure is good. Life is hard so you should enjoy yourself when you can. This meant clothes, dancing, and plenty of style. Advertisers directly attacked Victorian values. That is plain in the Modess campaign that took on a whole series of issues of the 1920s and dismissed the upholders of traditional views. Consider another ad in the Modernizing Mother campaign, "Don't Fuss, Mother, This Isn't So Fast." The daughter takes her mother for a ride in a speedboat. In the parlance of the day, a girl who was fast broke the sexual rules. She went beyond flirting and petting. Mothers and daughters had for years argued about whether wearing skirts at the knee, rolling stockings below the knee, taking off her corset at a dance, smoking cigarettes, using rouge and lipstick made the daughter look fast. How many of those daughters who said "Don't Fuss, Mother" had remonstrated that what they wanted to do wasn't "so fast"? Modess endorsed their side of the argument with this ad on the right:

Private collection of John McClymer.

Speed! Life is all a-tingle at twenty. The girl of today travels without an anchor. There's too much fun ahead for thought of fear—too many prizes to be won to be satisfied with common things. Do older people really object—are they not just as eager in spirit to escape drabness and drudgery and feel again the thrill of being young?

The modern young woman of the Modess ads bore no visible resemblance to the working girl. Students of advertising have shown that almost all of the faces and names in the ads suggest northern European origins. Blacks appear, except when the ads explicitly target them, only as menials. Immigrants from southern and eastern Europe show up rarely, and then as sources of danger. To the extent that an advertiser wanted millions to identify with the imaginary consumer in an ad, racial, ethnic, and working class features disappeared. Affluent consumers would not identify with any figure so marked. Yet these ethnic and racial communities are invisibly present, in the customs and activities the lily-white figures in the ads are shown engaging in. The excluded had captured the privileged.

V
Marketing Fantasy

On September 10, 1924, Earl Carroll, producer of Broadway shows that he entitled *Vanities* and spiced with glimpses of nudity unthinkable even a very few years earlier, displayed in his production 108 young ladies wearing only peacock feathers and bearing peacock fans. They were supposed to represent the beautiful creatures following the Queen of Sheba as she enters King Solomon's court. Carroll's extravaganza did not sit well with the New York district attorney. Since the death of the legendary censor Anthony Comstock, the city had become far more permissive about what could and could not be shown on the stage. But the "Peacock Dance" threatened to make the censorship laws meaningless: something had to be done. Two detectives from the Vice Squad attended the opening night performance. The next morning the district attorney demanded that Carroll either drop the number entirely or clothe the performers. Carroll refused. That night, a police officer stood in the wings of the Earl Carroll Theatre under orders to stop any display of nudity. For this purpose he brought a blanket. The policeman did not have to wait for the Peacock Dance. The opening number featured Kathryn Ray in the buff swinging upside down on the pendulum of a huge clock. Onto the stage raced the officer, who attempted to cover up the startled Ray with his blanket. She broke free and dashed across the stage with the law in hot pursuit.

It was a scene straight out of a Keystone Kops two-reeler. Max Sennett, the king of slapstick movie comedies, had dressed his Kops in the uniform of the New York City police, even down to the bowler hats. The audience, believing this scene was part of the show, shrieked with laughter. When stagehands finally rescued Ray by carrying her offstage—still followed by the determined police officer—the customers leapt to their feet in applause. The curtain fell.

Earl Carroll took the stage to address the audience. No, he explained, what they witnessed had not been part of the show. The censors intended to prevent him from presenting the entertainment he had advertised and they had purchased tickets to see. What did they want? They could see the revue as the Board of Censors wished or

72

as he had created it. The censors lost this vote in a landslide among the public, and the show went on. The next morning, another police officer observed a group of teenaged boys stopping in the lobby of the Earl Carroll Theater to ogle a poster of the same Kathryn Ray. This member of the force later testified that the picture had been a corrupting influence on them. He promptly went inside the theater to demand that Carroll remove it and others of a similar sort. Carroll again refused. The policeman arrested him on a charge of endangering the morals of minors. Despite the show's run of another 438 performances, Carroll had to stand trial on November 10, 1924 for displaying obscene posters in the lobby.

Carroll read a prepared statement in his defense. In the course of his comments he pointed out that the Board of Censors had acted in a reactionary manner. He went on to recall the profanity in *What Price Glory?*—a play about trench warfare—as an example of art besieged by censorship. Yet Carroll's statement attempted to justify a show far less exalted than could be mustered for a play as serious as *What Price Glory?* "I have always staked my name, my reputation, and when I had it, my money," he declared, "on the conception of what people wanted to see." The producer added that he never pretended that the *Vanities* had any higher purpose than giving the audience what it craved: titillation.

The three-judge panel of the Court of Special Sessions retired to consider its verdict, which, it announced, would be based strictly upon a question of fact: Were the images immoral? "We have examined the exhibits that are specimens of nudity and find they are not sufficient to hold the defendant. We find the defendant should be acquitted."

The Revue as a Sign of the Times

Edmund Wilson, later acclaimed as one of the nation's most insightful critics and literary historians, took the *Follies* revues quite seriously. Writing of the 1923 performances of the Ziegfeld *Follies*, he observed:

> [T]here is a splendor about the Follies. It has, in its way, both distinction and intensity. At the New Amsterdam, the girls are always young— the *mis en scene* [direction] nearly always beautiful. And there is always one first-rate performer. Just now it is Gilda Gray. She is not the official American Girl; she embodies a different ideal: an ideal which was probably created by the vibrant and abandoned Eva Tanguay and which has produced the jazz baby of the years since the war. . . . she is the semi-bacchante of Main Street.

Gilda Gray's proficiency in performing the "Shimmy" aside, Wilson was drawn back to the *Follies* because of the way it packaged "such fantasy . . . as the busy well-to-do New Yorker has been able to make of his life." At its core Wilson found a particular kind of sexual daydream:

> Mr. Ziegfeld has now "Glorified the American Girl" in a very real sense. He has studied, with shrewd intelligence, the American ideal of womanhood and succeeded in putting it on the stage. In general, Ziegfeld's girls have not only the Anglo-Saxon straightness—straight backs, straight brows, and straight noses—but also the peculiar frigidity and purity, the frank high-school-girlishness which Americans like. He does not aim to make them, from the moment they appear, as sexually attractive as possible, as the Folies Bergères [in Paris], for example, does. He appeals to American idealism, and then, when the male is intent on his chaste and dewy-eyed vision, he gratifies him on this plane by discreetly disrobing his goddess. He tries, furthermore, to represent, in the maneuvers of his well-trained choruses, not the movement and abandon of emotion, but what the American male really regards as beautiful: the efficiency of mechanical movement.—*The New Republic*, April 1923

Who was this chaste, dewy-eyed goddess? Her name was legion. One whom Wilson's description pictured almost exactly is Dorothy Flood, seen here in a portrait by Ziegfeld's official photographer, Alfred Cheney Johnston.

In "A Tribute to Florenz Ziegfeld" Gilbert Seldes, whose *The Seven Lively Arts* (1924) provided an early and perceptive appreciation of jazz, silent movie comedians, comic strips, and other new art forms erupting in the popular culture, agreed with Wilson on the "mechanical" precision of a successful revue. The revue "shows a mania for perfection; it aspires to be precise and definite, it corresponds to those *de luxe* railway trains which are always exactly on time, to the millions of spare parts that always fit. . . ." A jazz melody or a symphonic composition "may sound from the orchestra pit, but underneath is the real tone of the revue, the steady incorruptible purr of the dynamo." This becomes the "one and only point where the revue touches upon art."

A New Yorker who attended a revue could not romance all one hundred or so beauties on stage. An unlucky few fell for a particular girl. Stanley Joyce, the most notable, because most unfortunate, was Peggy Hopkins' third husband, and his one-year marriage with the decade's most celebrated "gold digger" cost him at least two million dollars. A press agent, Will Page, devoted several chapters of his *Behind the Curtains of the Broadway Beauty Trust* (1927) to recounting stories of rich men taken for large sums by the gold diggers of the chorus. According to Page, one admirer of Gilda Gray tossed a diamond bracelet worth $100,000 onto the stage in a gesture of appreciation. Page quickly put the story in every newspaper he could. The incident, by his accounting, made Gray a star. Most of the men in the audience, however, did not become enamored of one performer. Instead they embraced the fantasy that another critic, Joseph Wood Krutch, identified. What did King Solomon do with his seven hundred wives, Krutch wondered. He could not have been on intimate terms with many of them. He kept the others around, Krutch surmised, to stage his revues. The fantasy of having any women he wanted became a problem only when a customer pursued one specific performer. Better to have all one hundred beauties in his dreams and go to revues.

A Complementary Fantasy

Wilson and his contemporaries regarded the revue strictly as a purveyor of male fantasies. And the shows themselves confirmed their sense. Everything about the *Vanities* from the beautiful women to the dance numbers to the costumes fed masculine longings. But the revues offered women a fantasy too—the dream of becoming a chorus girl.

Every week Ziegfeld received hundreds of photographs sent by women from all over the country, hoping to be in the *Follies*. J.P. McEvoy, a comedy writer who worked on many *Follies* shows, described the "calls" Ziegfeld would issue periodically: whoever wanted to try out should appear on the New Amsterdam stage at about 11:00 a.m.

> Long before that all the streets leading to the New Amsterdam would be blocked with flocks of girls all sizes, shapes, weights and ages. Shopgirls and home girls, girls from small towns and big towns, chorus girls, models, girls from burlesque, vaudeville and the movies, debs from Park Avenue homes and hostesses from taxi-dance halls—all the girls who ever worked for him before, and practically all the girls from all the shows then running in New York. For every girl in the show business or out wanted to be known as a Follies girl . . . the stage manager would line the girls up in rows stretching clear across the stage, and row after row would march down to the footlights and stand there until Mr. Ziegfeld had looked them over. . . . After they stood for a few minutes looking out into the dark theatre, they were dismissed and the next line marched up to the footlights—"He Knew What They Wanted," *Saturday Evening Post*, September 10, 1932

James S. Metcalfe, writing in *Theatre Magazine* in April 1921, noted the endless supply of chorus girls for what seemed an unlimited demand. Why did so many women seek work in the chorus? "Because," he wrote, "of its adventure, its romance, its possibilities matrimonially, its temptation to feminine vanity, its apparent gayety and freedom of life—all this accounts for the why of the chorus girl in her countless numbers."

Oscar Hammerstein II and Jerome Kern made fun of this in *Show Boat* (1927) with a song entitled "Life Upon the Wicked Stage." But stories of chorus girls, rich businessmen, midnight suppers, and movie offers filled the newspapers and magazines despite Hammerstein's lyrics suggesting that the midnight suppers were few and many consisted of cold sandwiches.

Will Page's *Behind the Curtains* supplies a textbook example of this publicity. In 1925 two Ziegfeld Girls asked Ziegfeld for a vacation. All of their wealthy admirers, they explained, had gone to Palm Beach and they had various invitations to social functions. He lost both of his girls but won lucrative publicity.

Ziegfeld also publicized the number of his "girls" who achieved further success in the movies or made advantageous marriages. An article in the *Pictorial Review* of May 1925, called "What Becomes of the Ziegfeld Follies Girls?", boasts pictures of several former *Follies* chorus members who became Hollywood stars. Their number includes Marion Davies, Mae Murray, and Nita Naldi, who played opposite Rudolph Valentino in several films, including *Blood and Sand*. Who knows how many young women came out of the theater with dreams of vamping Rudolph Valentino? And how many fantasized about being the center of attention at the swank Royal Poinciana Hotel in Palm Beach at the height of the January season? Or of marrying a wealthy stockbroker or a successful tycoon?

Titillation and the Censor

Wilson and Seldes each in his own way insisted that the revue said something important about American popular culture. What Carroll and his colleagues on Broadway understood, beyond the American fascination with machine-like precision, was a country ripe for titillation. It appeared everywhere in the popular culture—in petting parties, in movie posters, in Mae West's stunning Broadway success *Sex*, in the newspaper stories circulated about Peggy Hopkins Joyce and other Follies girls, and in advertisements of all sorts. But what should titillation signify for historians? No one confused the *Vanities* with the plays of Eugene

A lobby card for a 1929 film starring Myrna Loy as Nubi; found on EBAY

O'Neill. Nonetheless the omnipresence of sexual images illumines an important aspect of modern American life, the selling of fantasy. Designing, packaging, and marketing fantasy provides the central component of the consumer ethos that came into its own in the 1920s and continues to help define American popular culture.

It would doubtless disturb censors to recognize that they did their part in spreading that ethos. If Carroll should matter to the historian, so should the censor. Despite his eloquent denunciation, Carroll needed the censor. How else could his productions achieve notoriety and generate wealth? Someone, as Carroll put it, had to express "the old compulsions, the old dominations."

John Roach Straton, pastor of the Calvary Baptist Church in New York, led the religious campaign against decadence in the modern theater. One scholar writes that Straton "perhaps comes closest to the 'ideal type' of the fundamentalist moral reformer." In the spring of 1920 he launched an exposé of vice in the Times Square area and published *The Menace of Immorality in Church and State*. Earlier in that year, in the February issue of *Theatre Magazine*, he issued an open letter to theater customers called "The Trouble With The Modern Theatre": "Perhaps the saddest fact of all is, that the stage is the only place where a stain upon a woman's personal character seems to enhance her popularity and success." At stake, according to Straton, was "Anglo-Saxon civilization," the "three greatest foundation stones" of which "are the home, the purity of womanhood and the sanctity of the Sabbath." These "are the three things which the theater most directly and constantly attacks and tries to undermine."

There was something going on in the lives of millions of ordinary people that the revues captured, though only a fraction of those millions ever saw one, and that Straton and other defenders of the moral order deplored. The furor over proper bathing attire offers a good illustration.

Bathing Beauties, Bathing Costumes, and Beach Censors

Unknown model and photographer, Santa Monica, California, ca. late 1920s; found on EBAY

Any male looking for a "leg show" could, as Earl Carroll pointed out, simply head for the nearest beach where "our young people in their unafraid companionship preach and practice a freedom formerly unknown." The photograph to the right shows the model wearing a one-piece bathing costume, an outfit that religious leaders (including the Pope), local communities, and parents had all campaigned against through much of the decade. Of all of the changes in women's appearance throughout the period, and the "modern young woman" looked very different from the "new woman" of the 1880s, none generated more concern or provoked more efforts at censorship than this beachwear. The controversy provides us with a way of grasping some of the ways in which women chose to be modern—beach censorship failed because women insisted upon wearing it—as well as some of the ways they defined their new freedom.

Under the banner headline WARS ON BATHING "SIRENS," the *New York Times* for October 5, 1925 reported that the "village of Valley Cottage in Rockland County is up in arms over the invasion of flappers, who during the last season paraded the roads in their one-piece bathing suits." Residents formed the Valley Cottage Community League to urge Governor Al Smith to send state police to patrol the village and enforce the ban on one-piece suits. The hamlet of Valley Cottage lacked a police force of its own. In its absence a kind of vigilante justice prevailed. League spokesman Vito Pascal told the reporter: "Several times during the Summer the wives of some of our members ran out into the roads with switches and paddywhacked these sirens back into their bungalows." Another "wrong crowd" overran Monmouth Beach in New Jersey, so some of its residents charged. A judge, however, refused to uphold their complaints. "Judging from the popularity of the bathers' parades staged at some of our seashore resorts," he ruled, "the modern bathing beauty is not so uniformly objectionable to the eye to justify the exercise of the injunctive powers of this court in excluding bathers from the streets of a seashore resort."

These battles continued for the rest of the decade before the censors finally gave up. By then, vast numbers of young people had flouted regulations concerning modest attire in hundreds of communities all across the country despite the arrest of thousands and the imposing of fines against thousands more. All were the object of impassioned indignation that poured from pulpits and editorial pages, not to mention the cottages of Valley Cottage in Rockland County, New York. Their brazen defiance was matched by their determination. And they won out. This is noteworthy because it is the one area of controversy where the advocates of censorship did not succeed. Nudity, even the merest hint thereof, disappeared from the Broadway stage when New Yorkers elected Fiorello LaGuardia mayor in 1932. A revivified Hays Office, vigorously backed by the Catholic Church's Legion of Decency, enforced a stringent Production Code in the movies beginning in 1934. But the bathing skirt and stockings went the way of the bustle.

There was more to the controversy than the desire of swimmers to pursue their favorite pastime unimpeded by skirts and stockings. Many, perhaps most, of the women who adopted the new bathing costume could not even swim. They flocked to beaches to bathe in the sun, not the water. Even more significant, is that they came to be seen. They sought, in the parlance of the day, to be "bathing beauties," a term taken from the movies. Local entrepreneurs began to drum up business by staging bathing-beauty contests at local resorts. Beauty contests themselves had been popular for decades. The innovation was the parade of contestants in bathing costumes.

Here She Is . . .

The contests generated, of course, much the same prudish recoil that the one-piece bathing suit produced but with a difference. Horror at the degree of exposure that had become common at the beach spelled prudery pure and straight. Beauty contests, to the contrary, connected bathing suits with the celebration of superficiality, the notion that a judge's idea of beauty conferred some sort of virtue on the winner. The very act of judging, moreover, required absurdities of invention. Here is a recollection from the illustrator Norman Rockwell, who wrote of his stints in Atlantic City in "36—24—36 WOW!" in his autobiographical *My Adventures as an Illustrator*. He gives one of the few first-hand accounts of the early beauty pageants. The judges were all well-known artists and illustrators, among them Howard Chandler Christy and James Montgomery Flagg. Rockwell's version of the event notes that they all worried about how to judge the contest. The Chamber of Commerce gave them no instructions, "so we talked it over among ourselves." One judge came up with a plan.

> . . . we'll give each feature — eyes, nose, lips, etc. — and each part— legs, shoulder, neck, etc. — an ideal score of ten points, and then we'll grade each feature and every part of every girl, add up the scores, and the girl with the higher score wins. Well none of the rest of us could think of anything better so we tried the system.
>
> The judge who had thought it up had a wonderful time measuring all the girls — bust, waist, hips, etc. But unfortunately his system didn't work.

A press report at the time makes the judging less random than Rockwell would remember. "Joseph Cummings Chase, one of the jury of artist experts who participated in the difficult task of picking the winner [in 1923], [said] 'Miss Campbell is possessed of great vivacity and an inherent shyness that constitute a wonderful combination. She is typically American and altogether an ideal type. Her forebears for ten generations have been American born.'" Miss Campbell, in short, precisely fit the description of the American Girl Edmund Wilson credited Ziegfeld with glorifying every year. Chase's reference to the winner's forebears underscores the influence of eugenics upon the popular culture of the decade. The judges, it seems, considered only a Nordic ideal of beauty.

The beauty contests the reformist magazine *Outlook* declared on September 10, 1924, to be "the vulgarest thing in America."

We can think of nothing better designed to develop a false point of view in the minds of the youthful contestants . . . than the notoriety, which is given them in press and film. These contests lack the wholesomeness of athletic contest, for victory is given for something which has no relation to achievement or skill. They set up Mack Sennett as a standard of customs and manners; they touch nothing they do not degrade

In 1927 the National Council of Catholic Women called the contests "a backward step in the civilization of the world." The *Washington Star* thought so, too. The *Boston Post* termed the contests "exhibitions of feminine semi-nakedness before crowds of ogling men."

Even Mary Katherine Campbell, who won the Inter-City Beauty Contest in 1922 and 1923 and thus the title "Miss America," and was runner-up in 1924, announced in an article for *Collier's* magazine of February 14, 1925, that there would be "No Beauty Shows for My Daughter": "From what I have seen of beauty shows and beauty contests," she wrote, "there is a fascinating glamour about them, but it is that of Fairyland with an artificial foundation."

Most beauty contestants, and winners, could expect no more than the thrill of being admired, and that satisfied them. But in an era of commodified fantasy, the dream of a greater prize loomed. Perhaps Hollywood would notice. And for some contestants, that dream became reality. The first to succeed was the 1925 Miss America, Fay Lumpier. Lasky-Famous Players, later to become Paramount Studios, decided to produce a film on the pageant, *The American Venus*, and cast Lumpier as the winner. The studio also hired a number of other contestants to play her rivals for the title. Given Hollywood's importance in creating the "bathing beauty," this scheme seemed appropriate.

A Whiff of Scandal

Charges by the New York City newspaper, the *Graphic*, that the pageant had been fixed so that Lanphier would win the Miss America contest for the next two years and led to its being discontinued after 1927. Yet in 1928 the *Graphic* admitted when taken to court that there had been no basis in fact for its accusations. Lasky-Famous Players wanted to feature whoever won the title. And the eagerness of the contestants to get into the movies, demonstrated by the willingness of many of them to play themselves in the film, made unnecessary any fear on the part of the studio that the winner, whoever she turned out to be, would refuse its offer. The *Graphic* attempted yet another scandal story, about an attempt by Earl Carroll to rig part of the competition leading up to the Atlantic City Miss America pageant. The city's Chamber of Commerce, which had always complained that the contest lost money, decided in 1928 that the negative publicity was

Ford Sterling plays a judge and Louise Brooks a contestant in *An American Venus,* 1925.

harming the image of the resort as a place where families could enjoy themselves and ceased participating in the pageant. It reversed its decision, in 1933, as a means of coping with the impact of the Great Depression. Now officially called the "Miss America Contest," the reborn pageant had much stricter rules about eligibility and judging.

The contestants in *The American Venus* stood on various pillars, dressed in low-cut, backless dresses, as the judges examined them from every angle just as Norman Rockwell remembered. The judges also took turns peering through a peephole. As in the revues, the male fantasy allowed the pick of a bevy of beautiful women. The complementary daydream, for the young women in the audience, envisioned Hollywood and stardom.

An interviewer of Louise Brooks

Malcolm H. Hettinger in *Picture-Play* for August 1926 interviewed Louise Brooks:

Here is inspiration for young America, for high-school belles, misses' sizes. And here, perhaps, was a chance to get a message from Louise. "What, Miss Brooks, are the chances for a young girl, fairly pretty, fairly intelligent, to come to the city, and make good?"

A breathless silence preceded her reply.

"The chances," said Louise, "are what she takes."

Brooks would prove over the course of her career that she fit what the politician George Washington Plunkitt called an "honest crook," an opportunist with no effort at hypocrisy. In that, she risked puncturing the male version of the revue fantasy, the dewy-eyed innocence to which Edmund Wilson attributed

Louise Brooks had been in George Whites's *Scandals* and then Ziegfeld's Follies for two years. This is a portrait of Louise Brooks in costume for the *Follies,* found on EBAY

much of the charm of chorus girls. Louise refused to pretend. She had taken her chances. So had tens of thousands of others who became chorus girls during the heyday of the revues. So did more thousands who took the risk by going to Hollywood seeking to break into the movies. They were still the exceptions. The great majority of young women did not even enter a bathing beauty contest. But lots of them did go to beaches where their costumes contributed to a change in the American view of the "undressed angle," as contemporaries sometimes phrased the New Standards.

The Peers as the Authority

Young people went to the beach with friends. And their bathing attire conformed to an ongoing series of collective judgments. Petting was an activity controlled by peers. Couples went to petting parties where they and their peers defined the meaning of "going too far." Popular dances became so because of pressure and agreement. Gilda Gray thrilled Edmund Wilson with her version of the Shimmy in the 1923 *Follies*, but when young people danced to "I Wish I Could Shimmy Like My Sister Kate," peer sensibility determined how frenetic the choreography would become. Different sets of peers decided in varying ways. At some colleges louder and hotter music played than at others. On one campus, perhaps, hemlines rose to the knee; at another, just above or just below. That hardly mattered. What troubled their elders was the realization that young people looked to one another to establish limits or practices previously set by grownups.

Beach censors ran athwart of this shift in popular moral thinking. William Jennings Bryan, by the 1920s well established as the champion of traditional evangelical beliefs and values, liked to declare that he cared much more about the Rock of Ages than about the age of rocks. As he had so often, Bryan articulated something millions felt. They wanted their faith to be a rock, an unchanging and indestructible source of moral guidance. To such people, the rise of the peer group as the monitor of morality destroyed the very possibility of moral behavior.

However different in detail, the myriad decisions made by the peer groups had much in common. All gave some legitimacy to the pursuit of pleasure. All conferred some measure of approval to titillation as a form of sexual play. Hemlines rose everywhere. Dance steps incorporated shaking hips, kicking legs, and freedom from corsets. Cole Porter merely exaggerated in his 1934 song "Anything Goes."

> In olden days a glimpse of stocking
> Was looked on as something shocking,
> But now, heaven knows,
> Anything Goes.
> . . . .

The world has gone mad today
And good's bad today,
And black's white today,
And day's night today,
When most guys today
That women prize today
Are just silly gigolos

. . .

And though I'm not a great romancer
I know that I'm bound to answer
When you propose,
Anything goes. . . Anything goes!

"Good girls" still did not "go all the way." But they went a lot farther than previous standards had allowed. Earl Carroll got it right when he compared his revues with "our young people [who] in their unafraid companionship preach and practice a freedom formerly unknown." What he and other Broadway producers, along with their counterparts in Hollywood and on Madison Avenue, sought to package was titillation. The market stretched ahead virtually boundless.

Marketing Fantasy I: Hollywood

Movie lovers, film scholars, and historians all acclaim *Sherlock, Jr.*, a comedy in 1924 starring Buster Keaton, as one of the most insightful explorations into the ways movie fantasies entrance. The film unfolds as a movie about watching movies, a fantasy about fantasies. Buster Keaton, a character simply called "the Boy" in the subtitles, nearly loses "the Girl" when his rival, "the Sheik," steals her father's watch, pawns it, and plants the pawn ticket in Keaton's pocket. Falsely accused and disconsolate, Keaton resorts to his work as movie projectionist. He tries reading a book about becoming a detective but falls asleep. His dream self then climbs out of his body and sets out to solve the crime, not the theft of the Girl's father's watch, but the theft of jewelry taking place in the film he is projecting. His dream self walks up to the screen and steps into the action, or tries to. The Sheik, a villain in the movie being shown, throws him out. Buster watches for another chance and succeeds in entering into the movie within the movie. The Boy is completely ineffectual; but the detective he becomes on the screen, the brilliant Sherlock, Jr., manages to become the master of every situation. Seeking to prove his own innocence, the Boy attempts to follow the Sheik but learns nothing. Sherlock Jr., single handedly foils a criminal gang led by the Sheik.

Back in the Boy's real world, the Girl believes in his innocence. She visits the pawnshop, gets a description that exonerates the Boy, and then, as the evil Sheik passes the shop window, secures an eyewitness identification. Off she goes to the movie theater to tell the Boy the good news. With his rival out of the way, he realizes he should romance the Girl. But what should he do? Both are shy. The movie within the movie is about to end but not before its hero embraces its heroine, and the Boy follows suit. The Girl melts into his arms. On the screen the hero gives the heroine a passionate kiss. The Boy flinches and settles for a peck on the cheek. The film is about to end. But in the fade-out we see the Boy, the Girl, and their several children. The finale shows the Boy looking bewildered.

Sherlock, Jr. is one of the very few movies to explore how the medium works, including how it plays upon the imaginations of the viewers. A series of sight gags allows the audience to see the difference between film and reality. When the Boy first steps into the movie within the movie, he initially cannot adjust to the rapid shifts from scene to scene and finds himself, for example, trying to dive into a lake only to wind up in a snow bank. Having established the difference, Keaton then undercuts it toward the end of his film. The awakened Boy takes the images on the screen as a realization of reality. How do you kiss a girl? The movie shows him, step by step.

The film provided its viewers with exactly what the Boy himself sought, a temporary break from ordinary life. For them, the primary fantasy revolved around "Boy gets Girl" despite the efforts of the Sheik and the Boy's own shyness and clumsiness. This formula Keaton used again and again as did Harold Lloyd, another popular comedic star. It was one of several recurrent movie fantasies. Filmgoers imagined themselves going to faraway places, having romantic encounters with impossibly beautiful lovers, catching desperados, matching wits with criminal masterminds, rescuing damsels in distress or being rescued. These daydreams formally submitted, much of the time, to Victorian proprieties, as the enormous popularity of movie star Mary Pickford attests.

But even when movies did portray Victorian values in a positive way, conforming to what would-be censors considered wholesome or decent, another level of fantasy associated with the stars themselves undercut the ostensible moral message. Pickford's highly publicized affair with the actor Douglas Fairbanks, his divorce, their grand estate of Pickfair celebrated in movie magazines, the comings and goings of their famous friends like Charlie Chaplin, countered the screen image of "America's Sweetheart." Or more precisely, her glamorous off-screen life dominated her persona as screen icon. "America's Sweetheart" did not live at "Pickfair" or own a substantial share of United Artists.

Many films openly undermined Victorian beliefs. Mack Sennett's Keystone Kops films, a source for much of the visual vocabulary of silent comedy, led the way. Filled with chases of every kind, bathing beauties, and stock characters, his two-reelers poked fun at everyone and everything. Wives henpecked husbands. Husbands ogled young women. The police never caught the right man. Judges never served justice. This became the moral universe of the silent comedy. In it the hero, usually small of stature and not handsome—Harold Lloyd, though short, wore glasses on screen to undercut his good looks—routinely falls in love with a pretty girl but is too shy and awkward to win her. Instead a smarmy rival threatens to gain her affections. Through the sheerest dumb luck, the hero performs a series of amazing acrobatic stunts and foils his rival. Lloyd's *Safety Last*, in which he climbs up the side of a building and hangs on to the bent hand of the clock at the top, is the classic example. His character too is simply called "the Boy." His Everyman status was also essential for the fantasy to work. At the fade-out "the Girl" gazes lovingly into his eyes. Virtue again finds its reward. But only as a result of a series of unlikely happenstances.

Still other films dispensed with Victorian notions altogether. Valentino led the way. In *The Sheik* he carries Agnes Ayers off into the desert; in *Son of the Sheik*, he mistakenly believes that the beautiful dancing girl Yasmin, played by Vilma Banky, has betrayed him. For revenge he rapes her. Why did so many women flock to the film? The fantasy, as in *Gone With The Wind* when Rhett Butler carries a struggling Scarlet O'Hara off to bed, consists of being ravaged but by a dream lover. In both films, the heroine looks blissful afterwards. In such a fantasy the woman in the audience could imagine performing acts her usual inhibitions would prohibit. If forced, she would be guiltless. And if the one committing the act were Valentino or Clark Gable, she could give morality a welcome rest.

The Tarzan movies, inspired by the writer Edgar Rice Burroughs, provided another sort of fantasy, a sexual Garden of Eden before the Fall. Beautiful Jane Porter accompanies her father on safari in Africa, where she encounters the Ape Man. Although a British aristocrat by birth, he is a perfect creature of nature, having been raised by gorillas. Tarzan rescues Jane, several times, from foes animal and human, and carries her off to his home in the trees. There she instructs him in the rudiments of language and he teaches her the ways of the wild. Soon Jane's garb becomes as abbreviated as Tarzan's. They swing on vines, swim in jungle pools, and explore the delights of sex. Of course, beasts and villains intrude. Yet there is no doubt that the two consummate their relationship. And Jane's decision to remain with Tarzan, without the benefit of a clergyman's blessing, forms the happy ending. *Variety* 's review of *Tarzan and His Mate* (1934), the second to feature Olympic swimmer Johnny Weissmuller and Maureen O'Sullivan, captures much of the series' appeal:

> It may be silly, but it continues to be fascinating, this "Tarzan" theme. In *Tarzan and His Mate*, second of the Metro series with Johnny Weissmuller, the monkeys do everything but bake cakes and

the very human elephants always seem on the verge of sitting down for a nice quiet game of chess; yet the picture has a strange sort of power that overcomes the total lack of logic and (probably most important) it is an extraordinarily beautiful photographic specimen. Picture will doubtless draw business.

Tarzan No. 1 ended with Tarz and the white girl from England at peace in their jungle kingdom. They're again at peace as No. 2 ends, but in the 92 minutes between the two fade-outs they're almost in pieces, several times. . . . There are gory battles between bands of natives to liven up the proceedings when Tarzan isn't fighting some jungle beast that is just about to devour his mate.

Why did such preposterous stories have such appeal? Swinging from trees, battling lions, defeating villains, romancing the beautiful Jane—all fed a common male fantasy of perfect virility. Women in the audience could dream of throwing off all of the inhibitions parents and pastors had sought to instill. Jane shed more than her clothes. She threw aside all of the conventions of courtship. There was nothing coy here, and she exhibited as much eagerness as Tarzan to explore the delights of sex. And Tarzan, in between his improbable feats of strength, proves a very attentive lover.

Simply going to the movies became a fantastic, romantic event. Even the architecture of the theater reflected the theme of fantasy. In 1922 Grauman's Egyptian Theater opened in Los Angeles and his Chinese film emporium followed a few years later. Theaters in other cities adopted similarly fanciful and exotic themes. Some resembled French chateaux; others evoked the Ottoman Empire at its height. Whatever the architectural style, theaters in large cities resembled palaces in size and opulence. New York's Roxy held over 6,000. Other theaters had their own hospital wards and exercise rooms. Bathrooms became lounges with hovering attendants offering towels. Moviegoers entered what Walt Disney would later dub a magic kingdom. They could imagine themselves, for a few hours, in imperial China or on one of Sinbad's voyages or at a Newport "cottage" of a millionaire.

Even after returning home, they could still recapture the fantasy. Studios manufactured stories about their stars almost as energetically as they turned out films. These filled the fan magazines like *Photoplay*, *Screenland*, and dozens of others. Readers devoured stories about movie stars as avidly as they attended their films. Few cared about their relationship to reality. In the magazines, everyone looked beautiful, every dress exquisite, every motorcar brand new and chauffeur driven. Stars cavorted in nightclubs, partied in mansions, and devoted their time to worthy causes while still showing up on the set on time for a shooting at dawn looking fresh and well rested.

Yet in stories about Hollywood, studios encountered competition.

Gossip columnists and other writers created a darker layer of fantasy. In these accounts screen stars defied the Volstead Act, experimented with narcotics, engaged in illicit sex, wrecked automobiles, and even committed murder. Fans devoured these stories, too. One of the earliest is "The Sins of Hollywood: An Exposé of Movie Vice," by the Hollywood Publishing Co. in 1922. In it a former *Photoplay* editor retailed gossip about a host of Hollywood figures after thinly disguising their identities. Rudolph Valentino, for example, became Adolpho. Roberts then described him as a gigolo working in dance halls. Movie magazines quickly saw the profit in the scandal market. In *SHADOWLAND* for November 1921 appeared an article by the novelist Theodore Dreiser, "Hollywood: Its Morals and Manners, Part One: The Struggle on the Threshold of Motion Pictures." In it he explained the "casting couch." Women coming to Hollywood soon learned "of the general assumption of those connected with the work, the males in particular, of course, that all women connected with the work are potentially, if not actually, of easy virtue. Therefore, if they resent this and still linger about the scene, ambition or not, the responsibility is at least in part theirs. . . . They are by no means innocents or lambs being led to the slaughter. And not a few relish the personal and emotional freedom which life in this realm provides."

Movie fans swallowed both the pieces that extolled every actor and actress as a paragon of virtue and the gossip that painted stars as, in Dreiser's words, "mentally liberated from most of the binding taboos which govern in the social realms from which they emanate." Each, like the different movie genres, offered its own sort of fantasy.

If impressionable young people, especially women, went to the movies several times a week, poured over fan magazines, and turned actors and actresses into participants in their fantasy lives, surely moral standards would crumble. Young men and women would absorb the same false sense of glamour as beauty pageant contestants. So reasoned the advocates of censorship. Hindsight tells us that, like prohibition, censorship was often worse than the vices it attempted to suppress. Better Mae West's scandalous play *Sex* on Broadway than efforts to censor the works of Eugene O'Neill. Better Mae West's *doubles entendres* in *She Done Him Wrong* than the prudery of the Motion Picture Production Code.

At the same time, proponents of censorship asked some important questions: Was indulging in fantasy through film an innocent way to banish your troubles? What if the fantasy involved flouting moral conventions? Fans of the actor Wallace Reid, for example, did not rush out and become opium addicts any more than devotées of Mary Miles Minter, a suspect in the murder of Director William Desmond Taylor, suddenly began to fall in love with wife deserters old enough to be their fathers. Even in the matter of hemlines, it is by no means clear that they rose faster in the movies, or sooner. Yet movies fostered to a major shift in the way ordinary people thought about moral issues by playing a part in two important developments: the validation of pleasure as a goal of human life and the presumptive innocence of fantasy. Men did not take to wrestling lions, women did not begin swinging on vines. But moviegoers did daydream about guiltless sexual indulgence. It was pleasurable. It did not do any harm. Advocates of censorship believed that the immoral should also be unthinkable because titillation did change peoples' moral standards, not by argument but by permitting imaginary transgressions.

Marketing Fantasy II: Madison Avenue

Fantastic as the movies, the fan magazines, the beauty pageants, and the revues all were, they formed part of the New Era of capitalism. They made money, particularly the movies. They all designed, packaged, and marketed one of the core products of the interwar years, escapism. Advertising offered the same temporary surcease.

Like many of the ads of the era, that on the right emphasized what the text called "the art of gracious living." Fashionably dressed, relaxing over coffee after dinner in a luxurious restaurant, a beautiful woman and her unseen companion enjoy a cigarette. She epitomizes, we learn from the text, one of those "fortunate people who seem to be born with a flair for living." Like her friends she has an instinct for lovely clothes, fine food, good books; and she smokes Camels. The advertisement does not suggest that, by smoking Camels, the consumer would join the class of the fortunate. Such people are born that way. In the same issue, another ad, this one for Selby's Shoes, makes the same point. "The Gifted Women," those "charming creatures who are the outstanding personalities in any gathering," are unfailingly drawn to Selby's new Arch Preserver shoes. Would purchase of the same product make the buyer "gifted" or "charming" or "outstanding?" No. Such ads insisted on an innate inequality. The fortunate, the gifted, set the styles. They formed an aristocracy of taste.

Another drawing, appearing in the *Saturday Evening Post*, featured the Broadway star Gertrude Lawrence. "Even her dearest enemy," the text reads, "would concede that Gertrude Lawrence is one of the smartest women who ever stepped across a stage or

Above is an image cropped from a Camels cigarette ad published in the *Delineator* magazine in 1929. John McClymer's private collection

a drawing room." Naturally, it continues, "she went to Paris twice a year to buy her clothes from the finest *couturier*," in this case Lucien Lelong. He also designed her Elgin watch. Elgin had signed up a number of Paris designers. As a result, "the usual situation is reversed." You did not have to go to Paris. "Paris has come to you" at your local jewelers where you can purchase an Elgin watch in your own price range. Everything about the image and text emphasizes that Miss Gertrude Lawrence rests several cuts above the common run of humanity.

Most prominent is the elongated figure the illustrator has given her. One observer notes that Lawrence would have had to be over seven feet tall for the drawing to be anatomically accurate. Next comes the assurance that everything she chooses is the best. Even her "dearest enemies" concede that. And why dearest enemies? Gertrude Lawrence's talent and taste inspire envy. Nothing in the ad suggests that you can become as smart as she. You can, of course, buy an Elgin watch which, the ad tells you, sells from $15 to $650. Nothing in the text implies that the $15 watch will be as nice as the $650 one.

Another ad proclaims that 102 New York and Boston debutantes use Woodbury soap. The text rhapsodizes on their dancing to the "seductive strains of the latest jazz." Handsome men gather round to pay "sophisticated compliments" and offer "delicious invitations." These ladies live a dazzling existence. And they have to look just so. So they must enter upon every engagement alert, starry-eyed, and—most important—with beautiful smooth skin. How do "these engaging young creatures" manage? They use Woodbury Soap and so could you. A fifteen-cent cake of the soap will last up to six weeks. That makes it affordable to anyone. These debutantes have the money to buy any soap and the leisure to discuss beauty products with experts. If they choose Woodbury's, you can trust their judgment. Debutantes are born with a flair for food, fashion, and fun. This accounts for the emphasis in the advertisement on numbers: 102 debutantes chose Woodbury's. This was more than half of those surveyed. Other soaps could claim, on average, only half a dozen debutantes.

Another Woodbury's ad, featuring the same product and again using the debutante motif, shows a young woman in an evening gown taking "that last lingering look in the mirror." Young society girls,

Above: Woodbury Soap ads invite the consumer into the glamorous world of the debutante.
Both ads appeared in *The Ladies Home Journal*; they are re-produced in the Rolland Marchand Collection at the University of California at Davis.

whether from conservative Philadelphia or jazz-loving New York or the romantic cities of the South, all choose Woodbury soap and by substantial margins. No male admirers appear in the accompanging illustration. A common prop in advertisements for beauty products, a mirror, completes the image. Many ads stressed the anxiety looking into a mirror could induce. "Most men ask 'Is she pretty?' Not 'Is she clever?'" a 1924 Palmolive ad notes, as a woman gazes at her reflection. From an early age when little girls read *Snow White and the Seven Dwarfs*, they knew that the mirror tells the tale of who is truly beautiful. Taking that "last lingering look" mirrors what all women presumably do before heading off to a night out. But the woman in the illustration is not Everywoman. She is beautiful, well-born, perfectly groomed and coiffed. Her reflection shows a skin radiant with fresh beauty. The ad does not preach equality. It offers fantasy. Imagine yourself heading off to a ball wearing the most gorgeous gown, certain to be the belle of the evening.

By Way of Conclusion

Fantasy became a consumer good in the interwar period even as Madison Avenue used it to sell other consumer goods. This marketing of fantasy formed a core component of the new ethos of consumption that triumphed, albeit unevenly, in the 1920s and carried over into the 1930s. New Era capitalism required a new ethic that sanctioned the immediate gratification of desire. Pleasure became an end in itself. Restraint ceased to be virtuous. It is difficult, even now, to grasp the magnitude of the change. For the first time in American cultural history the marketplace and religion came into conflict. Previously, the traditional Judeo-Christian virtues reinforced the lessons of the market. Consider Andrew Carnegie's advice on "The Road to Business Success;"

> There is one sure mark of the coming partner, the future millionaire; his revenues always exceed his expenditures. He begins to save early, almost as soon as he begins to earn. No matter how little it may be possible to save, save that little. Invest it securely, not necessarily in bonds, but in anything which you have good reason to believe will be profitable, but no gambling with it, remember. A rare chance will soon present itself for investment. The little you have saved will prove the basis for an amount of credit utterly surprising to you. Capitalists trust the saving young man. For every hundred dollars you can produce as the result of hard-won savings, Midas, in search of a partner, will lend or credit a thousand; for every thousand, fifty thousand. It is not capital that your seniors require, it is the man who has proved that he has the business habits which create capital, and to create it in the best of all possible ways, as far as self-discipline is concerned, is, by adjusting his habits to his means. Gentlemen, it is the first hundred dollars saved which tells. Begin at once to lay up something. The bee predominates in the future millionaire.

The businessman of the 1920s who personified the cultural hero of the hour, paid as much attention to spending money as to making and saving it, a phenomenon symptomatic of other changes. Temperance had been a mark of good character. Carnegie warned that drinking meant a sure road to ruin for a young man in business. In the interwar years, however, the smart set gathered for cocktails nightly before dinner or the theater.

The furor that such a shift in popular moral thinking occasioned did not focus upon the underlying incompatibility of New Era capitalism and traditional Judeo-Christian moral teaching. To frame the issue in such terms would have been virtually impossible for contemporaries. The recent Red Scare had fused capitalism and Americanism. "The business of America is business," President Coolidge supposedly proclaimed. Meanwhile, the marketplace actually openly challenged religious values, implicitly extolling itself for its capitalist success in providing pleasure and fantasy. Surely the fusion of enjoyment with capitalism, which as everybody knew was America, moral, and godly, spoke well for both. The connection remains in an American creed that found its articulation early in the twentieth century.

VI

Fundamentalism and "the Acids of Modernity"

"I don't know any more about theology than a jack-rabbit does about ping-pong, but I'm on the way to glory."—Billy Sunday

By 1920, many evangelical Protestants thought of themselves as besieged. Biblical scholarship, sometimes called the "higher criticism," had demonstrated that the books of the Old and New Testaments do not form a single continuous account of God's dealings with humankind. The four canonical gospels, *Matthew*, *Mark*, *Luke*, and *John*, for example, existed for a time along with others that early Christians regarded with as much devotion. The process of determining which to include in the New Testament had taken generations; it involved much theological argument but no attempt to trace the historical origins of the texts.

The new scholarship of the late nineteenth and the early twentieth century did exactly this. In the process it revealed both the diversity of the traditions that had come together in the Bible and the difficulty of deciphering what specific passages might mean. Both were devastating developments since they called into question the literal interpretation of the Bible that Martin Luther, the sixteenth-century founder of Protestantism, had insisted on. "Here I stand" was his famous refusal to accept the rulings of the Pope, if they conflicted with scripture. Whatever the Bible said was true. And for understanding it a devout heart was as important as any knowledge. Therefore the good Christian regularly read the Bible as the spread of literacy in Protestant countries accompanied translations of scripture from Latin into native languages. Protestants tried to base all important decisions on what it taught. The historical study of the Bible, by calling into question the believer's ability to understand the Word correctly, threatened the very basis of Protestantism. Developments in science, notoriously in the case of evolution but just as disturbingly in geology, also made a literal reading of much of the Bible intellectually irresponsible. How were evangelicals to respond?

Some religious leaders known as modernists sought to find ways

92

to understand scripture in the light of new knowledge. This meant abandoning the belief in miracles, the virgin birth of Jesus, and a literal Second Coming along with the conviction that biblical prophecies could clarify current events or current events could clarify prophetic writings. Modernism might put an end to what a hymn calls the "Old Time Religion." Like Billy Sunday, many evangelicals would not, could not, adapt faith to modern scholarship. They became fundamentalists, people who identify Christianity with a literal understanding of the Bible, belief in Jesus as God and in the redemptive character of his death and resurrection, his return at the end of days, and a Last Judgment. If modernizers moved away from any of these fundamentals, traditionalists believed, they ceased to be Christians.

Accommodation, in the judgment of fundamentalists, came with too high a price. J. Gresham Machen, a professor at Princeton Theological Seminary, wrote in *Christianity and Liberalism,* published in 1923: "The liberal attempt at reconciling Christianity with modern science has really relinquished everything distinctive of Christianity, so that what remains is in essentials only that same indefinite type of religious aspiration which was in the world before Christianity came upon the scene."

What modernists particularly gave up was the certainty that Jesus was their personal savior. Evangelicalism had achieved its great influence over American life by means of the revival, which especially during the Second Great Awakening in the decades before the Civil War brought the conversion experience of being "born again in the spirit." Millions found salvation through it. Whoever sought to accommodate Christianity with historical and scientific findings turned away from revivalism and from conversion.

Fundamentalism came with a price as well. Believers had to choose ignorance over knowledge. They had to insist upon doctrines that contradicted well-established facts. Evolution provides the most obvious example. Fundamentalist Bible study also required the believer to avoid learning anything about the historical origins of scripture.

Historians have not explored this choice. Most have simply dismissed fundamentalism as the religion of a lunatic fringe. Scholars who do take it seriously treat fundamentalists as people sincerely seeking the truth. But fundamentalism begins in a commitment to willed ignorance. Fundamentalists genuinely believe in the lack of error in the Bible, to be sure, and in a variety of other doctrines. Most also believe in what they call creation science, the attempt to reconcile the geological record with a literal reading of the account of creation in Genesis. Doing so, though, entails blocking out, rather than considering, the massive evidence collected by biologists for evolution and their explanations of how change in species occurs. For this willed rejection of evidence historians let off fundamentalists too easily, perhaps thinking that the reason why fundamentalists reject it is a personal mater in which schools should not intrude. Tolerance thus also becomes the enemy of scholarship.

Fundamentalism was caught between the experiential knowledge of salvation, so often gained in a revival, drawing on assumptions about a specifically describable plan of salvation, and scientific knowledge about the character of the historical and the biological past, whatever their natural or divine origins. Suddenly, they became irreconcilable. The conviction gained in a revival or in a church service or in solitary prayer lost none of its force after the split. Conversion continued to change believers' lives. Believers knew Jesus was their personal savior. They also knew that, as the Reverend Bob Jones said in founding his university in South Carolina, scientific and historical knowledge would shake their faith. The choice of faith in the literal details of scripture necessarily required believers to close their minds on an array of issues. Any open discussion on matters ranging from medical research to choosing books for the local library could threaten faith. Fundamentalists from the outset had to adopt a fortress mentality. This has had profound implications for American history and culture.

One symptom of the crisis in evangelicalism in the 1920s was the effort on the part of fundamentalists to purge several mainstream churches of modernists. Another, closely related, was the Scopes Trial in Dayton, Tennessee. John Scopes was a teacher charged with violating the state's Butler Act that prohibited the teaching in public schools of "any theory that denies the story of the Divine Creation of man as taught in the Bible, and to teach instead that man has descended from a lower order of animals."

Still another sign of the degree to which fundamentalists considered themselves under siege was the belief in the imminence of the Second Coming among evangelicals: the notion that the end of the world is at hand. From the 1870s on, it became a touchstone of faith for millions. The related appeal to fundamentalists of the Ku Klux Klan, which had its own vision of a coming final struggle, what the Book of Revelations calls Armageddon, indicated a profound unhappiness about the directions in which American society was moving. At the same time membership in evangelical churches continued to grow. Crisis with growth is a paradox worth investigating.

Evangelicalism offered believers a coherent way of understanding experience. At its heart were notions of grace and of sin. American children learned at mother's knee that, as the New England Primer had put it, "In Adam's fall we sinned all." But the revival, the experience of conversion that came with the sincere acknowledgment of the convert's own sinfulness and the acceptance of God's grace, made it possible to triumph over sin. The notion of triumph is critical. Evangelicals did not simply believe, as their Anglican and Puritan forebears had, that they were saved through divine grace. They believed that grace transformed them. In the doctrine of Perfectionism, formulated by the great nineteenth-century revivalist Charles Grandison Finney in his *Lectures to Professing Christians*, Christians found assurance that they could conquer sin. The drunkard could stop drinking; the adulterer become faithful; the slaveholder free his slaves. The sinner could stop using the name of the Lord in vain, observe the Sabbath, be truthful. This notion of conquest over sin unleashed an enormous energy in the converted. They could remake themselves. And since society in their minds was simply a collection of individuals, they could remake it as well. The very character of evangelicalism before the Civil War dictated that its adherents be reformers. Revival converts provided much of the impetus behind the abolition movement. They organized Sunday Schools and social service agencies like the Young Men's and Young Women's Christian Associations. Reform meant eradicating sin: the sin of intemperance, the sin of slavery, prostitution, gaming, violations of the Sabbath.

The Monkey Trial
Darrow: "What do you think?"
Bryan: "I do not think about things I don't think about."
Darrow: "Do you think about things you do think about?"
Bryan: "Well, sometimes." [Laughter.]
—from Clarence Darrow's examination of William Jennings Bryan during the Scopes Trial of 1925

Contemporaries regarded the "Monkey Trial," as the trial of John T. Scopes for violating the Butler Act was sometimes called, as a climax in the ongoing struggle between fundamentalist Christians and their adversaries. William Jennings Bryan had championed the evangelical cause his whole adult life. He challenged modernists within his own Presbyterian Church; he crusaded for prohibition; and in the 1920s, he divided his time between efforts to persuade state legislatures to adopt laws prohibiting the teaching of evolution and a campaign to promote Florida's real estate. Clarence Darrow, a long-time champion of agnosticism and perhaps the most celebrated defense attorney of the era, offered his services to Scopes. In an odd twist he called Bryan as a defense witness and Bryan accepted eagerly. This put the two technically on the same side, and they were in fact insofar as both the defense and the prosecution wanted a conviction. Why Bryan wanted a conviction is obvious enough. He supported the Butler law. The reason the American Civil Liberties Union, which had advertised in the Tennessee press for a teacher willing to challenge the law, wished for a conviction is that Scopes's forces might then get the case appealed on the ground that the Butler law violated both the Tennessee and the federal Constitution. The Supreme Court had not yet ruled on whether the Fourteenth Amendment restrains states from violating freedom of speech and religion in the same way that the First Amendment does; such a decision would be a major victory for civil liberties. Darrow accepted this legal strategy but intended to bring in scientists and theologians to testify against the fundamentalist understanding of the origins of creation and humanity; the prosecution did not want testimony about evolution. Its lawyers contended, and the judge ruled, that the issue before the court was a simple question of fact: Had John T. Scopes violated the Butler Act? Testimony about evolution was irrelevant.

Why, then, did the antagonists Bryan and Darrow enter in effect into their bizarre collaboration to confront each other in court? They did so for a purpose that the two of them, as attorneys, should have known to be out of place in a courtroom. Darrow wanted to attack the antievolutionists; Bryan wanted to uphold the Old Time Religion, and judging by the increased number of "Born Agains" Bryan beat Darrow (which is not the conventional interpretation). So they turned the trial into an argument that belonged not there but in biological laboratories and on the bookshelves of scholars in the languages and history of the Old Testament.

Scopes probably had not violated the Butler Act. He taught biology only as a substitute teacher and, when approached about volunteering to challenge the law, he observed that he could not remember whether evolution had come up during those classes. (Equally noteworthy is that it was Dayton's economic and civic leaders who persuaded him to challenge the law. They saw it as a way of drawing attention to the town.) But the legal details that the trial was supposedly all about soon became inconsequential to the trial as a drama. Darrow had called Bryan as an expert witness on the Bible. This should have been inadmissible, as the judge rightly ruled the following day. But on that blistering July day in 1925 Bryan ignored objections made by other members of the prosecution legal team, including Tennessee's attorney general, and volunteered to testify. There would be a bare knuckles battle between the best-known upholder of traditional evangelical Christianity and the village agnostic.

Darrow's cross-examination of Bryan lasted several hours. It was broadcast live over the radio to much of the country. The Associated Press account, which reported much of it word for word, appeared in newspapers nationwide the following day.

During the exchange over Noah's Ark as reported by the AP, Darrow challenged his witness:

Darrow: "You believe the story of the flood to be a literal interpretation?"
Bryan: "Yes."
Darrow: "When was that flood?"

Bryan: "I would not attempt to fix the date. The date is fixed, as suggested this morning."
Darrow: "About 4004 B.C.?"
Bryan: "That has been the estimate of a man that is accepted today. I would not say it is accurate."
Darrow: "That estimate is printed in the Bible [i.e., the Bible Bryan introduced into evidence]?"
Bryan: "Everyone knows, at least, I think most of the people know, that was the estimate given."

At this point, the prosecution team objected. Darrow, it pointed out correctly, was cross-examining his own witness. This objection failed because, as the Associated Press noted:

Bryan . . . assured the court that he desired the defense attorney to be given latitude, "for I'm going to have some latitude when he gets through."
Arising, he addressed both the court and the crowd: "These gentlemen have not had much chance. They did not come here to try this case. They came here to try revealed religion. I am here to defend it and they can ask me any questions they please."

Bryan's appeal to the people had the desired effect. They cheered on their champion.

The press report continued:

Applause from the spectators brought an interchange of remarks between the attorney and the witness which concluded with the declaration of Darrow that "you insult every man of science and learning in the world because he does not believe in your fool religion."
Another objection came from the attorney-general [of Tennessee], who asserted that Darrow was making an effort to insult the witness. Judge Raulston of nearby Gizzards Cove did not wish to be purely technical and allowed the examination to continue.
The effort to establish the date of the flood was continued, Bryan asserting that the Bible gave the date as about 2340 B.C.

Darrow: "You believe that all the living things that were not contained in the ark were destroyed?"
Bryan: "I think the fish may have lived."
Darrow: "Outside of the fish?"
Bryan: "I cannot say."
Darrow: "No?"
Bryan: "Except that, just as it is. I have no proof to the contrary."
Darrow: "I am asking you whether you believe it."

Bryan: "I do."
Darrow: "That all living things outside of the fish were destroyed?"
Bryan: "What I say about the fish is merely a matter of humor."
Darrow: "I am referring to the fish, too."
Bryan: "I accept that, as the Bible gives it, and I have never found any reason for denying, disputing or rejecting it."

Bryan's jest is worth noting. We normally associate any humor in the trial with Darrow's sarcasm. But Bryan felt quite in control of the situation, comfortable enough to joke.

Darrow: "But the Bible you have offered in evidence says 2340, something, so that 4200 years ago there was not a living thing on the earth, excepting the people on the ark, the animals on the ark and the fishes? Don't you know there are any number of civilizations that are traced back to more than 5000 years?"
Bryan: "We know we have people who trace things back according to the number of ciphers they have. But I am not satisfied they are accurate."
Darrow: "You are not satisfied there is any civilization that can be traced back five thousand years."
Bryan: "I would not want to say there is because I have no evidence of it that is satisfactory."
Darrow: "Would you say there is not?"
Bryan: "Well, so far as I know, but when the scientists differ from 24,000,000 to 860,000,000 in their opinion, as to how long ago life came here, I want them to be nearer, to come nearer together, before they demand of me to give up my belief in the Bible."
Darrow: "Do you say that you do not believe that there were any civilizations on this earth that reach back beyond five thousand years?"
Bryan: "I am not satisfied by any evidence that I have seen."
Darrow: "I didn't ask what you are satisfied with; I asked if you believe it?"
Bryan: "I am satisfied that no evidence I have found would justify me in accepting the opinions of these men against what I believe to be the inspired Word of God."
Darrow: "And you believe every nation, every organization of men, every animal, in the world outside of the fishes. . . ."
Bryan: "The fish, I want you to understand, is merely a matter of humor."

Of course many scholars assert that archaeological evidence proves the continuous existence of civilizations over six thousand years or longer. But scientists often disputed with one another over dates.

Bryan would stick with the Bible, especially since the scientists could not agree. He used an old trick here. He switched from the dating of artifacts, about which there was little dispute, to dating the emergence of life, about which there was a good deal. But Darrow was not about to abandon his main line of questioning because of the trick.

> Darrow: "Don't you know that the ancient civilizations of China are six or seven thousand years old, at the very least?"
> Bryan: "No; but they would not run back beyond the creation, according to the Bible, six thousand years."
> Darrow: "You don't know how old they are; is that right?"
> Bryan: "I don't know how old they are; but probably you do. I think you would give the preference to anybody who opposed the Bible, and I give the preferences to the Bible."
> Darrow: "I see. Well you are welcome to your opinion. Have you any idea how old the Egyptian civilization is?"
> Bryan: "No."
> Darrow: "Do you know of any record in the world, outside of the story of the Bible which conforms to any statement that it is 4200 years ago, or thereabouts, since all life was wiped off the face of the earth?"
> Bryan: "I think they have found records."
> Darrow: "Do you know of any?"
> Bryan: "Records relating [to] the flood, but I am not an authority on the subject."

With Bryan's response that "I think you would give the preference to anybody who opposed the Bible, and I give the preferences to the Bible," the issue was fairly joined. Bryan's attack was not against the scholarship but against the motives of its sponsors. Darrow believed the scientists and historians because their findings undermined a literal interpretation of the Bible. The problem with this argument is that it missed the main point or, more exactly, conceded it. Decades of careful research had generated findings that were incompatible with a literal interpretation of scripture. Darrow's argument was that Bryan willfully chose ignorance, that neither he nor any other fundamentalist dared study archaeology or geology or a range of other subjects, for all feared what they would discover. This Bryan seemed to confirm, when he switched from fact to motive, his and Darrow's. In response to another question, this one about the history of religions, Bryan replied: "I have all the information I want to live by and to die by,"

> Darrow: "And that's all you are interested in?"
> Bryan: "I am not looking for any more religion."

Darrow: "You don't care how old the earth is and how long the animals have been here?"
Bryan: "I am not so much interested in that."

Bryan's answers drove home Darrow's argument. Bryan's was a "fool religion" incompatible with serious thought. Instead of meeting this argument, Bryan continued to rely upon rhetorical tricks. He got a cheer from the onlookers when he said he was more interested in the "Rock of Ages" than in "the ages of rocks." The confrontation came to a climax with this exchange:

"The purpose [of this interrogation] is to cast ridicule on everybody who believes in the Bible, and I am perfectly willing that the world shall know that these gentlemen have no other purpose than to ridicule every person who believes in the Bible," declared Bryan. "We have the purpose of preventing bigots and ignoramuses from controlling the education of the United States, and you know it, that is all," fired back Darrow.

The two faced each other on the platform. The witness asserted:

"I am simply trying to protect the Word of God against the greatest atheist, or agnostic, in the United States. I want the papers to know that I am not afraid to get on the stand in front of him and let him do his worst. I want the world to know that agnosticism is trying to force agnosticism on our colleges and on our schools and the people of Tennessee will not permit it to be done."

H. L. Mencken, one of the most caustic and influential journalists and social commentators of the day, summed up the view of many outside of the fundamentalist camp in an article in *The Baltimore Evening Sun*, September 14, 1925.

I do not know how many Americans entertain the ideas defended so ineptly by poor Bryan, but probably the number is very large. They are preached once a week in at least a hundred thousand rural churches, and they are heard too in the meaner quarters of the great cities. Nevertheless, though they are thus held to be sound by millions, these ideas remain mere rubbish. Not only are they not supported by the known facts; they are in direct contravention of the known facts. No man whose information is sound and whose mind functions normally can conceivably credit them. They are the products of ignorance and stupidity, either or both.

Some writers have attempted to soften the harsh characterization of Bryan offered by Mencken, who covered the trial, and sealed Mencken's view in the popular imagination by the film *Inherit the Wind*. Bryan did not personally believe some of the literal interpretations of scripture he defended that day, they argue. And his objections to evolution rested, to a considerable extent, upon his opposition to Social Darwinism, generally understood to be the conviction that governments should not intervene to help the poor or disabled and often associated with imperialism and eugenics, both of which Bryan opposed. But Bryan did not stake his public case against Darwinism on these grounds. The issue as he posed it was the incompatibility of Christianity with the theory of evolution, and he did so not just in Dayton in 1925. In an article published in the *New York Times* in 1922, he had written:

The objection to Darwinism is that it is *harmful*, as well as groundless. It entirely changes one's view of life and undermines faith in the Bible. . . . If a man accepts Darwinism, or evolution applied to man, and is consistent, he rejects the miracle and the supernatural as impossible. He commences with the first chapter of Genesis and blots out the Bible story of man's creation, not because the evidence is insufficient, but because the miracle is inconsistent with evolution. If he is consistent, he will go through the Old Testament step by step and cut out all the miracles and get rid of all the supernatural. He will then take up the New Testament and cut out all the supernatural—the virgin birth of Christ, His miracles and His resurrection, leaving the Bible a story book without binding authority upon the conscience of man.

Historians commonly see the Bryan who took on Darrow as a semblance of his former self. This hindsight is informed by H. L. Mencken's vitriolic reporting at the time and then reinforced by the play and movie *Inherit the Wind*, especially the scene in which the Darrow character tells the Mencken figure that he has been unfair. This had been a great man, a champion of good causes. It was necessary to defeat him but not to belittle him.

Bryan had done great things. In addition to championing the cause of family farmers and workers, he led the fight against the American conquest of the Philippines. He resigned as secretary of state to protest what he considered President Wilson's deviation from the policy of "strict neutrality." And even though he would die suddenly a few days after the trial ended, Bryan was not in 1925 a shadow of his former self. He was still one of the premier orators of the day and a resourceful as well as experienced debater. If Darrow made him look the fool, it was because he chose to support a cause that was insupportable: He refused to acknowledge that it needed any support beyond his continued insistence that he believed it and that was that. To that extent, Bryan's posture was that which fundamentalists have maintained ever since.

Bryan's efforts to demonstrate that the theory of evolution was a mere "hypothesis," unsupported by compelling scientific evidence, were, as many noted at the time, intellectually feeble if not dishonest. His argument that evolution "has no place for the miracle or the supernatural," however, was perfectly sensible. Anyone who did accept the theory of evolution as applied to human beings would, if consistent, have to dismiss the first chapter of Genesis. On that much, Bryan was on strong grounds. Such a critic would then go on to dismiss much of the rest of scripture, "leaving the Bible a story book without binding authority upon the conscience of man." Bryan and Darrow were in full accord about this. Of course, not everyone is consistent, Bryan added. Many who held evolution to be correct nonetheless held on to traditional Christian beliefs or at least to some of them. They cultivated what a historian has labeled "split-level minds." Or—this was at the heart of the modernist controversy of the 1920s—they attempted to find ways of reconciling science with faith in the Bible as the word of God.

Harry Emerson Fosdick, pastor of the First Presbyterian Church in New York City, answered Bryan in the *Times*. Fosdick was a leading modernist. His response drew upon Biblical scholarship as much as upon science.

Indeed, as everybody knows who has seriously studied the Bible, that book represents . . . the view of the physical universe which everywhere obtained in the ancient Semitic world. The earth was flat and was founded on an underlying sea (Psalm 136:6; Psalm 24:1-2; Genesis 7:11); it was stationary; the heavens, like an upturned bowl, "strong as a molten mirror" (Job 37:18; Genesis 1:6-8; Isaiah 40:22; Psalm 104:2), rested on the earth beneath (Amos 9:6; Job 26:11); the sun, moon and stars moved within the firmament of special purpose to illumine man (Genesis 1:14-19); there was a sea above the sky, "the waters which were above the firmament" (Genesis 1:7; Psalm 148:4) and through "the windows of heaven" the rain came down (Genesis 7:11; Psalm 78:23); beneath the earth was mysterious Sheol where dwelt the shadowy dead (Isaiah 14:9-11); and all this had been made in six days, each of which had had a morning and an evening, a short and measurable time before (Genesis 1). . . .

One who is a teacher and preacher of religion raises his protest against all this [Bryan's defense of literal interpretations] just because it does such gross injustice to the Bible. There is no book to compare with it. The world never needed more its fundamental principles of life, its fully developed views of God and man, its finest faiths and hopes and loves.

Bryan and his followers, Fosdick noted, hated evolution because they feared "that it will depreciate the dignity of man. Just what do they mean? Even in the Book of Genesis God made man out of the dust of the earth. Surely, that is low enough to start and evolution starts no lower." This is a fine rhetorical sleight of hand but evades the question of purpose, so central to Bryan's position. On this, Fosdick wrote:

> So long as God is the creative power, what difference does it make whether out of the dust by sudden fiat or out of the dust by gradual process. . . . Were it decided that God had dropped him from the sky, he still would be the man he is. If it is decided that God brought him up by slow gradations out of lower forms of life, he still is the man he is.

Fosdick assumed that "God is the creative power." Bryan saw no basis in Darwinism for that assumption. Nor could he see how anyone could hold that the Bible could provide "fundamental principles of life" or "fully developed views of God and man" or the "finest faiths and hopes and loves" without believing it was the revealed Word. On what basis could anyone believe in its "fully developed views of God and men" if its account of human creation was false?

The Fundamentals

Non-believers had no use for Bryan. He was, Darrow claimed towards the end of the cross-examination, an ignoramus, a bigot. Mencken was equally vituperative. Yet non-believers found more cogency in Bryan's position than in Fosdick's. This did not lead to any kind words for Bryan. But it did lead to a number of glowing reviews for J. Gresham Machen's book on fundamentalism.

Machen's work marshals evidence to show that the early Christians thought Jesus was the Messiah, that they accepted him as the Son of God, that they regarded his Resurrection as a fact, and that they believed that by his death he had redeemed mankind from sin. They believed, that is, in the "fundamentals." It was perfectly possible to reject these doctrines, Machen pointed out, and still be decent, even devout. But the religion that remained was not Christianity.

As a scholar, Machen had no serious rivals among the modernists and no equals among the fundamentalists. His "brilliant polemic" did indeed demonstrate how far from traditional Christianity the modernists had moved. Yet his attempt to answer in the affirmative the question "whether first-century religion can ever stand in company with twentieth-century science" fell short. His failure sprang from the same source as his success in routing the modernists, his scholarship.

A careful, conscientious scholar, Machen acknowledged that the gospel accounts of Jesus' life were written two generations or so after his death. Those accounts could not stand as exact transcriptions of what Jesus had said and done. They represented rather what some early Christians believed he had said and done. Proving that they believed in his Resurrection, as a result, was a straightforward matter. It would start with the Pauline Epistles as the earliest documents, written within several years of Jesus' death by someone (not all, necessarily, by the historical Paul) who had known a number of the original apostles. Historical research, however, could not demonstrate that the beliefs revealed in these letters were true. For this, Machen had to employ a series of rhetorical questions on the order of "Shall we imagine that the people who created this vast movement were deluded on this central question?" Fundamentalism rested upon belief in the accuracy, word by word, of scripture in its earliest languages. Yet as a conscientious scholar, Machen accepted the historical evidence that the gospels contained not the actual words of Jesus but versions current among some Christian communities forty to seventy years after his death.

Machen's appeal to non-believers like Mencken lay in demonstrating to their satisfaction that modernism was an exercise more in wishful thinking than in theology. Machen, wrote Walter Lippmann, "goes to the very heart of the matter . . . when he insists that you have destroyed the popular foundations of religion if you make your gospel a symbolic record of experience, and reject it as an actual record of events." Machen himself, however, had acknowledged that the Gospels constituted not "an actual record of events" but rather a record of early beliefs. Was that any better than "a symbolic record?" Fundamentalists did not think so. They did not embrace Machen's ideas. Nor did they follow his example of basing their theological positions on historical research. They instead insisted that the Gospels were "an actual record of events," and they rested their case upon the very fact of their insistence.

The Loss of Faith in a "Converted Nation"

Bryan carried on the reform tradition within evangelical Protestantism. He believed in the continuing possibility of a Converted Nation. That belief had informed his famous Cross of Gold speech that won him the Democratic nomination in 1896. The forces seeking to "crucify mankind upon a cross of gold" were sinners. So too the advocates of an American empire in the Philippines and, later, the instigators of the nation's entrance into the World War. Most evangelical spokesmen did not follow Bryan's lead. They turned away from reform, prohibition excepted. Many adopted the view that Jesus would soon return and that there would follow a climactic struggle between good and evil.

One historian suggests reasons for the appeal of this belief. For some it may be "a hedge against the fear of death." The believer will not die. Instead Jesus will return and the saved will be gathered in the "Rapture." Others may be drawn by the promise of "momentarily meeting departed loved ones in the air at Christ's return." More still may be attracted to what another historian calls "the psychology of deliverance, the confidence that current toils, frustrations, disappointments, pains, or difficulties might be immediately eliminated by the appearance of Jesus Christ."

Belief in the imminence of the Second Coming offered believers, and continues to offer, a way of explaining their lives. It was, and is, a theological expression of despair with prevailing social conditions, on the one hand, and of a sense of entitlement on the other. It is the same combination to be found in the appeal of the Ku Klux Klan of the 1920s. "My own group has a special claim to having the dominant say in the way American society works. At the same time, other groups have pushed mine aside." Why did this expression of despair and entitlement become so central to conservative evangelical Protestantism?

Despite successes in much of the nineteenth century, when many of them were in the front ranks of abolitionism and the temperance movement, evangelicals had come to doubt that they could effectively shape American society. Rapid urbanization, industrialization, and the influx of ever-increasing numbers of immigrants, many of them Catholics and Jews, transformed the United States in ways the evangelicals had not anticipated and did not approve. A deeper problem was that evangelical Christianity as a frame for understanding everyday experience worked less and less well.

That steel workers had to work on the Sabbath in the early 1920s constituted a moral issue. So did setting six- and seven-year-old children to working in coal mines. But could the Carnegie Steel Company commit a sin? Was it a sin to employ children? To allow your own children to work? Did economic necessity cancel out the sin? Evangelicalism gave no answers to such questions. Probably most of its adherents did not even ask them. But they define a strange world in which evangelicals now had to live.

The boys in the photograph on the next page worked as nippers and mule drivers. Mules pulled the coal from the face of the seam back to where steam-powered cars were set up to move it to the surface. Nippers opened mine doors so that the mules and their driver could pass through. A number of evangelicals sought to develop a morality, known as the Social Gospel, keyed to the industrial, pluralist society that such photographs revealed to them. They became known as liberals. The Social Gospel, popularized by Walter Rauschenbusch in *Christianity and the Social Crisis* (1908), needed to move beyond a literal reading of scripture to find a basis for this theology. This alarmed many evangelicals. It was wrong, they argued, to import political ideas into belief. Seek your salvation in the original four gospels and work out your politics without claiming they constitute a fifth.

Bryan thought it was possible to apply evangelical principles to the reform of modern problems. This could make him seem to be an

At the close of day. Just up from the shaft. All work below ground in a Penn-sylvania Coal Mine. Smallest boy, next to right hand end is a nipper. On his right, in Arthur, a driver, Jo on Arthur's right is a nipper. Frank, boy on left end of photo, is a nipper, works a mile underground from the shaft, which is 5000 Ft. down.—Photograph by Lewis Hine [his caption] of young boys, circa 1910. Library of Congress.

adherent of the Social Gospel. He was not. He approached the gold standard, imperialism, and other issues in very much the same way that an abolitionist had attacked slavery. Bryan did not think he was living in the "last days." And he retained the optimism that had once characterized evangelicalism. America could be redeemed. Many did not think so any longer. Dwight Moody and then Billy Sunday did win converts by the millions. All faithfully promised to forsake alco-hol, card playing, and dancing. Did America thereby become a holier place? A mere glance at the daily newspaper would reveal the dis-couraging truth. As the vision of the Converted Nation evaporated, evangelicals had to choose. They could continue to battle Satan or they could struggle against evils like child labor where the sin was plain but the sinner hidden behind the legal process of incorporation. Carnegie Steel was not about to approach the anxious bench.

In his Old Time Religion sermon Billy Sunday, no more a Social Gospeler than a modernist, put the matter with characteristic direct-ness. "The way to salvation is not Harvard, Yale, Princeton, Vassar or Wellesley. Environment and culture can't put you into heaven with-out you accept Jesus Christ." In another sermon, Sunday explained:

Some folks do not believe in miracles. I do. A denial of miracles is a denial of the virgin birth of Jesus. The Christian religion stands or falls on the virgin birth of Christ. God created Adam and Eve without human agencies. He could and did create Jesus supernaturally. I place no limit on what God can do. If you begin to limit God, then there is no God.

Sunday's insistence that either the Bible is literally inerrant or "there is no God" made no logical or theological sense. But Sunday was uninterested in the existence of any God but the one of his own faith. If fundamentalist faith was wrong, God did not exist. It is not recorded whether Sunday ever got a chance to explain that to an orthodox Jew or a Unitarian.

Sunday made clear both his disdain for mere learning and his conviction, much as Walter Lippmann put it in *A Preface to Morals*, that "without complete certainty religion does not offer genuine consolation":

> People are dissatisfied with philosophy, science, new thought—all these amount to nothing when you have a dead child in the house. These do not solace the troubles and woes of the world. . . .
>
> Go to some dying man and tell him to pluck up courage for the future. Try your philosophy on him; tell him to be confident in the great to be and the everlasting what is it. Go to that widow and tell her it was a geological necessity for her husband to croak. Tell her that in fifty million years we will all be scientific mummies on a shelf—petrified specimens of an extinct race. What does all this stuff get her? After you have gotten through with your science, philosophy, psychology, eugenics, social service, sociology, evolution, protoplasms, and fortuitous concurrence of atoms, if she isn't bug-

Billy Sunday brought his message to millions in the first decades of the twentieth century.—Billy Graham Center, Wheaton College

house, I will take the Bible and read God's promise, and pray—and her tears will be dried and her soul flooded with calmness like a California sunset.

Sunday's indifference to social problems addressed by the Social Gospel led a young Carl Sandburg to castigate him as a tool of capitalists seeking to exploit the poor:

When are you going to quit making the carpenters
build emergency hospitals for women and girls
driven crazy with wrecked nerves from your
goddam gibberish about Jesus—I put it to you
again: What the hell do you know about Jesus?

Go ahead and bust all the chairs you want to.
Smash a whole wagon load of furniture at every performance.
Turn sixty somersaults and stand on your nutty head.
If it wasn't for the way you scare women and kids,
I'd feel sorry for you and pass the hat. . . . .

You tell people living in shanties Jesus is going to
fix it up all right with them by giving them
mansions in the skies after they're dead and the
worms have eaten 'em.

You tell $6 a week department store girls all they
need is Jesus; you take a steel trust wop, dead
without having lived, gray and shrunken at
forty years of age, and you tell him to look at
Jesus on the cross and he'll be all right.

You tell poor people they don't need any more
money on pay day and even if it's fierce to be
out of a job, Jesus'll fix that all right, all right —
all they gotta do is take Jesus the way you say.

Sandburg mistook for conspiracy Sunday's indifference to reform efforts. Sunday was out to convert sinners, not improve their lives.

Evangelicalism and the "Acids of Modernity"
Walter Lippmann argued that the "acids of modernity" would make orthodox belief impossible. "The suppositions of traditional religion about how the world works have ceased to be consistent with our normal experience in ordinary affairs." Mere consistency, mere logic would force the would-be believer into doubt, Lippmann thought:

[W]hen daily experience for one reason or another provides no credible analogy by which men can imagine that the universe is governed by a supernatural king and father, then the disposition to believe, however strong it may be at the roots, is like a vine that reaches out and can find nothing solid upon which to grow. It cannot support itself. If faith is to flourish, there must be a conception of how the universe is governed to support it.

It is these supporting conceptions . . . that the acids of modernity have eaten away. The modern man's daily experience of modernity makes instinctively incredible to him these unconscious ideas that are at the core of the great traditional and popular religions. . . . With the best will in the world, he finds himself not quite believing.

Lippmann's analysis certainly fits the experiences of people in other modern nations. Across Europe churches have emptied. By 2000 only a minority of Europeans, twenty percent, said that religion "was important in their lives." About the same percentage said they prayed on a regular basis. Yet for the United States, Lippmann's prediction was flat wrong. There, over sixty percent said in the same survey that religion was very important and that they prayed on a regular basis. A 1996 Gallup Poll found that sixty-nine percent of Americans believed in angels; fifty percent thought they had a personal guardian angel.

Why are Americans so different? Why haven't the "acids of modernity" eaten through their faith?

In many cases they have. American Jews attend temple about as infrequently as the French go to Mass. American Catholics too have become less observant. A larger percentage attends Mass than in Europe, but the figure has been declining steadily. And according to unhappy conservatives in the American Church, all too many have become "cafeteria Catholics," putting this teaching on the tray, passing up that one. So, for example, Catholics engage in contraception as much as others in the population despite the hierarchy's denunciation of it as sinful. Indeed, most Catholics no longer hesitate to disagree with their bishops on subjects ranging from capital punishment to gay relationships. Their drift away from orthodox devotion is proceeding more slowly than that of European Catholics, but the overall dynamic is the same. The younger you are, the less likely you are to be observant in practice or orthodox in belief. Older Catholics grew up in a society in which anti-Catholicism still mattered. They identified with their church. Protestantism had been a greater challenge than modernity, and facing it with fortitude was an experience bracing to their faith. Now, if they pray privately in their own way, they no longer stand with the Church Militant. Many Protestant churches have experienced similar declines. There is, as Lippmann argued, a lack of fit between traditional teachings and modern life.

But not all churches are declining. Fundamentalist and other conservative evangelical congregations are growing rapidly. What, among Americans who have found the Lord in evangelical churches, makes them different from Europeans, and from their compatriots?

The answer lies with the Second Coming. The fastest growing evangelical movement, Pentecostalism, for example, is rooted in it. A 1997 survey conducted by the Associated Press revealed that twenty-four percent of all Americans expected the return of Jesus within their lifetimes. This is a faith resistant to science and scholarship, resistant equally to atheism, to modernism, and to a belief in a God revealed in sources other than scripture. No fact presented matters, for those facts are implanted by the forces of evil in an era preceding the Second Coming. For its adherents, this belief explains both their despair at the alien values of the media and the consumer ethos and their joy at being the chosen of the Lord.

VII
"Speaking in Tongues": Sister Aimee Mcpherson and the Pentecostal Revival

In the course of the twentieth century and the beginning of the twenty-first, tens of millions in the United States and hundreds of millions around the world have experienced a religious phenomenon known as Pentecostalism. The word derives from the ancient term for "fiftieth day," on which, so relates a passage in the Acts of the Apostles, the followers of Jesus preached in words that all the hearers, no matter what their native language, could understand. Pentecostals experience Baptism in the Spirit, speak in tongues, attend healing services where they witness or receive miracle cures. Pentecostalism is the fastest growing form of Christianity in the country and one of the fastest globally. It is difficult to estimate the numbers who have embraced it since it is not a single denomination. Most experts estimate that at least twenty million Americans are Pentecostals of various denominations. The figure may be too low because many Methodist and Baptist congregations have adopted Pentecostal beliefs and practices. Pentecostal influence has even reached the Catholic Church in the form of charismatic services including faith healing. This new faith constitutes a new American revivalism. Its influence on American life, though often ignored, is profound.

This Is That (1919), the first autobiography of the Reverend Aimee Semple Mcpherson—Sister Aimee or just "Sister" to millions—describes "a drama enacted under power of Holy Spirit" during her eastern summer tent revival campaign in 1917 in Washburn, Maine. She was just beginning her ministry. This early "illustrated sermon" in Washburn portrays her message as well as her extraordinary success in getting it across. It is based upon one of the parables in the gospel of *Matthew* (Chapter 25: 1-13).

The Drama of the Wise and Foolish Virgins

One night a drama was all worked out in the Spirit, showing forth the ten Virgins, going first with white robes to meet the Bridegroom. They said:
"He delayeth His coming; let us rest."
At first some argued that all should keep awake, for He would come, would come quickly; but finally all were asleep.
Suddenly a loud cry –
"Behold! The Bridegroom cometh! Go ye out to meet Him!" Then all the virgins opened their eyes, and examined their lamps in alarm. The five sisters enacting the part of the wise virgins dance for joy because of the oil, but the foolish begged the wise to share their oil with them. The wise said it was impossible, and sent the foolish to buy oil of Him who had to sell.
Then followed a scene where the foolish knocked at an imaginary door and haggled long over the price they would have to pay for the oil; they wanted to pay only a price which would not inconvenience them or cost a sacrifice, but the man who sold asked for all to give one hundred per cent sacrifice before they could obtain oil. At last the foolish went away, only to find that the wise had been taken up to meet the Lord; then they fell down and tore their hair and wept aloud.
This was followed by a ringing, warning appeal to all to make full surrender, pay the price, buy oil now, for the Bridegroom is at the door.
This was only one of the many wonderful messages and dramas worked out in our midst which were beyond description.

The Bridegroom is Jesus. The virgins are awaiting his Second Coming. The wise have their lamps filled with oil. The foolish do not. Nor are they willing to pay the price, that "one hundred percent sacrifice" of worldly things. This is a detail Sister added. While the virgins are haggling, the Bridegroom comes. The foolish are too late, while "the wise had been taken up to meet the Lord." "Taken up" is Sister's invention too. In *Matthew* we read: "And while they went to buy, the bridegroom came; and they that were ready went in with him to the marriage: and the door was shut." "Taken up" is a reference to the Rapture, the gathering of the Saints in the air described in the *Book of Revelations*.
Despite these variations, Sister Aimee's play hews to the moral of the

gospel parable: "Watch therefore, for ye know neither the day nor the hour wherein the Son of man cometh." "When is He coming?" McPherson asked in her 1921 booklet, *The Second Coming of Christ.* "What is to be done must be done quickly for soon, O soon, will the prophecy be fulfilled wherein our Lord shall reign upon the throne of David."

Within a few years Sister would become the most popular preacher of the day, surpassing even Billy Sunday. Her message was Pentecostalism. The largest Pentecostal church calls each of its congregations an Assembly of God. But many ministers, among them Sister Aimee, founded their own denominations. Hers is the International Church of the Foursquare Gospel, and today it claims over two million members worldwide. Historians of religion agree that Sister Aimee contributed nothing theologically to the new revival. Her importance lay in being its most brilliant and successful exponent.

On January 1, 1923, Sister Aimee opened the Angelus Temple in Los Angeles. Every Sunday evening she preached an illustrated sermon. These far exceeded in grandeur the first one in Maine. Sister hired professional lighting experts from nearby Hollywood along with actors and actresses. Also from the movie studios came sets, wardrobe, and props. Sometimes the casts for these productions numbered in the hundreds. Occasionally Sister Aimee took a leading role. More often she was the narrator who explained to the congregation of more than 5,000 and the radio audience of at least ten times that many what the drama unfolding before them meant. How good were these productions? H. L. Mencken claimed to be unimpressed, as did other journalists who nonetheless wrote feature stories on McPherson in leading magazines. Charlie Chaplin, on the other hand, though himself immune to the power of the Spirit, found the performances entrancing. And crowds lined up hours beforehand to get in.

Sister Aimee has been a perfect subject for biographers. Hers is the classic American self-made success story. In addition, there is the mystery of her disappearance. In 1926 she claimed to have been kidnapped and held for five weeks before she managed to free herself. Then, she said, she walked twenty miles across Mexico's Sonora Desert just south of Arizona. There she was found. Had she been kidnapped? Her followers believed her. Everyone else, including rival clergy such as the Reverend Robert Pierce Shuler (or Rev. Bob as he preferred to be called), decried her story as a hoax. Why were her shoes and clothing in nearly perfect condition? Why had she not asked for water after such a trek? Where was the shack she was held in? In reality, Rev. Bob and others charged, she had run off to a "love nest" with her lover, Kenneth Ormiston, a worker at her radio station. The *Los Angeles Times* reporters assigned to the story turned up evidence that the sound engineer and a woman resembling Sister Aimee had rented a cottage in Carmel by the Sea. They also found witnesses who said they had seen the couple together at several hotels before the disappearance. The love nest story had legs, as newspaper people say; the continuous discovery of new details kept it on the front page for months. Scandal did not stop Sister from continuing her ministry. Equally likely is that her congregation and her radio audience grew.

As fascinating as McPherson is as a biographical subject, the focus upon her personal qualities takes away from a more significant story. Sister Aimee is most important not for her notoriety but for her success in popularizing Pentecostal beliefs and shaping the practices of this new revival. She exemplifies its rejection of modernity in the form of evolution and other products of modern scholarship and its simultaneous embrace of modern media like radio and film. Hers was one of the first electronic ministries. Where she led, the Reverend Oral Roberts, the Reverend Jerry Falwell, and others would follow.

As she liked to point out, McPherson had started with no resources beyond the conviction that the Lord wanted her to preach. She dropped out of high school in a small farming community in Ontario and in 1908 married a preacher, Robert Semple. They moved from one Canadian town to another until they discerned that the Lord wanted them to do missionary work in China. This was a common Pentecostal ambition. Many believed that their ability to speak in tongues would eliminate the chore of learning Chinese. The Spirit would speak through them and, even though they themselves would not understand what they were saying, potential Chinese converts would. This did not happen. Once in Hong Kong, the couple contracted malaria. Aimee and her unborn child survived; Robert Semple did not. The twenty-year-old Aimee went to New York in 1910, where her mother was working with the Salvation Army. Marrying Harold McPherson, she attempted to settle down as a wife and mother. They had a son. Aimee loathed her new domestic life. And according to *This is That*, she felt very guilty that she did. Her husband and mother-in-law took turns telling her that she had everything she could possibly want. She did not. She did not have the opportunity to preach. She described herself as hysterical:

> My nerves became so seriously affected that the singing of the teakettle upon the stove or the sound of voices was unbearable. I implored the little one [her daughter Roberta, whom she had been carrying when she had malaria] to speak in whispers. I hated the sunshine and wanted to keep the shutters closed and the window shades drawn tightly.

She tried to shake off her "lethargy and depression" with household tasks. "Such a fever of restlessness came upon me that it seemed as though I must wear the polish off the furniture and the floors by dusting them so often." Doctors recommended surgery. Prevailing medical doctrine held that a hysterectomy, the removal of the uterus, would cure hysteria. Aimee followed their advice, but her depression continued.

Then appendicitis struck. Aimee was in the hospital recovery room writhing in agony. She was dying, she knew. Once again the Lord summoned her to preach: "WILL YOU GO?" She was going to go, one way or the other, Aimee later wrote; so she said yes. Immediately the pain abated. Within a few weeks Sister was a new woman. Late one night she kept her promise. She bundled up the two children and caught a train for Canada and the family farm. She deposited the children with her parents and set off for a nearby camp meeting. She was on her way. She was twenty-seven, had no formal theological training and no affiliation with any denomination. Within a few years Sister Aimee was one of the most successful revivalists in the country. She held tent meetings up and down the east coast and in Canada. She started a monthly magazine, *The Bridal Call*, as a way of staying in touch with participants in her meetings and of raising money.

Sister went wherever she believed the Lord wished. And she went in the sublime confidence of the completely committed. Whatever she needed would be given her. She traveled in the "Pentecostal Gospel Car." On its sides were painted in gold "Judgment Day is coming," "Get Right With God," and "Where will you spend eternity?" When Aimee decided she needed a newer and larger auto for a cross-country trip, the Lord provided it in the form of donations from the faithful subscribers of the *Call*. So too with food and even a tent. Sister was on her way to Philadelphia for a great assembly of Pentecostal believers in the summer of 1918. She needed a larger tent. But she didn't have the money. And the military had gobbled up the available supply during the World War. "Each time I went to the Lord," Aimee wrote, "He would say: 'it is all right. You shall have your tent.'"

> When we arrived in the city of our summer's work, there was the very tent of my dreams and prayers, in an attic store-room of a downtown building, all tied up in bags, poles and stakes complete, ready for erection. Hallelujah! . . . [It would be] worth twenty-five hundred dollars today, and could be had at eighteen hundred cash, but I felt that fifteen hundred dollars was all the Lord wanted us to pay for that tent; and although at first they would not accept this, as the man stood in the door and read the sign, "Judgment day is coming, get right with God," his face became thoughtful and he said he would let us know later, and of course Father opened the way.

Aimee's husband would occasionally join her on the road but never for very long. Perhaps he could not reconcile himself to being overshadowed by his wife; perhaps he got tired of the hardships of travel. Sister Aimee often camped out in good weather and slept in the Gospel Car when it rained. Perhaps her husband told the simple truth when he said he wanted a quiet, conventional family life. In any case he filed successfully for divorce. The parting was not amicable. Tracked down by a reporter during the days of Sister's disappearance in 1926, her ex-husband would make it clear he believed the love nest stories and commented that her new lover "will be dropped like a hot penny by Aimee as soon as she has obtained all the help from him he is able to give to her cause." As for himself, "I do not wish to come in contact with her in any way, shape, or form" even though that meant that he never saw his son Rolf.

Sister taught that whoever is baptized in the Spirit experiences the same gifts as had been granted the apostles on the original Pentecost, including speaking in tongues. When a believer prayed for it, Sister joined in. Then, without warning, the believer would fall to the ground. McPherson always placed straw around the altar at the rear of her tent to cushion the fall. The seeker would lie there, often twitching violently, before getting up and testifying in tongues. Outsiders called Pentecostals "Holy Rollers." *This Is That* provides numerous descriptions of the Baptism in the Spirit. Here is one from the 1918 meeting in Philadelphia:

[I] had just turned to go into the big tent . . . when something fell with a thud and a shout to the ground behind me, and all the people began to run and shout. Hastening back to see what it was, I found [a] Methodist class leader lying on his back under the power—no, I should hardly say on his back, either, for he was really just on his head and heels, his body raised up from the ground by the power and his feet going round and round.

Before we could reach him he was shouting in tongues and praising the Lord as the Spirit gave utterance. After a time he bounded to his feet and went around the tent leaping and praising God.

Such reactions as falling to the ground and crying out had characterized American revivalism from the start. Jonathan Edwards, who helped launch the First Great Awakening in the 1730s and 1740s, understood that more conservative ministers and church members might take that kind of behavior as signs of hysteria rather than salvation. He did not encourage such things, he wrote, but sometimes the experience of the Lord is so powerful that all the believer can do is shout or fall.

Speaking in tongues, on the other hand, had not been a regular part of American revivalism, and certainly not considered proof that the Christian was baptized in the Spirit. That belief originated on January 1, 1901. Charles Fox Parham, a former Methodist pastor, had assigned the students at his Bethel Bible College in Topeka, Kansas, to search out the meaning of the biblical phrase, baptized in the Spirit. One of them, Agnes Ozman, fell, shook, groaned, and started speaking in an unknown tongue. Soon other students had the same experience. Later Parham too was baptized in the Spirit. He set about formulating a theology to explain what had happened. This was the "latter rain," the special dispensation on the eve of the Second Coming. It is based upon Parham's reading of chapter two of the Acts of the Apostles (King James Version):

Acts.2
[1] And when the day of Pentecost was fully come, they were all with one accord in one place.
[2] And suddenly there came a sound from heaven as of a rushing mighty wind, and it filled the entire house where they were sitting.
[3] And there appeared unto them cloven tongues like as of fire, and it sat upon each of them.
[4] And they were all filled with the Holy Ghost, and began to speak with other tongues, as the Spirit gave them utterance.
[5] And there were dwelling at Jerusalem Jews, devout men, out of every nation under heaven.
[6] Now when this was noised abroad, the multitude came together, and were confounded, because that every man heard them speak in his own language. . . .
[14] But Peter, standing up with the eleven, lifted up his voice, and said unto them, Ye men of Judaea, and all ye that dwell at Jerusalem, be this known unto you, and hearken to my words. . . .
[17] And it shall come to pass in the last days, saith God, I will pour out of my Spirit upon all flesh: and your sons and your daughters shall prophesy, and your young men shall see visions, and your old men shall dream dreams. . . .

Parham was untroubled that his experience did not parallel that of the apostles on the original Pentecost. On that occasion the miracle had been that everyone heard in his own language what the apostles were saying. Parham had no idea what he was saying when he spoke in tongues, and neither did anyone else. Occasionally someone might claim that the speaker was using a known language. One woman told Sister that she had been preaching in perfect Spanish. The gift lay in her total ignorance of that language.

While almost always the tongues are unknown to the listeners, the speech is clear. There are distinct words and sentences. Students of linguistics have long been interested in the phenomenon. They are unanimous in thinking that the tongues are not languages. Instead they are combinations of sounds drawn from the speaker's native tongue. An English-speaker talking in tongues, for example, never uses sounds common to African languages but unknown in English. This finding dovetails with what experts have discovered about how children acquire language. Babies start out making virtually all of the sounds used in human languages as well as some used in none. Gradually they limit their repertoire to sounds common to the language of their parents. Adults trying new languages often experience difficulty correctly pronouncing words because they have forgotten sounds that they had used as infants.

Interpretation was a second gift, and much rarer. Sister had received it. So when someone at her revival meetings began to speak, she would translate into English what the new saint was saying. Since it was the Spirit speaking through her, the message was prophesy.

Charles Fox Parham set about spreading the word. In 1906 he was running a Bible Training School in Houston. One of his students was William Joseph Seymour, who because he was black had to sit outside the classroom and listen through the open door. After a month or two, the Reverend Seymour moved to Los Angeles to lead a small congregation. His preaching about Baptism in the Spirit proved highly controversial, and he was locked out of his own church. For a while he preached in a private home. Then he and his flock moved into a former African Methodist Episcopal Church on Azusa Street. Within a few weeks people from all over, white as well as black, were flocking to the church. This was at first a product of word of mouth enthusiasm. Soon Seymour began publishing *The Gospel Faith*, distributing it free to some 50,000 subscribers. In its first issue he offered this description of the work:

[T]he meetings begin about ten o'clock in the morning and can hardly stop before ten or twelve at night, and sometimes two or three in the morning, because so many are seeking, and some are slain under the power of God. People are seeking three times at the altar . . . we cannot tell how many people have been saved, and baptized with the Holy Ghost, and healed of all manner of sicknesses. Many are speaking in new tongues and some are going on their way to the foreign fields, with the gift of the language.

The *Los Angeles Times* and other papers described the revival very differently. In its April 18, 1906 issue, on the front page, a header read:

Weird Babel of Tongues
New Sect of Fanatics Is Breaking Loose
Wild Scene Last Night on Azusa Street
Gurgle of Wordless Talk by a Sister
[C] lasped in his big fist the colored brother holds a miniature Bible from which he reads at intervals one or two words—never more. After an hour spent in exhortation the brethren present are invited to join in a "meeting of prayer, song and testimony." Then it is that pandemonium breaks loose, and the bounds of reason are passed by those who are "filled with the spirit," whatever that may be.

. . . [O]ne of the wildest of the meetings was held last night, and the highest pitch of excitement was reached by the gathering, which continued to "worship" until nearly midnight. The old exhorter [Seymour] urged the "sisters" to let the "tongues come forth" and the women gave themselves over to a riot of religious fervor. As a result a buxom dame was overcome with excitement and almost fainted.

Undismayed by the fearful attitude of the colored worshipper, another black woman jumped to the floor and began a wild gesticulation, which ended in a gurgle of wordless prayers which were nothing less than shocking.

"She's speaking in unknown tongues;" announced the leader, in an awed whisper, "keep on sister?"

Seymour conducted these services every day for three years. They were a mix of African American religious practices and the new theology. Seymour's Apostolic Faith Mission was something new, or at least uncommon since the first days of the revivalism early in the nineteenth century: a church where blacks and whites worshipped together and the leader was black. "The color line was washed away in the blood," declared Frank Bartleman, a white convert who wrote an account of the revival at the Azusa church. Racial segregation was worsening everywhere in the first decades of the new century. But at Seymour's church all were brothers and sisters.

What Seymour brought to Pentecostalism was the call and response style of preaching and singing characteristic of black Christianity. People called out "Amen!" They yelled "Hallelujah!" in gratitude and joy. Both preaching and singing were highly rhythmic. Believers swayed in time to the music and clapped their hands. Black worship supplied powerful forms for the expression of the Pentecostal experience. Glen A. Cook testified in the November 1906 issue of *The Gospel Faith*:

I could feel the power going through me like electric needles. The Spirit taught me that I must not resist the power but give way and become limp as a piece of cloth. When I did this, I fell under the power, and God began to mold me and teach me what it meant to be really surrendered to Him. I was laid out under the power five times before Pentecost really came. Each time I would come out from under the power, I would feel so sweet and clean, as though I had been run through a washing machine. . . . My arms began to tremble, and soon I was shaken violently by a great power, and it seemed as though a large pipe was fitted over my neck, my head apparently being off. . . . About thirty hours afterwards, while sitting in the meeting on Azusa Street, I felt my throat and tongue begin to move, without any effort on my part. Soon I began to stutter and then out came a distinct language, which I could hardly restrain. I talked and laughed with joy far into the night.

Sister Aimee, who polished what Seymour had developed, also preached to integrated congregations. One of her first triumphs was in Corona, New York. She responded to a request from "a colored lady" to lead a revival. Like the gatherings at Seymour's Azusa Street Church, the meetings quickly attracted whites. On her southern tours Sister made a point of telling her white converts that the Lord had directed her to work equally hard for the salvation of "black pearls." Of a revival in Key West, Florida, in 1918, she wrote, "it was impossible to keep the white people away."

So for the first time in the Island the white and colored attended the same place of worship and glorified the same Lord side by side. We arranged seats for the white people at the sides, reserving the center for the colored people, but so interested became the people in the meetings that reserve was a thing unknown.

Seymour healed. So did Aimee. Here is Seymour's account from the September 1906 *Gospel Faith*:

Mrs. J. Kring was healed of cancer of the lungs on August 8, after the doctor had given her up. One lung was entirely closed up. When she was prayed for, the Lord immediately touched her body and healed her. She shouted for an hour with strong lungs, and is the happiest woman you ever saw.

———

A mother brought her son to the Mission to be healed of epileptic fits. He is about twenty-one years old and has been suffering for years, like the boy that was brought to Jesus whom the devil had often caused to fall into the fire and into the water. The boy was so wracked in mind and body that he was in a semi-conscious condition. Bro. Batman, who is called to Africa [as a missionary], prayed for him, asking the Lord to cast the demon power out of him and give complete healing. The boy rose up from the floor and witnessed that the work was done and went home rejoicing.

Declared Sister Aimee from *This Is That*:

A preacher came on crutches not believing that the Lord could heal as in days of old, and in answer to prayer God healed him instantly, in the middle of the meeting and he ran about the tent, dancing without his crutches and shouting: "Why, the Lord still heals! He heals as in days of old!"

A little girl with a paralyzed leg and a stiff knee was brought by her parents, for healing. One leg was two inches shorter than the other. The Lord instantly healed her and she was able to bend her knee and the limb was lengthened and became as [the other] one.

One girl who came to the altar to seek her baptism, wore a heavy steel truss around her waist and running down both sides of her limb, it fastened at the bottom of a heavy shoe and strapped down her withered, helpless limb. The Lord baptized her in the Holy Ghost and healed her limb. She removed the truss, brace and shoe, and walked up and down, perfectly strong and without pain. Her mother wept and saints shouted. Surely we have a right to shout with such a wonderful Jesus.

Neither Seymour nor McPherson attempted to keep track of these cures. Unlike the Catholic Church, which also teaches the possibility of miraculous healing, they did not bring in medical experts to examine the patient. They did not do long-term follow-ups to see how the cure was progressing. There was no need. Believers could see with their own eyes what had happened. And the Bridegroom was coming. Why worry about what would be the situation five years from now? Early Pentecostals lived in expectation of Christ's imminent return.

Most important is that both Seymour and McPherson insisted that God was as likely to choose a woman as a man to deliver a message, as likely to choose an African American as a white. Quakers believe this as well. But in the early twentieth century, at least, other Protestants as well as Catholics and Jews emphatically did not. Woman ministers were rare. All rabbis along with all priests, of course, were men. And churches were segregated, in fact if not according to doctrine. The races did not worship together. Black and white Pentecostals did. And their services drew heavily upon African American practices.

Where Seymour and McPherson differed was in the degree of control Sister Aimee managed to exert over her meetings. At the Azusa Street church everyone was free to do anything. As a result, Christian Scientists, spiritualists, and others competed with Seymour for the congregation's attention. Seymour preached very little. Instead he would read a word or two from scripture and implore his listeners to take the reading to heart. McPherson, in contrast, made sure that the Christian Scientists and others stayed out of her tent. Of a meeting at Onset Bay in Rhode Island she wrote:

[Our] new tent was pitched in the Holiness Camp ground, and though the battle was hard, Jesus gave victory. The war against spiritualism, Christian Science, and demon powers was hot and heavy, but we sang and preached the blood of Jesus until the break came and the Lord poured out His Spirit.

Most of the millions who embraced Pentecostal beliefs and practices were not very well educated. H. L. Mencken seized upon this as the reason for the new revival's appeal. Aimee succeeded so brilliantly in Los Angeles, he wrote, because it contained the largest concentration of morons in the country. Less sarcastically, he noted that few who attended Aimee's services could even hope to understand evolution or the Higher Criticism. That somewhat milder comment was true, but it is far from providing an adequate explanation of the rapid growth of Pentecostalism.

One Pentecostal who could make sense of evolution was Sister Aimee herself. *This Is That* declares that, while in high school, she read essays on Darwinism as well as the works of Robert Ingersoll, the outspoken agnostic of the late nineteenth century. She challenged her teacher to explain the discrepancies between the Old Testament account of creation and the claims in her geography textbook that mountain ranges developed over tens of thousands of years. He could not answer. Aimee began to lecture her classmates on evolution. She was on her way to becoming something of a village atheist.

The Pentecostal preacher Robert Semple changed her life, not by answering her questions or refuting her arguments but by slaying members of his small congregation in the Spirit. He spoke in tongues. Aimee had yet to receive the gift of interpretation. No one at that meeting had. But the unintelligible message produced powerful results.

To me it was the voice of God thundering into my soul awful words of conviction and condemnation, and though the message was spoken in tongues it seemed as though God had said to me—"YOU are a poor, lost, miserable, hell-deserving sinner!"

Suddenly, questions about the ages of rocks, to use Bryan's phrase, no longer mattered. Aimee dropped out of school, married Semple, and threw herself into his ministry. She attended all of his meetings, prayed with whoever "tarried at the altar" seeking the Baptism of the Spirit, and began to preach herself. Aimee had seen clearly that modern knowledge and fundamentalist Christianity were incompatible. She chose ignorance and ecstasy. And power.

Power appears in accounts by Pentecostals of their baptisms almost as often as Spirit. They feel it. It courses through their bodies and throws them to the ground. It stumbles out of their mouths in tongues. It fills them with joy. It cures the sick. Pentecostals know it is real. How can they doubt their own senses? In all of these respects their testimony resembles that of the converts of Charles Grandison Finney during the Second Great Awakening in the nineteenth century or of Jonathan Edwards during the First in the eighteenth. Some of them too had fallen to the ground and rolled about. They felt lifted out of themselves, enveloped in a blinding white light. They talked of the intense joy. The difference is that Pentecostals not only feel the power, but exercise it. Earlier converts had been passive. They surrendered to the Lord. So do Pentecostals, but then they bound to their feet, and the Spirit speaks through them. They prophesize. They see visions of Christ's crucifixion or of the Second Coming. People listen transfixed, even if nobody knows what they are saying, including themselves. Most early Pentecostals did not have very much money. They did not hold important jobs. If they were black, and many were, they faced insult and discrimination. The power of the Spirit filled a void in their lives. So did the ecstasy of the meetings. Physicians and psychologists explain speaking in tongues and faith healing as mental phenomena that take physical expression, but among believers that is irrelevant. For them the intensity of the experience is convincing enough; explanations offered from outside that experience cannot touch it. The "acids of modernity" cannot dissolve the certainty that you are baptized in the Spirit.

Up through 1919 Sister Aimee retailed salvation. She prayed by the side of seekers for baptism. She laid hands on the faithful seeking cures. She drove the Gospel Car and distributed uncounted numbers of pamphlets at every stop. That changed with her decision that the Lord wanted her to build a great house of worship. She went from saving souls one by one to creating religious fantasies for the masses. She went Hollywood. She wrote, produced, staged, and sometimes starred in religious extravaganzas. She built Angelus Temple, where 5300 at a time could attend a service. It opened in 1923. Aimee ac-

Angelus Temple, Los Angeles.

quired radio station KFSG (Kall Four Square Gospel) the following year and oversaw its programming, which included live broadcasts of all the Temple services in addition to children's programs and serials, one featuring the "Lone Evangelist."

People came to the Temple seeking entertainment as well as salvation. Aimee's challenge was to transform into a series of weekly programs—illustrated sermons, healing services, baptisms—the fervor of a tent meeting that might run for days and bring direct contact between the revivalist and the believer. Part of the fervor of the tent meetings sprang from their spontaneity. The revivalist did not know who or how many would be slain in the Spirit. But in Angelus Temple, where all the services were broadcast live over KFSG, Sister had to produce baptisms, cures, and salvation on a relentlessly tight schedule. And she did.

> During our trip the first part of 1927, while [I was] preaching in the Municipal Auditorium in Denver, twenty-eight hundred persons responded to a single altar call. They swept like a human flood and flowed all over the platform, all over every foot of space they could find or we could find for them in the front of the hall. So eager were they to get down on their knees, that they so overloaded the platform that the manager of the building protested loudly, fearing the platform would not bear the weight of the people who rushed the altar.—*In the Service of the King* (1927)

Disenchanted ministers who left the Foursquare Gospel Church charged that Sister used plants within the audience. She stationed students from the Temple's Bible School in the main auditorium. Then, when she issued an altar call, they would lead the way, encouraging others.

Aimee took on the challenge by borrowing more from Hollywood than lighting technicians and props. She turned herself into a star. That meant glamour. On the road, living out of the Gospel Car, Sister had cared little about her clothing or appearance. Most of the space in the auto was occupied by the tents and by tracts. And Aimee did not hesitate to join in when the tents had to be put up or taken down. She seems not to have thought about herself except as an instrument of the Lord. That too started to change in 1919. In that year Sister informed readers of *The Bridal Call* that the Lord had promised her a house in Los Angeles. He had, in fact, showed her a vision of the very house. Donations flowed in. One believer gave a suitable parcel of land. Others provided free labor. Soon "the House the Lord built" was ready. It was the first time Sister discerned that the Lord wished her to enjoy modern creature comforts. There would be other such revelations.

About the same time Aimee made a discovery. If she wore the right sort of clothes, had her hair done a certain way, used the correct cosmetics, she had "it." "It" is the title of a story by Elinor Glyn. She wrote of "that nameless charm, with a strong magnetism, which can only be called 'It.'" Essentially it is sex appeal, garnished with personality. Clara Bow starred in the movie *It* in 1922 and was thereafter known as the "it" girl. Sister, taking on the character of a movie star, began to preach in evening gowns. The Rev. Bob proclaimed his disapproval, but the people who came to the Temple loved her. She drove around Los Angeles in a sporty roadster or in a chauffeured limousine. She brought her clothes from Paris designers. She attended parties with other celebrities. Adjoining the Temple she built a second lavish home. The faithful, in Los Angeles and around the country, paid and did not question. In 1929, for example, Sister determined that she needed a new seven-passenger Cadillac. Or more exactly, she discovered that the Lord wished her to have it. She was always going from place to place on Temple business and had to conserve her strength. A new, more comfortable car would enable her to do God's work more effectively. She paid $5000 for the Cadillac. Then Aimee dedicated it to the Lord. Temple faithful could attend and place a contribution on the hood and receive the personal thanks of Sister. Enough did to pay off the car. The messenger was becoming as important as the message.

Among the categories of religious fantasies that Aimee produced was the belief that through her the Spirit would heal. Reach out your hand, Sister instructed her audience, and place it on your radio. The power of the Spirit coursed through the radio waves. Each week testimonials were sent in. If you were a faithful listener, sooner or later you would hear of someone suffering from just the same symptoms as you who had experienced a miracle. Non-Pentecostal clergy protested. Elder Ben M. Bogard, pastor of the Antioch Missionary Baptist Church in Little Rock, debated Sister Aimee on the subject. "[M]iracles and divine healing, as taught and manifested in the Word of God," he insisted, "ceased with the closing of the Apostolic Age." This was the orthodox Protestant view, dating back to the Reformation, while Rome preached that miracles still occurred. But Pentecostals believed that since original sin had brought sickness into the world, the crucifixion of Christ has redeemed humanity from illness as well as sin. Bogard was so sure he had won the debate that he published the transcript. Sister Aimee simply continued her services. And her radio audience grew.

For the illustrated sermons, which were more popular even than the healing services, two long ramps led from the back of the Temple to the stage. One Sunday evening Sister roared down one on a motorcycle. She was dressed in the uniform of a California State trooper. "Stop!" she called out. "You're speeding to ruin!" By her own account, one of the most powerful of these sermons took place in

1927. Sister had held a special service for the sailors of the Pacific fleet two weeks earlier. Now she noted as she began that, a few days before, there had been a fire on one of the ships and several sailors died. "Who knows?"Aimee said. "Some of those brave boys who were here last Sunday? And—who knows—perhaps in God's divine mercy, some of them were saved?" Then, she reports *In the Service of the King*, a sailor came up to her and asked to "deliver a message for his 'buddy' who had met death in the explosion." Sister gave her assent. "Friends," he said:

[Y]ou all remember what happened in this Temple a week ago last Sunday night—you all know how Sister McPherson wore a little white sailor's cap in honor of us boys, and how she preached the illustrated sermon with the ships, the lighthouse and the rock with the Cross up here on the platform. You know how hundreds of us boys listened to her and how some of us cried when she had finished, how we came down these aisles and how we knelt here at the rail.

My buddy was in that explosion. . . . He was here that Sunday night. He said he hadn't been to church before for years. . . . [H]e felt she was speaking to him, as she pictured us all adrift on the sea of life without compass or guide, he answered the altar call and took Jesus Christ on board the ship of his life as Pilot.

Then the sailor asked to lead a hymn. "Tell Mother I'll be there/In answer to her prayer. /This message, blessed angels, to her bear;/Tell Mother I'll be there." He asked the congregation to join in. "They tried," but "the song was not sung—it was sobbed out of hearts melted by that simple story." To her altar call: "Come on. Let's all be there—come on!" Aimee wrote, "Ah, how they came! In an instant the aisles were overflowing, the altar space jammed."

McPherson told stories in her sermons. Some came from scripture, some from her own experiences, and some from accounts given by her staff. An operation as large as Temple Angelus required many assistants. To answer inquiries, volunteers took turns in the Prayer Tower of two hours each, twenty-four hours a day. Radio listeners and *Bridal Call* subscribers wrote in special requests, often in great detail. Aimee wove some of their letters into her sermons. The Temple also ran a Commissary. Members of the congregation were asked to bring a donation for the poor, not in cash but in kind. Commissary workers occasionally wrote touching stories about particular people they had assisted with food or clothing. If they were touching enough, they appeared in one of Sister's sermons instead of *The Bridal Call*. These sermons anticipated one of commercial broadcasting's biggest successes, "Queen For A Day," in which contestants would compete over who had the saddest story. The winner then got a series of prizes, usually household appliances. Audiences, it appears, love wallowing in other people's grief, a fact of human nature Sister made use of.

McPherson embodied two components of the Pentecostal appeal. One is the intense relationship at the local revival between the preacher, the Spirit, and the convert. This is the Pentecostalism of the Azusa Street revival. The other is the electronic ministry. Aimee created the fusion of salvation and entertainment that continues to characterize televangelism. When you tuned in KFSG you could listen to an orchestra playing hymns that Sister had adapted from popular songs like "It Ain't Gonna Rain No More, No More" or hear a band concert. You might hear touching melodrama or the exciting adventures of the Lone Evangelist. Pentecostals were not supposed to patronize commercial entertainment, including radio programs in general. But with Sister's programming, you could have your entertainment and still be holy.

McPherson did not venture into politics. During the furor surrounding her story of being kidnapped, she did briefly call upon the Ku Klux Klan to silence her critics, whom she linked to the Catholic Church. But this was far from typical. Unlike Rev. Bob Shuler, who also had a radio station from which he routinely endorsed candidates and boosted the KKK, Sister stuck to salvation and requests for donations. She never became a United States citizen or expressed interest in a political campaign. With others convinced that Christ's Second Coming was imminent she shared the belief that the return of the Jews to Palestine would precede the Second Coming and so she did speak positively of Zionism and the Balfour Declaration of 1917, in which the British government pledged to support a Jewish homeland. But unlike the Reverends Jerry Falwell and Pat Robertson and other televangelists, she did not call upon the American government to assist in securing that homeland.

* * * *

The five weeks in 1926 during which McPherson went missing dominates most of her biographies. No one can know for certain what happened, but we can rule out her story. It is blatantly preposterous. No kidnapper would wait weeks before writing a ransom note. For a time it was assumed that Sister had died in a drowning accident. Then doubts began to awaken. People claimed to have seen Aimee. Such Elvis-sightings are common when a celebrity dies. But the newspapers treated them seriously. The stories sold papers. Next came the rumors about Kenneth Ormiston, the sound engineer with whom whispers had romantically connected Sister. An array of witnesses claimed to have seen someone resembling her at hotels where Ormiston had stayed. Before the investigations could go any further, McPherson showed up on the Mexican border. It is safe to infer that she had decided that time was shortening before someone located her. Better to turn up on her own, receive the heartfelt welcome home of the Angelus faithful, and return to her work.

A mystery is why Aimee had left in the first place. One of her earliest biographers suggests that she found running the Temple much less rewarding than her earlier revival work. The joy, she writes, was in the struggle. Once McPherson achieved her goals, the endless duties became work. Then too, Aimee had denied herself a love life. In 1925, when she was thirty-five, she met Ormiston. He was charming and interested in her as a person. He was not a Temple member, and she had no interest in making him one. Perhaps Aimee hoped to build a new life in which she would not always be on display. Perhaps. But McPherson was one of the most recognizable people in America. The chance that she could remain hidden for long was slim at best. So was the chance that she could live with her own conscience after abandoning her two children. As for finding contentment in a quiet domestic setting, she had tried that with Harold McPherson and suffered a nervous breakdown.

Much of the full story of Sister Aimee's disappearance will probably remain unknown. The mystery, however, should not overshadow the importance of her role both in spreading the Pentecostal message and in creating many of the enduring features of the electronic ministry.

VIII

Popular Culture and the Arts

Beyond Modernism

Love for sale,
Appetizing young love for sale.
Love that's fresh and still
    unspoiled,
Love that's only slightly soiled,
Love for sale.
 	
Who will buy?
Who would like to sample my
    supply?
Who's prepared to pay the price,
For a trip to paradise?
Love for sale.
 	
Let the poets pipe of love
In their childish way,
	I know every type of love
	Better far than they.
	
	If you want the thrill of love,
	I've been through the mill of
	    love;
	Old love, new love
	Every love but true love.
	
	Love for sale.
	Appetising young love for sale.
	If you want to buy my wares,
	Follow me and climb the stairs.
	Love for sale.
	Love for sale.

—Cole Porter, "Love for Sale," 1930

A search of the online All Music Guide turned up over 750 recorded versions of this Cole Porter song by artists ranging from Cannonball Adderly to Teddy Wilson. "Love For Sale," a song from Porter's Broadway musical *The New Yorkers*, is a classic example of the popular impulse in the arts. In writing appreciatively of jazz, comic strips, silent comedies, and other popular arts, Gilbert Seldes in *Seven Lively Arts* (1923) proved well ahead of his time. Few critics today would question his acumen in hailing Charlie Chaplin as a genius or in discussing the sophistication of jazz when most contemporaries, including W. E. B. Du Bois and several other black intellectuals, dismissed it as primitive. Being right about these matters also validates Seldes' central insight: that these endeavors carried links to everyday experience and exemplified a specific type of art.

Popular culture students aside, scholars pay little attention to Seldes. The recent *New York Modern* quotes him on jazz but contains

129

not a single reference to Cole Porter or to Irving Berlin, who wrote many sophisticated songs still popular today. Ruth St. Denis, a pioneer of what now is called Modern Dance, rates eleven mentions, Fred Astaire, whose movie musicals charmed two generations, none. George Gershwin's popular songs and musical comedies receive no mention, although his compositions for the concert hall and his opera *Porgy and Bess* are briefly discussed. In contrast, Charles Ives is treated at some length and hailed for bridging "the gap between art and vernacular music by combining avant-garde forms with popular expressions to democratize and modernize American music." Given this idea of music, it makes no sense to describe Ives as spanning the bridge between traditional art and vernacular music. Scholars usually assume that the vernacular cannot itself be art and therefore may at most become so only by some metaphorical equivalent of a bridge. Seldes was such a fan of Berlin that he compiled a catalogue of his published songs for *Seven Lively Arts*. *New York Modern* simply follows the routine scholarly assumption that serious American music proceeds out of the European symphonic tradition and ascends to the level of art only insofar as it does so successfully.

Art after World War I, most critics will claim, exists only in the form called modernism, which in music, painting, and architecture expresses itself in ways abstract and distant from the public. Non-modernists need not apply. Duke Ellington, Scott Joplin, and other African Americans merit exceptions to this rule of exclusion, in part for reasons of political correctness and partly because they had a deep and well-documented influence upon modernists, as demonstrated by Ives's interest in Joplin's ragtime tunes. A chapter in *New York Modern* on Harlem includes a lengthy, well-informed, and highly interesting discussion of jazz that is unconnected to the rest of the book. Jazz of course did not define itself in European musical traditions. Modern art, in contrast, arose out of nineteenth-century European art by a deliberate and adventurous overturning of it. Jazz is an anomaly, modern and artistic but outside any modernist category, at least until after World War II.

Jazz (originally jass) took its name from an African American slang term for sexual intercourse that probably originated in New Orleans brothels. One notion is that it was short for "jasmine," an inexpensive perfume favored by whores. Early jazz titles offer some idea of their creators' efforts to express the experiences of black people as well as their separation from European music: Lil Harden Armstrong's "Struttin' with Some Barbeque," which she recorded with her husband Louis Armstrong and his Hot Five; Armstrong's own "Gut Bucket Blues," also recorded by the Hot Five; "East St. Louis Toodle-Oo" by Duke Ellington and his trumpeter Bubber Miley and released by Ellington's orchestra under the name of the Washingtonians. This last piece give rise to Ellington's so-called "jungle" sound. The lyrics described unfaithful lovers in, for example, "St. Louis Blues"; the pleasures of dancing in tunes like "Cake-Walking Babies Back Home," a Clarence Williams original recorded by his own Hot Five; and the pain of color prejudice within the black community captured in "What Did I Do To Be So Black and Blue?" a Fats Waller and Andy Razaf tune created for Connie's Hot Chocolates and released by Louis Armstrong and his orchestra.

In both its audience and its roots jazz epitomizes the popular impulse in the arts. It remained frequently misperceived as primitive, even by its friends. But Duke Ellington, whose white manager Irving Mills introduced him to radio audiences as "the greatest living master of jungle music," in his 1927 recording of "Black and Tan Fantasy" (also composed with Bubber Miley) included a paraphrase of Chopin's "Funeral March" from the Second Piano Sonata. At the time, Ellington was playing the Cotton Club in Harlem. With its all-white clientele, Old South decor, dark-skinned waiters, and light-skinned chorus girls, the club enticed patrons with a fantasy in black and tan. Describing it in dirge-like musical terms shows a daring act of artistic courage, as does the use of Chopin in so-called jungle music. But that appropriation is not a modernist recasting of classical music for artistic effect. Ellington employed it because it worked.

In *New York Modern*, the authors echo the judgment reported by the African American writer Ralph Ellison that "while primarily a creative composer, [Ellington] was seen [by contemporaries] mainly in his role as entertainer." Ellington's brilliance, so runs this notion, enabled him to write important music despite the necessity of keeping a mass audience amused. This ignores Ellington's own view. Performing at clubs was not something he did so he could afford to compose. For decades after his royalty income would have given him the time to devote himself entirely to composition, he continued to tour. In fact, he sometimes had to subsidize the orchestra out of his royalties. Why didn't he forsake the road? Because, he insisted, music exists only when it is played. And that to him was not a private act. The listeners might be other musicians at "cutting contests," as jazz artists called competitions at rehearsals or after hours. They might be an in-crowd such as audiences at jazz festivals or dancers in a hotel in Fargo, North Dakota on a weekday evening in 1940. No matter. Ellington made no distinction between creative work and performance. The point was to reach people in one way or another. Perhaps they got up and danced or walked home humming. Some might come away understanding something about their own experience.

Ellington was, in the words of a *Downbeat* magazine essay, "a black genius in a white world." He was not alone.

The Harlem Renaissance

There was a terrible race riot in Chicago in 1919. Civil government collapsed; the Church fell down on the job; the school shrunk away;

social service agencies recoiled in their shell; publicists either suc-
cumbed to the hysteria or closed their otherwise vigilant eyes; the
good church people hid away to their holes of holiness. . . . The
break down in racial brotherhood was well nigh complete except for
the black and tan cabarets. Here white and colored men and women
still drank, ate, sang, and danced together. Smiling faces, light hearts,
undulating couples in poetry of motion conspired with syncopated
music to convert the hell and death from *without* to a little paradise
within.—Chandler Owen, "The Black and Tan Cabaret—America's
Most Democratic Institution," *The Messenger*, February 1925

Owen, co-founder of *The Messenger* with the labor leader A. Philip
Randolph, was one of the leading figures of the flowering of African-
American genius in the arts known as the Harlem Renaissance. And
despite his overall optimism that racial barriers were beginning to
fall, his essay pointed to a core dilemma in American life. Black influences in music, language, and style were becoming ever more powerful. Yet segregation and racial discrimination showed no signs of
weakening. Would white Americans go on copying African-American
dances, whistling African-American melodies, adopting African-American slang and still insist upon white supremacy?

For Owen the flocking of whites to black neighborhoods and the
clubs there proved that they were places "where people abandon their
cant and hypocrisy. . . . The little barracks of hypocrisy and the prison
bars of prejudice are temporarily at least torn down, and people act
like natural, plain human beings. . . . " But many whites went to Harlem
or the South Side of Chicago merely seeking thrills. They were, as the
slang of the day put it, "slumming." They wanted to listen to "jungle
music." They wanted to watch chorus girls who threw aside such inhibitions as *Ziegfeld's Follies* retained. And they wanted both to join in
the revels and to revel in their own superiority. The white lyricist Lorenz
Hart mocked such people in "The Lady Is a Tramp." His heroine refuses to "go to Harlem in ermine and pearls" just as she will not "dish
the dirt with the rest of the girls/That's why the lady is a tramp."

Yet though the black and tan cabaret was not a harbinger of a new
color-blind democracy, black artists made important and highly visible contributions to the emerging popular culture. These were most
obvious in music. In the mid-1920s Louis Armstrong joined Fletcher
Henderson's big band in New York City. Over the next two years they
invented the big band sound that dominated American music through
World War II. Henderson had to give up his band during the Great
Depression, but he became the chief arranger for Benny Goodman,
the "King of Swing." In the late 1920s Duke Ellington brought his orchestra to New York for an extended engagement as the house band
at Harlem's Cotton Club. It is impossible to calculate Ellington's in-

fluence. He was, in his own form of the highest praise, "beyond category." He did not write or play Swing. Instead, several years before that sound became popular, he wrote the playful "It Don't Mean a Thing, If It Ain't Got That Swing." He did not, like Count Basie, for example, play the blues. He reinvented the blues over and over, as elegant laments ("Mood Indigo," "Sophisticated Lady"), as symphonic works ("The Drum Is a Woman"), as religious affirmations ("Come Sunday"), and as joyful shouts ("Harlem Airshaft").

It was Armstrong, his friend Bing Crosby maintained, who taught a whole generation how to sing. He introduced the popular note. He sang the way ordinary people expressed themselves. Sometimes he was pure high spirits ("I'll Be Glad When You're Dead, You Rascal, You"), sometimes pure sorrow ("Why Must I Be So Black and Blue?"), but always without affectation. Where Armstrong led, other black singers followed, many of them women. The two most influential were Ella Fitzgerald and Billie Holiday.

Black musical influence flowed through many channels—recordings, live performances, radio programs and dance halls. One of the most pervasive but least studied is the animated cartoon. Here the pioneers were the Fleischer Brothers, Jewish immigrants from Austria who created a number of popular cartoon characters. Popeye was one, but he was not especially musical. Betty Boop was another, and she was. The Fleischers modeled the movements of their animated figures on real people. In "Minnie, the Moocher" the film begins with live action footage of Cab Calloway, who made the song his trademark, and his Cotton Club Orchestra (he had replaced Ellington as the club's headliner). Cab sings and dances the title song. When the animation begins, Betty and her father, a Jew from Austria, perhaps based upon the Fleischers' own father, are arguing. He insists that she follow the family custom and eat a traditional dish. Betty tearfully refuses. The scene is a thinly disguised parody of "The Jazz Singer." Like Jakie Rabinowitz, Betty decides to run away. Like Jakie, she runs toward jazz music. But unlike Jakie, Betty runs toward the real thing. No "Toot, Toot, Tootsie" for her. With her friend, the dog Bimbo, she runs off to the strains of "Minnie, the Moocher." Minnie, Calloway sings, had learned "to kick the gong around," to use opium, from her boyfriend "Smoky," whose drug of choice was cocaine. Although the cartoon does not show Betty taking any drug, she does, to the accompaniment of Cab's version of the song, find herself in a dream world. Her experiences, however, do not parallel Minnie's. Minnie dreamed that the King of Sweden "was giving her things that she was needin'." Instead Betty meets a ghostly walrus with enlarged lips who sings the song. Betty and Bimbo are terrified, as well they should be, for the walrus transforms itself into a spectral cat whose kittens suck it dry and into a prison guard who escorts skeletons to the electric chair, among other transmigrations. In all of these, the walrus/cat/guard moves like Cab Calloway. Finally, Betty and Bimbo run for their lives, pursued by various goblins and skeletons. Bimbo seeks refuge in the doghouse. Betty climbs into her own bed. The farewell letter she leaves for her parents obligingly shreds itself, leaving the message "Home, Sweet, Home." It is hard to estimate how many millions first saw a real jazz performance—from Armstrong, Caloway, or the bandleader and arranger Don Redman—in a Betty Boop cartoon.

Countee Cullen, Langston Hughes, and other African-American writers had a much harder time finding a mass audience. In part this was because while there were thousands of cabarets, only a handful of literary magazines were open to them. Owen and Randolph's *The Messenger, The Opportunity* of the National Urban League, and the NAACP's *The Crisis* published the bulk of the poems, short stories, and essays black writers created in the 1920s and 1930s. Few magazines with large white readerships would open their pages to African Americans. Book publishers were a bit more accommodating, but only a bit. Theater owners and producers were a bit less. The result was a variation on the core dilemma race posed: Would white America continue to marginalize some of its most talented and creative people while still coming more and more under their influence? Perhaps Countee Cullen expressed the paradox best when he observed:

Yet Do I Marvel

I doubt not God is good, well-meaning, kind,
And did He stoop to quibble could tell why
The little buried mole continues blind,
Why flesh that mirrors Him must some day die,
Make plain the reason tortured Tantalus
Is baited by the fickle fruit, declare
If merely brute caprice dooms Sisyphus
To struggle up a never-ending stair.
Inscrutable His ways are, and immune
To catechism by a mind too strewn
With petty cares to slightly understand
What awful brain compels His awful hand.
Yet do I marvel at this curious thing:
To make a poet black, and bid him sing!

Or perhaps the painter Hayden Palmer cought the paradox best in "The Janitor Who Paints," currently hanging in the National Gallery of Art.

This account does not intend to belittle modernism. Instead the aim is to call attention to a different sort of modern art, which Gilbert Seldes called "lively." Although he too took note of the distinction

Hayden Palmer, *The Janitor Who Paints.*

between great art and popular or lively art, and acknowledged the superiority of the great, Seldes insisted upon the validity of the popular. "Except in a period when the major arts flourish with exceptional vigour," he wrote, "the lively arts are likely to be the most intelligent phenomena of their day." For our time, "[We] must have arts which, we feel, are for ourselves alone, which no one before us could have cared for so much, which no one after us will wholly understand. . . . We require, for nourishment, something fresh and transient. It is this which makes jazz so much the characteristic art of our time and Jolson a more typical figure than Chaplin, who also [with Picasso] is outside of time."

Modernist and Modern

During the first half of the twentieth century modernism and the popular largely defined art in the United States. Although they inevitably influenced each other, each flourished as a separate medium. They differed in impulse and in ways of measuring artistic achievement. A leading characteristic of those differences is that modernist artists defined their work as attempts to break out of what they regarded as the constraints of European traditions. Popular artists proclaimed no such effort. They either drew upon non-Western sources, as in the case of jazz, or invented artistic conventions for new media, as in film and animation, or freely adapted European traditions to new uses: comic strips or illustrations for mass audience publications such as pulp novels. The musical comedy provides another example with its appropriations from opera and operetta. Modernist artists, moreover, disdained popular approval. At the Art Students League, a major teaching center of modernist painting, instructors sought to shelter their young students from the pressures of the marketplace. The poet William Carlos Williams maintained a full-time career in medicine and the composer Charles Ives kept a livelihood in business, and thereby each was able to pursue his own vision without compromise. Popular artists, in contrast, looked the marketplace to provide the very possibility for their art. The magazine illustrator Norman Rockwell did not apologize for his popularity any more than did the musician Louis Armstrong or the songwriter George Gershwin.

Popular artists sought to express common experiences: working up the courage to kiss a pretty girl in "Gimme A Little Kiss, Will Ya, Hon" (introduced in a 1926 recording by Jean Goldkette and

Stuart Davis, "Abstract Vision of New York: A Building, A Derby Hat, A Tiger's Head, and Other Symbols" (1932).

his orchestra that featured Bix Beiderbecke, Jimmy and Tommy Dorsey, Frankie Trumbauer, and Joe Venuti—all white musicians who would achieve fame in the interwar years); finding a way into American culture, the theme of the first sound movie, *The Jazz Singer*. Modernists also incorporated features of daily life, often explicitly within American settings. But they treated more somber themes, such as alienation in the modern city or the powerlessness of the individual. And they approached such subjects not by identifying with the average man or woman but by expressing their highly individualistic and sometimes abstract vision.

"I paint what I see in America," declared Stuart Davis; "in other words I paint the American Scene." The dark building here is the brand new Empire State; the derby (shown twice) presumably was intended to evoke Al Smith, then president of the Empire State Building Corporation, and his Brown Derby campaign for the presidency in 1928. The tiger's head, a reference to Tammany Hall, also recalls Smith, its most illustrious sachem or leader. Other symbols lend themselves to easy recognition. The gas pump at the left center is straightforward like the tire in the lower center. Not so the "H" [Harlem?] just beyond the face in the Moon. This was not art for the common man and woman. It was for people in the know.

In the early twenties when Seldes wrote and creativity in the arts, both modern and popular, flourished, Charlie Chaplin with Buster Keaton and several other actors in silent comedies consciously set about creating a new art form for mass audiences. Chaplin's "Little Tramp" is an Everyman, as are the characters played by Keaton and Harold Lloyd. In film after film they portrayed the little guy wrestling with the challenges of ordinary life—trying to land a

Charles Chaplin.—Courtesy, Library of Congress.

job, to win the girl, to succeed and impress. Arrayed against them loom villains, larger, stronger, richer, and often more handsome than they. Set against them too is the force of circumstance. Bad luck dogs them. Yet they never lose heart. Movies generated an immediate relation to their public. A Van Gogh could go entirely unrecognized for his entire career, only to be acclaimed a genius later. A filmmaker had to produce hits. If paying customers did not flock to see the pictures, the studio heads would hire someone else. This, in fact, happened to Keaton. Several of his films, now considered masterpieces, flopped. That spelled the end of his creative independence.

Comic Strips

Comic strip artists similarly depended upon instant acceptance by a mass public. Their work appeared in daily and Sunday papers precisely because people bought one paper rather than another for the funnies. To lose touch with the buyers was to evaporate. Strips that succeeded did so because they resonated with the imaginations of the readers.

Seldes' own favorite George Herriman, creator of "Krazy Kat," did not hold the broadest appeal. More in demand was Billy DeBeck's "Barney Google" strip. Barney, a lover of sporting events, especially horse racing, lives with a disapproving wife who, according to the hit song composed about the series, is "three times his size." The real

"Bringing up Father," November 19, 1918, from the Halloway Pages.
http://home.comcast.net/-cjh5801a/Jiggs.htm

love of his life, however, is "Spark Plug," a race horse so slow that, as an exasperated Barney once says, he "wouldn't even make a good pot of glue."

George McManus' "Bringing Up Father" ran in far more papers than "Krazy Kat." It related the story of Jiggs, a former construction worker who is now rich but most at home in his old surroundings: he would often be pictured sitting on a steel beam and chatting with other workers. His wife Maggie, very much to the contrary, is determined that they now move only in high society. The strip combines social history with satire at Maggie's social pretensions. "Bringing Up Father" explores the rise of the children of immigrants who achieve wealth and determine to be accepted by the Anglo American elite. The daughter is Maggie's triumph: pretty, babbling trivia with her social peers on the phone and sheltered from her parents' ethnic background. Though Maggie wins most of the couple's encounters, McManus' sympathies are planted on Jiggs' side of the struggle between his fidelity to his working-class origins and his wife's money-fed social climbing. The strip's popular impulse also comes from the artist's highly accessible visual style, unlike the weird landscapes of "Krazy Kat."

"Moon Mullins," a strip detailing the misadventures of a sometime prizefighter and his younger brother Kayo, explored some of the same themes. Moon (short for "Moonshine") is also Irish American. So is the "Yellow Kid," the yellow-gowned infant onlooker in what most commentators have considered the first comic strip. The mischievous heroes of "The Katzenjammer Kids" are German. Though the kids are marooned on a desert island with their father, the strip offers yet another portrayal of an ethnicity recognizable in American society.

Comic strips almost by definition remained purposefully short-lived. They were of and for their era, art that contemporaries alone could fully appreciate, both fresh and unpretentious. Their ephemeral quality provided part of their appeal.

Jazz too had a large public, but did not so greatly depend on mass acceptance. Musicians and composers did not need to have a succession of hits to keep their jobs. And the proliferation of radio stations and record companies in the twenties meant that jazz artists could find listening publics large enough to pay the bills even if they attracted only a tiny fraction of the millions who flocked to see Chaplin's latest film or turned to the comics every morning to see the latest encounter between Maggie and Jiggs.

Modernist vs. Popular Art: Distance vs. Accessibility

Modernist artists typically came from middle or upper-class backgrounds. Many of them had studied at the best schools and frequently benefited from travel abroad. So did some popular artists like Cole Porter and the lyricist Oscar Hammerstein II. But more often than not, popular artists came from immigrant, working-class backgrounds or the African American community. Most of them lacked formal art training or had to cut it short to support themselves. Both jazz and film emerged from the nether reaches of society. Initially a novelty patronized by the urban poor, movies were made by immigrants and their children for people like themselves. Yet within a few years, moviemakers succeeded in creating films that combined enormous popular appeal and great emotional depth. They would go on to invent new, ever more elaborate techniques for conveying the subtlest shades of meaning while their films remained available to a mass audience.

Accessibility is essential to the popular impulse in art. In this it stands at several removes from modernism. After crediting Charles Ives with covering "the gap between art and vernacular music," *New York Modern* remarks:

In turning his back to New York's entertainers and other artists, Ives gained the freedom to compose radically new music, unencumbered by popular taste or musical convention. And, like his music, Ives remained uncorrupted by commerce or fellowship, but also obscure and remote, his artistic isolation a testament to the modernity of his music and his personal eccentricity.

George Gershwin also composed "radically new music." But far from "turning his back to New York's entertainers," he wrote his *Rhapsody in Blue* at the suggestion of the bandleader Paul Whiteman and played the piano at its premier. Nor did he see commerce as a source of corruption or popular taste as a burden. For Gershwin artistic isolation would have meant failure, not integrity. Following the success of his *Rhapsody*, he sailed to Paris in the hope of studying with the composer Maurice Ravel. In this too he stood at the opposite pole from Ives, who sought to create an American music independent of European influence. Gershwin did not aspire to write American music. Ravel declined to take him as a student, pointing out that Gershwin had already developed his own artistic voice and urging him to develop it. Gershwin took the advice and composed *An American in Paris*, the great product of his stay in France. He already was what Ives sought to become, an American original. He continued to write for the concert hall but also for the Broadway stage and, once sound was introduced, for the movies. And however innovative his songs, he did not set himself against the musical traditions of the nineteenth century. Like his idol Berlin, Porter, Kern, Richard Rodgers, and other popular musicians, Gershwin borrowed unabashedly from operetta composers like Rudolph Friml. His music was modern but not modernist. And the music remained intrinsically American because he drew upon all of the musical possibilities open to him. Ives's idea of developing American music matched William Carlos Williams' vision of an American poetry. Both sought to mine the nation's past and recast it in avant-garde terms. But neither looked to the people as a suitable public and neither saw public indifference to their work as a sign of artistic failure.

The Uses of Surroundings

Joseph Stella's vision of New York remains one of the most celebrated modernist works of the 1920s. It captures the overwhelming vastness of the modern metropolis, the sensory overload residents and visitors alike have to cope with and in *The Brooklyn Bridge* particularly, the beauty of its constructed environment. The work rejects literal representation, especially in the second panel, Broadway, in which geometrical shapes and color replace buildings and lights. Stella, like Ives and Williams, drew material from the life about him but distanced himself from that life by employing techniques associated

Joseph Stella, "Voice of the City of New York Interpreted," 1920 panel. *The Brooklyn Bridge.*

with avant-garde abstraction. Popular artists did not routinely turn to urban settings for inspiration, as did their modernist counterparts. Norman Rockwell, easily the most popular of all, portrayed small town life and family scenes in most of his work. Illustrators of pulp magazines, monthlies that contained a complete novel for only a dime, often used cosmopolitan backdrops but rarely portrayed cityscapes. *The Shadow*, which began in 1931 and may have been the most popular of all the mass publications, provides one example. So too others like *The Spider*, another long-running pulp series, and *Spicy Detective*, itself successful enough to spin off *Spicy Western* and several other magazines. Drawn to appeal to male customers, the pulps featured large-breasted women in torn dresses, evil-looking villains, many of them stereotypically of foreign origin, and intrepid heroes. Background drawings rarely featured a skyscraper. Illustrators working for ad agencies, on the other hand, often used skyscrapers, bridges, and other aspects of city life, especially when the theme of the advertisement promoted the future.

"Up to the Minute Merchandising and Manufacturing Methods Enable Certain-teed to give Extra Value in All its Products. Unhampered by precedent—but tempered by the experiences of many productive years, Certain-teed, today, is in a stronger position to serve you than ever before."

The text used in the ad below for Certain-teed building products offers a commentary on the illustration. A giant figure pushes time

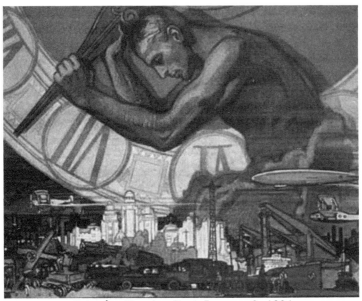

Saturday Evening Post, January 2, 1926

"Trend to What and Where" in *Everybody's Business* by Floyd W. Parsons, May 12, 1932, p. 3.

ahead while beneath it planes and a zeppelin soar past skyscrapers, derricks, and an oil well.

In "Trend to What and Where," the past gives way to the future. The camel driver and charioteer evoke the one while the speeding train, racecar, airplanes, and zeppelin all forecast the other. The beams of light streaming down suggest that all is right with this new world. Here the force impelling the rapid forward movement is the abrasive wheel, used to cut machine tools and parts. The smokestacks in the distance represent the giant kilns used in making the wheels. By employing similar imagery in *Advertising Age* for Dec. 21, 1926, Bernarr Macfadden advertised his magazines, which included *True Stories*, *True Detective*, and a number of bodybuilding and physical culture publications. The Chrysler Building (see the illustration on p. 143) defines the New York skyline as an ocean liner and a speeding passenger train intersect while an airplane and a zeppelin move across the sky. Yet again, golden rays illumine the new day allied to an outline of the United States on the globe.

Macfadden's ad combines almost as much visual complexity as Stuart Davis' *Abstract Vision of New York: A Building, A Derby Hat, a Tiger's Head, and Other Symbols*. Its symbolism is more apparent, as befits an ad, and it shows a preoccupation with speed as well as massiveness.

Abstract Motion became as common a theme in popular depictions of the city as the future. And the facile association between motion and that future proclaimed progress. The melding of motion, the city, and the future appears in much of the modernist art dealing with the city as well, but the work of Stella and Davis and their colleagues also suggest bewilderment and alienation. Their cityscapes rise vast and impersonal. They present no human figures. Edward Hopper, another modernist who often painted urban scenes, did include people but accentuated their lack of connection with one another. *The Nighthawks*, his most famous painting, depicts several customers sitting in a diner late at night. They make no eye contact with one another. Neither Hopper nor any of his modernist contemporaries used the cliché of a golden sky or a sunrise to suggest serenity.

Both modernist and popular artists sought a visual language for their times, but the popular artists worked within the commercial constraints dictated by the role of advertising in the new consumer culture of the era. According to James Montgomery Flagg, a highly successful illustrator who sold his first picture in 1890 at the age of twelve and composed the celebrated "I Want *You*" poster of Uncle Sam, "the difference between the [illustrator and the modernist artist] is that the former knows how to draw, eats three square meals a day and can pay for them." Illustrators had to get across a specific message to specific groups. And like other popular artists, they needed commercial success if they wanted to be employed. The visual language they developed, moreover, had to work in tandem with the written copy: "Not Yesterday . . ." had to complement "Paced Ahead of Changing Times, this Editorial Technique proves its Fundamental Vitality . . . MacFadden . . . did much to foster liberality by creating a new Editorial Technique. . . . The Times have simply caught up with this dynamic Technique." The Certain-teed ad showing the giant pushing time ahead had to complement "Up to the Minute Merchandising and Manufacturing Methods Enable Certain-teed to give Extra Value in All its Products. Unhampered by precedent—but tempered by the experiences of many productive years, Certain-teed, today, is in a stronger position to serve you than ever before."

Paced Ahead of Changing Times, this Editorial Technique proves its Fundamental Vitality

Yet another defining contrast between modernist and popular art is the latter's role in guiding the imagination. Certainly Hopper's *The Nighthawks* haunts many. But only people with a grasp of the history of modern art can even identify Stuart Davis or Joseph Stella. Almost everyone not only knows the name Norman Rockwell but can call to mind a number of his most famous covers. The vast majority of commercial artists lacked Rockwell's renown but may have done even more to define modern life for millions. Their countless illustrations for ads, magazine covers, sheet music, and posters supplied the images that people conjured up when they thought of the city, mechanization, progress, and the good life.

"Modern Dance" and Popular Dancing

Nothing better illustrates the influence of the popular in art in shaping the imagination than to contrast the dancers Fred and Adele Astaire with Ruth St. Denis and Ted Shawn.

In 1933 Ruth St. Denis wrote of the dance of the future that it

will no longer be concerned with meaningless dexterities of the body. . . . Remembering that man is indeed the microcosm, the universe in miniature, the Divine Dance of the future should be able to convey with its slightest gestures some significance of the universe. . . . As we rise higher in the understanding of ourselves, the national and racial dissonances will be forgotten in the universal rhythms of Truth and Love. We shall sense our unity with all peoples who are moving to that exalted rhythm.

Early in the century, Ruth St. Denis and Ted Shawn had taken up the banner of Isadora Duncan and set out to create a modern dance free of the "meaningless dexterity" characteristic of classical ballet. St. Denis chose mythic figures from a variety of cultures and interpreted their stories through dance. Like Duncan, St. Denis achieved a measure of public attention and the patronage of some rich admirers. Martha Graham, a student of St. Denis and Shawn and a dancer in their Denishawn troupe, carried on "Miss Ruth's" ideas. Unlike many other modernist artists, St. Denis and Shawn did not dream of creating an American dance. Their aspirations stretched considerably

Ruth St. Denis. Private collection of John McClymer.

farther toward the creation of a universal, timeless dance, a "divine dance," as St. Denis put it. The resulting dances themselves, however, had specific cultural roots. Some lay in vaudeville. St. Denis began her career when only thirteen, as a "skirt dancer," a performer whose steps lifted her skirts enough to titillate male audiences with glimpses of thigh. The producer David Belasco discovered her and proceeded to change her name from Ruthie Denis to Ruth St. Denis, and featured her, and her legs, in his own productions. Shawn also had a vaudeville background, devising an act modeled upon that of the popular dance team Vernon and Irene Castle. He popularized the tango. Other roots lay in St. Denis' admiration for the French actress Sarah Bernhardt, who had starred in several productions as Cleopatra. But mostly the innovations were inspired by Isadora Duncan and her fascinating idea that allowing the dancer's intuitions to direct the movements could reveal profound truths. Gauzy costumes and bare limbs helped.

Before she met Shawn, St Denis had brought her ideas to vaudeville but with limited success. She fared better with New York society ladies for whom she gave private performances and organized lessons. This played itself out after several years and St. Denis returned to vaudeville. She and Shawn formed the dance troupe Denishawn. Their characteristic combination of exoticism with hints of eroticism drew enough interest for the troupe to carry on for several decades. During this time St. Denis and Shawn trained numerous dancers ranging from Graham and Doris Humphrey to Louise Brooks.

"Top Hat, White Tie, and Tails" by Irving Berlin
I just got an invitation through the mails:
"Your presence requested this evening, it's formal
A top hat, a white tie and tails.
Nothing now could take the wind out of my sails
Because I'm invited to step out this evening
With top hat, white tie and tails.

I'm puttin' on my top hat
Tyin' up my white tie
Brushin' off my tails
I'm dudin' up my shirt front
Puttin' in the shirt studs
Polishin' my nails.

I'm steppin' out, my dear
To breathe an atmosphere that simply reeks with class
And I trust that you'll excuse my dust when I step on the gas.
For I'll be there
Puttin' down my top hat
Mussin' up my white tie
Dancin' in my tails.

Fred Astaire began performing in vaudeville at the tender age of six with his seven-year-old sister Adele. Successful as child dancers, the Astaires made the transition to adult roles, opening on Broadway in *The Nine O'Clock Revue* (later renamed *Over the Top*) in 1917. By the early 1920s both had become major stars on the New York and London stages and in 1924, they opened in George and Ira Gershwin's *Lady Be Good*, in which Fred introduced through dance both the title tune and "Fascinatin' Rhythmn." After long runs on Broadway and the West End of London, the Astaires starred in 1927 in another Gershwin show, *Funny Face*. In this show Astaire performed a solo number, "High Hat," in which he first wore the formal evening clothes that would become his trademark.

Personal collection, John McClymer

Fred and Adele appeared together for the last time in 1931 with another hit, *The Band Wagon*. Adele left the theater to marry into the British aristocracy, and Fred starred in one last Broadway show, *The Gay Divorcee*, by Cole Porter, before turning to the movies. Astaire introduced "Night and Day," which Frank Sinatra called the finest American song of the twentieth century.

While St. Denis and Shawn sought inspiration in ancient mythologies, the Astaires followed the lead of Vernon and Irene Castle, basing their act on the popular music and the dance steps of the day, including tap. When they moved on to musicals, they developed a new kind of number fusing dance and song. For the Astaires, dancing meant business, show business. When theatergoers went home from *The Gay Divorcee* humming "Night and Day," their mind's eye carried away Fred Astaire's dancing and their ears his singing. This was unquestionably the effect of art of a very high order that St. Denis and Shawn would not recognize as remotely like their own.

A Popular Sense of "Class"

To the public, Astaire personified grace. He also defined class. A preoccupation with "class" characterized much popular art in the interwar years. In this sense class refers not to social position but to being classy, a word that people of the 1920s used along with "smart" a term of high phrase. The title of H. L. Mencken's *Smart Set* magazine captures the idea. Harold Ross' *The New Yorker* also catered to readers who wished to be thought smart. Ads, even for toilet paper, played off, and preyed on, this desire to be smart.

> —that atmosphere of elegance and refinement—those necessary little appointments, noticed but not discussed, which contribute so much to the comfort and well-being of guests and family. ScotTissue has made a place for itself in well-conducted homes. It is the choice of discriminating women everywhere because of its hygienic purity and safety. . . . *Saturday Evening Post*, Sept. 11, 1926, p. 186

Having class meant knowing how to act and what to prize, and purchase. It required a measure of affluence but not vast wealth. And it emphatically did not depend on a privileged background. Most of the popular arbiters of class—Mencken, Ross, Astaire, Berlin—came from working class or lower middle-class backgrounds. Cole Porter and F. Scott Fitzgerald aside, they had not attended Ivy League schools. Class used in this popular sense spelled achievement.

Fitzgerald turned this notion upon its head in his most critically acclaimed novel, *The Great Gatsby*. By largely unspecified illegal dealings, Gatsby (originally Gatz) has risen from working class origins to become a figure sought after by Long Island society. In ease and manner, he is eminently smart, a perfect embodiment of class. But his quest to win the heart of Daisy Buchanan ends tragically. The novel when first published did not sell well, perhaps because it so directly challenged the dream that anyone could achieve class.

Berlin's lyrics showed him more in the mode of the times, particularly the lines "I'm stepping out, my dear/To breathe an atmosphere that simply reeks with class." The use of "reeks" injects a note of self-parody that sets up "I'll be there/Puttin' down my top hat/Mussin' up my white tie/Dancin' in my tails." The goal here was not to win Daisy Buchanan's heart, a prize scarcely worth Gatsby's devotion according to the novel's narrator. Nor did it echo Maggie's misguided attempts to become part of the Four Hundred in George McManus' comic strip "Bringing Up Father." The goal simply was to enjoy yourself with a certain grace and ease. Consider the revised lyrics to Berlin's "Puttin' On the Ritz":

> Have you seen the well-to-do
> Up and down Park Avenue
> On that famous thoroughfare
> With their noses in the air
> High hats and narrow collars
> White spats and lots of dollars
> Spending every dime
> For a wonderful time

Now, if you're blue
And you don't know where to go
Why don't you go where fashion sits
Puttin' on the Ritz

Dressed up like a million dollar trooper
Trying hard to look like Gary Cooper
Super-duper

Come, let's mix where Rockefellers
Walk with sticks or "umberellas"
In their mitts
Puttin' on the Ritz.

Tips his hat just like an English chappie
To a lady with a wealthy pappy
Very snappy.

You'll declare it's simply topping
To be there and hear them swapping
Smart tidbits
Puttin' on the Ritz.

Who was "puttin' on the Ritz"? Clearly the folks who did not live on Park Avenue, along with devotees of fashion. And, of course, the fellow trying to charm the "lady with a wealthy pappy"—even the Rockefellers who walked "with sticks or 'umberellas' in their mitts." Like "reeks" in *Top Hat*, "mitts" strikes the popular note. What could be better than to get all duded up? But, and this shows the Astaire characteristic at its best, you should not take yourself too seriously.

The Comic Impulse in Popular Art

Modernist artists sometimes aspired to wit of an ironic or sardonic sort. They aimed for the knowing smile. Popular artists sought the belly laugh.

This is obvious in the work of the "silent clowns," as the film critic and historian Walter Kerr has titled Chaplin, Keaton, and their colleagues. Silent comedy has become largely a lost art, almost as remote as Kabuki theatre. Seldes found elements of the timeless in Chaplin's movies; others now make the same claim for Keaton. Most comedy, however, belongs very much to its time. When Fanny Brice sang

I'm wearing second hand clothes.
Second hand hose,
That's why everybody calls me
Second Hand Rose.

> Even the piano in the parlor,
> Papa bought for ten cents on the dollar

the audience immediately understood the status owning a piano conferred in working-class families: thus the tragi-comic situation of "Second Hand Rose from Second Avenue."

> Even Jakie Cohen,
> He's the man I adore,
> He had the nerve to tell me
> He's been married before!

Comic strips aimed at timeliness as well. So did monologists like Will
Rogers. His quip—"I don't belong to an organized political party; I'm
a Democrat."—tickled the audience of his day, but would not mean
much to one today.

Irving Berlin started composing music by writing Yiddish-language
parodies of popular songs. And from "Oh, How I Hate to Get Up in
the Morning" to "Doin' What Comes Naturally," he continued to write
comic songs throughout his career. In the former, written for the First
World War revue "Yap, Yap Yapank" and performed by Berlin himself in "This is the Army," the rewritten version for World War II, he
promises

> Someday I'm going to murder the bugler.
> Someday, they're going to find him dead.
> I'll amputate his reveille
> And step upon it heavily
> And spend the rest of my life in bed.

Audiences empathized with the draftee longing for an extra hour or
two of sleep and with his wish to put an end to the bugle call that
interrupted his slumbers. They also appreciated the wit of describing
the longed-for homicide as amputating his reveille and rhyming that
with "step upon it heavily." Berlin's variation at the end of the song
drops "I'll amputate his reveille" and substitutes:

> And then I'll find that other pup,
> The one that wakes the bugler up,
> And spend the rest of my life in bed.

Like so many popular lyricists, Berlin routinely fused the literal—I'm
going to murder the bugler—with the fanciful: I'll amputate his
reveille. Berlin wrote the music for *Animal Crackers*, the Marx Brothers' Broadway success of 1925. George F. Kaufman wrote the book
on which the film is based, which features jokes such as Groucho's

describing a reward as "chickenfeed, a poultry thousand dollars." Kaufman went on to share a Pulitzer Prize with George and Ira Gershwin for *Of Thee I Sing*, a musical parody of presidential politics. And he continued to write for the Marx Brothers. In *Animal Crackers* Groucho complains to brother Chico about the exorbitant fee he and his orchestra receive. Chico attempts to explain by mentioning the time for rehearsal:

> Groucho: Well, how much do you charge without rehearsal?
> Chico: You could never afford it.

All of this, like their celebrated "Why a Duck" routine in which Groucho shows Chico a viaduct, features silliness but silliness of a very high order.

Freeman Gosden and Charles Correll launched "Amos 'n Andy" in March 1928 over what became, in part because of their success, the NBC radio network. The show created a sensation, at least with white listeners. Its popularity partially stems from Gosden and Correll's use of what could be easily mistaken for racial stereotypes. They are not. Like the Little Tramp, Amos and Andy represent Everyman. Amos, hard working, sensible, and reliable, is a family man. Andy, in pursuit of the ladies, dreams of quick wealth. In the two, listeners heard echoes of themselves. Comedy quickly became a staple of radio programming. Gosden and Correll wrote their own material. Not so Jack Benny, who helped initiate the practice of hiring a stable of writers to come up with the material needed week in and week out. Benny perfected the collaborative approach to comedy. There had been comedy teams for some time, like Gallagher and Sheen, in which the comics traded jokes. Here is an example:

> Customer: Waiter! These oysters are very small.
> Waiter: Yes sir.
> Customer: And they don't seem to be very fresh either.
> Waiter: Then lucky for you they're small.

But Benny helped create a different style of comedic exchange in which over the years members of his troupe, like the characters in "Amos 'n Andy," developed specific personalities. Every week listeners tuned in to hear the repartee between Jack and Rochester, his black valet and chauffeur, or Jack and Phil Harris, his hard-drinking bandleader, or between Jack and a host of other regulars. These exploited in endless variation a familiar set of jokes. Rochester's success with the ladies and Jack's failures, Jack's vanity about his blue eyes, Jack's compulsive miserliness, the frustration of his violin teacher with Jack's tin ear all became set pieces used in radio show after show. Rather than become stale, the comedy built as the audience came to know the characters. People tuned in just to hear Jack lose patience again with Rochester or hit yet another sour note.

Of Show Boat and Saints: A Conclusion

Much of what characterizes popular art came together in *Show Boat*, the 1927 production that, theater historians agree, redefined musical theater.

What makes *Show Boat* most memorable is its demonstration that a musical could take on themes like racism, miscegenation, and "passing." In evoking these, music and story fuse so that the songs are not interludes but directly advance the plot, as when Julie, "the prettiest leading lady on the river" and a mulatto passing as white, sings "Can't Help Lovin' That Man of Mine," a song "only colored folks" ever sang. *Show Boat* also consciously celebrates American popular song and popular entertainment from the 1880s through the 1920s. Cap'n Andy and his wife Parthy mirror Maggie and Jiggs in the wife's aspiration to reach a height of respectability the husband finds both silly and oppressive. Much of the trouble that afflicts the characters is firmly rooted in the world of the potboiler. Yet the first words the audience hears protest racial injustice. And when Magnolia confides with Joe, the black servant and husband of the cook, about her romantic problems with the new juvenile lead, there comes a stunning moment in the mating of art with popularity. "Better ask de river," Joe tells her before turning his spoken advice into "Old Man River," which brings down the curtain on Act One. The rest of the musical never quite reaches the heights achieved in that first act, perhaps because if "Night and Day" is not the finest song of the twentieth century, then "Old Man River" is.

Show Boat is a popular masterpiece. The story comes from a best-selling novel of the day. The music, written by Jerome Kern and Oscar Hammerstein II, drew directly on the vernacular styles of the preceding half-century. They aimed directly at commercial success with a hit and they got one. *Show Boat* continues to be performed regularly in revival, the popular equivalent to the operatic repertoire. But Kern and Hammerstein had a more noble goal. They condemned racism and made their white audience identify with African Americans and acknowledge a common humanity.

Contrast their work with *Four Saints in Three Acts*, the most successful modernist opera. The libretto, and presumably the misleading title (there are four acts), were by Gertrude Stein, who said of it:

> A saint a real saint never does anything, a martyr does something but a really good saint does nothing, and so I wanted to have Four Saints who did nothing and I wrote the Four Saints in Three Acts and they did nothing and that was everything. Generally speaking anybody is more interesting doing nothing than doing anything.

Two of the saints, Ignatius Loyola and Teresa of Avila, were based upon historical figures; their companions, Saint Settlement and Saint Chavez, are products entirely of the playwright's imagination. The imaginary saints indeed do nothing. But the two real saints, in reality if not in the opera, did quite a good deal. The immensely talented Virgil Thomson wrote the music. In early 1927, in his accounting, Gertrude Stein and he thought of writing an opera. He proposed that they base it on lives of the saints. Stein chose the Spanish saints Teresa of Avila and Ignatius Loyola. Neither Thompson nor Stein, he said, felt any concern that the two saints had never met in life. Why these two?

Miss Stein loved these saints because they were Spanish. I liked them for being powerful and saints. She had traveled a great deal in Spain, loved its landscape and its people; I had been brought up in Missouri among Southern Baptists and spent my youth as a church organist. So we made together, Gertrude Stein and I, an opera about the Spanish landscape and about the religious life. She gave me the libretto of "Four Saints in Three Acts" in June of 1927, and I completed the music in July of the following year.

It took six years before the opera was performed in Hartford, New York, and Chicago by a troupe calling itself "The Friends and Enemies of Modern Music." As Thompson proudly pointed out, the production "made theatrical history" because "an all-Negro cast should be received so warmly in a work that had nothing whatever to do with Negro life. I had chosen them purely for beauty of voice, clarity of enunciation and fine carriage. Their surprise gift to the production was their understanding of its obscurities, [they] moved in on it, adopted it."

The use of an all-black cast necessarily made a comment about the racial attitudes of the day. But the story in the opera itself has nothing to do with race and in subsequent productions most casts have been white. Though directed by John Houseman, who would go on to find success on Broadway, radio, and film, and drawing on the assistance of Frederick Ashton, soon to become the leading ballet choreographer of the day, *Four Saints in Three Acts* abjures production values—no elaborate sets, no gorgeous costumes. In all of this it adopts a classic modernist stance in contrast to the art of the preceding century. *Saints* aimed and succeeded at being as unlike a grand opera as Stein and Thomson could make it. Stein's contribution, in phrasings that might make sense if only some words were left out, gives lines like this: "No one chain is it not chain is it, chained to not to life chained to not to snow chained to chained to go and gone." The initial production ran for sixty performances, a record for a modernist opera, and there continues to be enough of an audience for occasional revivals. But *Show Boat*'s run lasted years, was released in three movie versions, and continues to be revived regularly.

Show Boat is grand opera in everything but the name. It has the sets, the costumes, the chorus, the dancers. It has raucous comedy and high tragedy. Above all, it has arias ("Old Man River"), choral works ("Misery's Comin'"), and love duets ("Only Make Believe"). As befitted a popular work, the words make sense both in their clarity of meaning and in their reporting of experiences that at least some part of an audience could relate to.

> You an' me, we sweat an' strain,
> Body all achin' an' racked wid pain—
> Tote dat barge!
> Lif' dat bale!
> Git a little drunk,
> An' you land in jail . . .

Unlike *Saints*, *Show Boat* inspired a host of other major works starting with *Porgy and Bess* and including *Carousel* and *West Side Story*, which draws frankly on Shakespeare as well.

Seldes' verdict clearly held for his own time: "Except in a period when the major arts flourish with exceptional vigour, the lively arts are likely to be the most intelligent phenomena of their day."

IX

A New Deal and a New Polity

Well before the Great Depression, divisions between well to do and poor were both substantial and, in public discussion, almost nonexistent. A hit song from a Broadway musical of 1929 unwittingly told the story.

In "Makin' Whoopee" Eddie Cantor recounts the sad tale of a young man who cannot wait to become sexually active. At his wedding he is so nervous "he answers twice." Within a year there is a baby, and he has become so entangled in domestic chores "he even sews." Yet his desire to make whoopee remains and his resultant philandering leads to a divorce suit.

> He doesn't make much money,
> Only five thousand per.
> Some judge who thinks he's funny,
> Says, "You'll pay six to her."
> "But, Judge, suppose I fail?"
> "Well, son, right into jail.
> You'd better keep her,
> You'll find it's cheaper,
> Than makin' whoopee."

The casual reference to $5,000 a year as "not much money" laid bare the gap between the two Americas captured in Margaret Bourke-White's photograph on the right. Only eight percent of the nation's families earned even that much. But cultural conflicts after the Great War muted class differences as they do

154

once again in the early twenty-first century. Several reasons for the political dominance of business over labor suggest themselves.

The failed strikes of the immediate postwar years left unions weakened and their workers discouraged. Membership declined steadily throughout the 1920s, as did the number of strikes. This was an ominous sign for the labor movement. Previously, membership had increased during periods of prosperity. Under such conditions, strikes had a greater chance of succeeding because workers could more easily find other jobs and because employers were eager to have their factories operating during good times. Another reason for the decline in labor militancy can be traced to the champions of class struggle, the socialists and other left-wing activists who came out of the war and the immediate postwar period bloodied and divided. Their opposition to the war had made them easy targets for wartime prosecution and harassment. Then the Red Scare of 1919 stigmatized all political movements on the left as variants of Bolshevism. As for the real American Bolsheviki, the members of the new American Communist Party, their meager numbers came chiefly from a handful of immigrant groups, particularly Finns and Russian Jews. Communists loathed socialists, who reviled them in return.

Still another reason for the popular trust in business is that the economic distress of the twenties disproportionately afflicted farm families, while much of the nation was experiencing good times. Prices for wheat and many commodities fell once wartime demand ceased. Some in Congress sought to help. The McNary-Haugen Bill, first introduced in 1924, would have prevented prices from dropping below prewar levels. It authorized the federal government to buy up surpluses that it could later sell on the international market. Initially, the bill lacked support among southern senators and failed. A revised version, which extended price protection to cotton and tobacco, did pass, but President Coolidge vetoed it. He feared an expanded federal bureaucracy and objected to its interference with the free market. Families that derived their living from work other than agricultural did not rally behind McNary-Haugen. They had economic worries of their own, though in most cases insufficient to spur political activism.

So most farmers found themselves thrown back on their own resources. They sought to survive by expanding production, bringing additional acres under cultivation; they invested in tractors, combines, and other equipment to improve yield per acre. Both initiatives increased their debt as well as their harvest. Adding grain to the market lowered commodity prices further so that even when farmers managed to sell more, their income did not rise. This in turn led to further attempts to increase production and to still greater debt. By the late twenties bankruptcies had become commonplace. Possessions of farm families sold at auction, often for pennies on the dollar. Then the dispossessed farmers had to start over, usually with no place to live, no credit, few possessions.

Trouble dwelt in some other sectors of the economy. Coal miners worked under unhealthy conditions for meager pay. Migrant labor continued vulnerable to exploitation, as did domestic workers such as housemaids. And black workers, of course, had little good to expect from society. But such portions of the workforce remained separate from the consciousness of the majority. It was widely assumed, even among much of the poor, that poverty was their lot—so easily assumed that their condition went unnoticed. They made up what a later social commentator would label the "invisible poor."

Class mattered in peoples' lives, defining which America they lived in. But widespread public awareness came only with the Great Depression, an economic disaster without precedent in American history. In response to fiscal catastrophe came the New Deal, as Franklin Delano Roosevelt called the policies his administration advanced. Many initiatives were frankly experimental and when they failed were abandoned. Others operated at cross purposes. None succeeded in restoring prosperity. But the New Deal programs did change the basic relationship between the federal government and society, allowing Washington to take on new roles. It regulated the economy; it protected the environment; it provided its citizens with pensions, unemployment compensation, and other entitlements; it promoted the mechanization of agriculture; it modernized rural areas. The New Deal reshaped the polity. Much of what the Roosevelt administration did addressed problems that had long pre-dated the Depression, but the turn from problems to disaster created the political crisis that made the New Deal possible.

The Crash

In practice governments routinely regulated economic activities, often at the insistence of corporations. But in major sectors of the economy, market forces operated relatively unimpeded. That was certainly the case with respect to the stock market. Prices had risen throughout the 1920s. At first, this reflected the expanding economy. Then, as new investors began to enter the market, stock prices went up regardless of the value of the companies issuing the stock. More people scrambled to get in on the Great Bull Market, aided by a risky credit arrangement called buying on margin (now termed leveraging). You put down ten percent on a stock purchase and borrowed the rest. When the price went up, you sold. Your stockbroker collected the balance of the purchase price plus interest and a fee. You pocketed the rest. The prospect was dizzying. Someone with $1000 could purchase one hundred shares of a stock at $100 a share or $10,000 worth. When the price went to $110, the investor sold for $11,000. After repaying the $9000 borrowed and interest and broker fees, the investor's $1000 had become $1600 or more, a sixty-percent profit realized in a matter of weeks even though the stock itself had gained only ten percent.

Stories abounded of previously ordinary people who had suddenly become millionaires.

When the bubble burst, the ranks of millionaires abruptly thinned. Brokers called in the loans. Investors had to sell their stock in order to meet these calls. Suddenly the number of sellers exceeded willing buyers. In October 1929 stock prices fell sharply, well below the price at which investors could salvage any of their initial investment. They were almost all wiped out. Some of the brokerage houses that had extended too much credit disappeared as well. For when they called in the loans, investors defaulted, and they ended up holding large blocks of stock that they could sell only at staggering losses. Eighty-nine percent of the value of the market evaporated in a matter of days.

The market crash did not cause the Depression. That had deeper roots. But the crash did trigger the hard times of the thirties by deepening a drop in demand already under way.

By 1922 consumer demand had become the primary source of economic growth. Yet the comparatively low wages of most working families severely limited their ability to consume. The percentage of the population able to buy a Cadillac or a Ford or a vacuum cleaner or a refrigerator for cash did not change over the course of the decade. Such things sold because buying on the installment plan became more popular, and consumer debt soared. One immovable obstacle prevented permanent growth. Wages rose only marginally. They had not increased with productivity: with the amount of goods and services produced by the average worker per hour. And in the twenties most farm income was already in sharp decline along with wages in soft coal mining and other selected industries.

Demand leveled off after 1927 and began to fall. People then postponed discretionary purchases indefinitely. As demand fell so did production and prices. Thereupon, so declared modern capitalist theory as articulated by the eighteenth-century economist Adam Smith, the market should have begun correcting itself. Once the economy reached a new equilibrium, once prices fell low enough to allow even the wretchedly poor to buy consumer goods, the recovery would begin. So held conventional wisdom. And so, apparently, thought President Hoover, at least through 1930 and well into 1931. But conventional wisdom was wrong. Although prices went down, consumers continued to postpone buying. This made sense for two compelling reasons. One is that so long as prices continued to fall, you could simply wait. Smith had imagined an economy that supplied basic needs for food, clothing, shelter, and some entertainment, and not much more. He did not foresee a time when much of what people bought was discretionary: a refrigerator, for example, to replace an old icebox. Such things a consumer could put off buying. The other reason why people did not take advantage of the fall in prices is that as more and more people lost their jobs or had their hours reduced, it did not make sense to go into debt, especially to buy something they did not need to have or to invest in companies that were close to failing.

Economic downtowns had occurred before, some quite severe. They were viewed as a normal phase of the business cycle, the term economists gave the periodic swings from prosperity to depression and back. Below is a graph that charts the gross national product (GNP), the sum of goods and services in the United States, between 1890 and 1940. The GNP dropped by seven percent during the severe business slump of the early 1890s. It dipped even more sharply in the years 1920 to 1922. Then came a relatively brief period of Republican prosperity. The economy did not grow so rapidly as it had during the early 1900s, and two minor downturns took place, but the good times were real. Earlier bad times had ended quickly. The depression of the 1890s ran the longest, lasting from 1893 to 1897. But recovery started as early as 1895. Other recessions had been even briefer. So President Hoover and his advisors in 1930 and 1931 were historically justified in predicting that the severity of the Great Depression would soon abate. But the Great Depression of the 1930s was different. The economy did not contract as in previous recessions. It collapsed. The gross national product fell by more than thirty percent. Worse is that the economy did not recover.

By the end of 1931, after job losses started to mount, many lost faith in the president's assurances. Hoover as secretary of commerce had been identified with Republican prosperity. He campaigned in 1928 on the promise that the United States stood on the verge of elim-

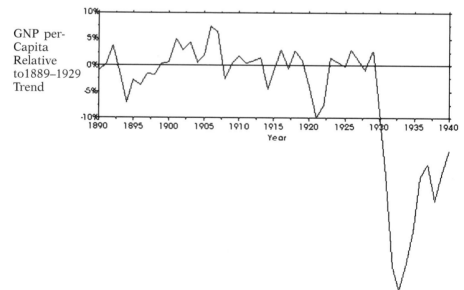

From J. Bradford DeLong, *An Economic History of the Twentieth Century*, online at http://www.j-bradford-delong.net/TCEH/Slouch_title.html

inating poverty. As trust in the Republican formula for prosperity waned, agitation over class and economic inequities replaced some of the cultural battles over religion and gender and sexuality, and the possibility for sweeping change emerged.

Three calamities, one political, one natural, and the other fiscal, show how rapidly events forced the shift to class-based politics. All three spotlighted problems the Depression did not so much cause as bring to the fore. The three also create a context for understanding the lasting import of the New Deal. They established its agenda.

The Bonus March of 1932

Back in 1924 Congress had approved a bonus of $1000 to all World War I veterans, payable in 1945. As hard times worsened, many veterans demanded that they get the money immediately. Quite apart from pleading the urgency of their need, veterans argued that the infusion of several billions of dollars into the economy would provide a stimulus benefiting everyone. President Hoover and the United States Senate disagreed, probably wrongly. They feared that paying the bonus would cause a large deficit in the federal budget. A group of veterans in Portland, Oregon, who called themselves the Bonus Expeditionary Force (after the American Expeditionary Force that had fought in France during the war), began a march on Washington, D.C. in May 1932. Others joined them along the way until thousands were marching. When they reached the capital, they set up shantytowns, the largest of which sat on the mud flats next to the Anacostia River just outside the city. Others moved into vacant office space in Washington or into unfinished or partially demolished buildings.

By June about 25,000 people were squatting on Maryland's Anacostia flats in what had become the country's largest Hooverville, as

From the Herbert Hoover Presidential Library and Museum, West Branch, Iowa

such shantytowns were called across the country. Representative John Patman, a Democrat from Texas, introduced a bill for the immediate payment of the bonus. It passed in the House but lost in the Senate, where Republicans still had a majority. Veterans responded by holding a three-day Death March along Pennsylvania Avenue.

Rumors spread that Communists had organized the march. Disgruntled marchers also engaged in minor acts of vandalism against the automobiles of Republican senators and other symbolic targets. Additional rumors circulated, suggesting that many in the Bonus Expeditionary Force were not veterans, but criminals. No one knew how many in the BEF had served in World War I, for the people moving into the Anacostia Hooverville did not have to show discharge papers. President Hoover's pronouncements as he grew older and more conservative describe the marchers as doing the bidding of a conspiracy of Bolsheviks, Democrats, and irresponsible newspaper publishers.

Many of the marchers left Washington following the defeat of the bonus bill in the Senate, but about ten thousand remained. On July 28 the city's Police Commissioner Pelham Glassford attempted to evict the demonstrators living along Pennsylvania Avenue. A crowd milled about. The police shot two veterans. This prompted President Hoover to order the army to clear the streets. General Douglas MacArthur took charge. He removed the squatters within the city, and moved on the camps along the Anacostia River, deliberately ignoring the president's order not to do so. Hoover feared, correctly, the political costs of using the army against veterans and their families; and in any event he had a humanity he had earlier demonstrated in his organized relief programs for victims of the First World War and the upheaval in Russia. Either MacArthur or fleeing veterans set the Anacostia Hooverville on fire. Macarthur held a press conference in which he praised the president for having the courage to take decisive action. Meanwhile, the general blamed Communists and criminals for the march. Hoover's *Memoirs* observe that MacArthur had exceeded his orders but commend him for destroying the shantytown without killing anyone.

Hoover was correct in foreseeing that the episode would stir up class resentments and hatreds. Emotions throughout the country were high enough at any rate, as is reflected in the popularity of the song "Brother, Can You Spare a Dime?":

> They used to tell me I was building a dream.
> And so I followed the mob,
> When there was earth to plow
> Or guns to bear
> I was always there
> Right on the job.

. . .
Once in khaki suits
Gee we looked swell
Full of that yankee doodle dee dum.
Half a million boots went sloggin' through hell
And I was the kid with the drum!

Say don't you remember?
They called me Al.
It was Al all the time.
Why don't you remember?
I'm your pal.
Say buddy, can you spare a dime?
—Warner Bros., Inc (1932, E.Y. "Yip" Harburg and Jay Gorney)

Albert Potter; www.culturekiosque.
com/art/exhibiti/re1us04.htm

Bing Crosby recorded the tune in October 1932. Rudy Vallee soon did another recording. Both became enormous hits. Three years later Albert Potter crafted a linoleum print with the same title. It shows an unemployed man, newspaper rolled up in his pocket after another fruitless search through the want ads, panhandling in Manhattan. Death hovers between the Chrysler and the Empire State Buildings, the two most famous skyscrapers in the country. Broadway's neon lights, advertising the Follies, the Paramount Theatre, and the Edison Hotel, gleam behind the man's head, forming an ironic halo. At his feet, anonymous hordes of people swarm the streets.

Many Americans were familiar with the print; everyone knew the song, and the frustration it captured of people who had done all they could, only to find themselves without jobs, without homes, and without hope. The handling of the bonus marchers in 1932, like the government's response to the economic crisis, revealed a frightening fragility in the political system.

The inability to resolve the bonus question within the limits of conventional politics was symptomatic of the larger failings of the economy that for a decade had gone widely ignored. Now the government would have to convince the millions below the American standard of living that the federal government could and would respond to their needs.

The Banking Collapse

Most demoralizing was the near collapse of the banking system between late 1930 and early 1933. The banking disaster threatened everyone. Thousands of banks failed, at the cost of $2 billion in deposits. The $2 billion loss resulted in a thirty-percent decrease in the money supply. Credit dried up. Wages fell, as did prices.

One cause lay in the hard times in the agricultural sector during the 1920s. Bank failures had averaged about seventy a year in the first two decades of the twentieth century. During the twenties about six hundred banks a year went bust, most of them in rural areas. The rate increased again early in the 1930s. In late 1930 the bankruptcy of the Caldwell investment group of Nashville, the largest chain of banks in the South, set off a series of failures. The Caldwell banks had invested heavily in southern real estate. As land values sank, especially farmland, the banks found that they could no longer recover the value of mortgages through foreclosing. The failures were regional and did not spread to banks outside of the St. Louis Federal Reserve District. But during the spring and summer of 1931 in the Midwest another wave of bank closings occurred. A real estate boom in Chicago during the 1920s had led to a doubling of the number of banks in that city and to a mortgage market in which bankers abandoned caution. The depression brought a sharp fall in real estate values, rapidly increasing rates of defaults by borrowers, and oceans of red ink for the banks.

All told, the panics led to the closing of 2100 banks in less than three years, resulting in a failure rate somewhat higher than that of the 1920s. The worst seemed over by the start of 1932.

Then came the winter of 1932-33. Three thousand banks failed within a few months. Historians and economists are far from agreeing about the causes. But some facts are clear. One is that the panic coincided with the period between the presidential election in November and the inauguration in March. The voters had rejected both Hoover and the entire congressional Republican majorities. In addition, the financial strength of individual banks was virtually impossible for a depositor to assess. You might think your bank was safe. But the Caldwell banks had been the biggest in the South, yet they failed. Some of the Chicago banks that went under had been among the fastest growing institutions in the city only two years before. This created a dangerous popular psychology. If depositors could not be really sure their bank was sound, it seemed prudent to remove the deposits. Since banks earn money by loaning it out, even the healthiest bank could not survive if enough of its depositors demanded their money all at once. So once a significant fraction of a bank's customers starting making withdrawals, a run was on. It was simply irrational to leave your money in a bank on which others were making a run.

Might the Federal Reserve System have stepped in? Some economists, led by the Nobel laureate Milton Friedman, say it should have drastically increased the money supply to offset the funds removed from the economy by lost deposits. But the Fed's Board of Governors was in unmapped waters. And American currency was still tied to the gold standard, which limited to the nation's reserves of gold the amount of money the Treasury could issue. A new elastic currency awaited an economic theory yet be devised.

The authorities who did step in were state officials, beginning with Michigan in February 1933. They declared a bank holiday; that is, they closed banks in the state and restricted the amounts individuals could withdraw. Word of Michigan's action panicked depositors in neighboring states whose officials thereupon adopted similar policies. Within days banks in Ohio, Indiana, Illinois, and Pennsylvania were closed. Depositors all across the country streamed into their banks, hoping to get their savings out in time. Like the decision of the individual depositor, the policies of the state officials made sense as a fulfillment of their own responsibility to safeguard the banks in their states. Doing so, however, spread the panic and put the national banking system at risk. The new Roosevelt administration, which came into office as the run on the banks reached its worst, felt bound to apply the Michigan remedy to the entire country. On March 5, 1933, the day after his inauguration, Franklin Roosevelt closed all the nation's banks.

Bad as had been the stock market crash of October 1929, this banking disaster proved worse. The sufferers were savers, not Wall Street speculators. They were the people who had patiently set aside small amounts in the hope of buying a house or educating a child or having a nest egg for retirement—practitioners of the traditional wisdom of the middle class, working hard, watching their pennies, and saving for bad times. The run on the banks threatened the American Dream, that hard work and prudence would reward you with a better life for yourself and your children.

The failure of so many banks revealed an American economy dangerously underregulated. Each state had its own banking laws, but no effective federal agency regulated the banks themselves. In Nebraska, to cite one extreme, requirements for an institution's assets were set so low that the state had one bank for every thousand inhabitants. Most of these rural banks had far too little in deposits to survive an extended period of declining prices. And so they went bankrupt or, as injuriously to confidence and therefore economic health, seemed about to fail.

Too many rural and small-town banks were granting too many loans. The market, orthodox economics held, would correct this. But it did not. Many farmers and many banks went belly up. In seeking to avoid this fate, both took actions that threatened entire sectors of the economy and then the economy as a whole. Bankers tried to refinance bad loans, for if they refused they would have to foreclose and thereby force a public sale requiring them to acknowledge a loss. Keeping the loans on the books permitted them to list them in the asset column. So long as they stayed in that column, the bank appeared still to be in the black, an accounting fiction revealed as soon as enough depositors asked to withdraw their money.

Similar problems dogged urban banks. Most had invested heavily in home mortgages. The typical mortgage called for monthly interest payments. Then, at the end of the term of the loan, usually five years, the borrower had to repay the principal or renegotiate the mortgage. In 1930 borrowers and banks alike were squeezed. Housing prices, like prices generally, were falling. Properties on which borrowers had taken out $5000 mortgages, for example, might be worth only $3500 or less. But they still owed the banks the full amount. Only if borrowers paid the difference between the principal and the market value in cash would banks renew the loans. Many could not. Banks then repossessed their homes and, in an attempt to retrieve the institution's money, put them on the market. This drove housing prices down even further, and that in turn made it all the harder for the next person to renew a mortgage. Foreclosures were bad for both banks and borrowers. Borrowers lost their homes. But banks could not extend mortgages for more than the houses were worth, and borrowers could not come up with cash they did not have. The widespread availability of foreclosure bargains also crippled the market for new housing. Since few new houses were being built, construction jobs disappeared. The spiral quickened its downward pace.

Understanding the dangers of underregulation had been impossible prior to the Great Depression. Adam Smith's *Wealth of Nations* and the vast body of orthodox economics that followed rested upon a central belief: The marketplace, free of governmental interference, will create wealth more efficiently and more rapidly than if the government seeks to establish wages or prices or control production. Each individual acts on self-interest. As each pursues gain, the market itself will guarantee the overall success of the economy. The French phrase for non-interference, *laissez-faire*, became the great truth of economics. But before and into the depression years, self-interest harmed both the individual and the system. The self-interest of individual states recommended a bank holiday; and so, in neighboring states, confidence and banks fell. The self-interest of the consumer argued for putting off purchases until times improved; and so production fell, along with the same consumer's job. Concerning his own free-market system, Smith himself had recognized a significant exception: wages. Laws then effectively prevented workers from combining to secure higher pay. Employers, however, remained comparatively free to combine against workers. The state, Smith held, had a moral obligation to intervene. Smith's concerns about wages were lost in his larger message, as was his claim that government should provide for the needs of the defenseless poor—an idea that some ideologues today who think of themselves as Smith's disciples dismiss as socialism.

The Dust Bowl

The Dust Bowl, which also forced national attention on long-neglected urgent problems and helped set the New Deal's agenda, began in 1931 when a drought affected the Texas and Oklahoma panhandles, Kansas, and parts of Colorado and New Mexico. A very dry winter followed. Wind easily lifted the loose soil and hurtled it for miles—at one point all the way across the country and far into the Atlantic.

Year after year brought more of the same. Here is how *Time* reported the ongoing disaster:

Last week farmers in ten Midwestern States had sand in their beards, in their hair, in their ears, in their eyes, in their mouths, in their pockets, in their pants, in their boots, in their milk, coffee, soup and stew. Dust poured through the cracks in farmhouse walls,

Source: Arthur Rothstein, *Dust Storm in Oklahoma*, Farm Security Administration, Library of Congress.

under the doors, down the chimneys. In northwest Oklahoma a hundred families fled their homes. Every school in Baca County, Colo. was closed. In Texas the windswept hayfields were alive with blinded sparrows. Methodist congregations in Guymon, Okla. met three times a day to pray for rain. Originally confined to a 200-mile strip between Canada and Mexico, last week's dust storm suddenly swirled eastward over Missouri, Iowa and Arkansas, crossed the Mississippi to unload on Illinois, Indiana, Kentucky, Tennessee and Louisiana. With half the nation blanketed in silt, farmers everywhere were asking what was going to happen to the wheat crop—April 22, 1935.

Many family farmers had been hanging on by a hair's breadth before the storms. Income, already dangerously low, fell from just under $1000 in 1929 to a little over $350 by 1932. Many farmers had no choice but to abandon their land. Much of the migration was local, or from farm to town. Among longer journeys, California received the greatest number of refugees. The "emigrants tell the story," reported Paul Taylor in the *Survey Graphic* for July 1935:

"We got blowed out in Oklahoma. Yes sir, born and raised in the state of Texas; farmed all my natural life. Ain't nothin' there to stay for, nothin' to eat. Somethin's radical wrong," said an ex-cotton farmer encamped shelterless under eucalyptus trees in Imperial Valley. A mother with seven children whose husband died in Arizona enroute explained: "The drought come and burned it up. We'd have gone back to Oklahoma from Arizona, but there wasn't anything to go to."—"Lots left ahead of us"—"There is no work of no kind."—"It seems like God has forsaken us back there in Arkansas."

Like the panhandlers on the street, the natural catastrophe of the Dust Bowl inspired a classic song, Woody Guthrie's "Dusty Old Dust," which he later rewrote as "So Long, It's Been Good to Know Yuh." That version would become a standard during World War II, an anthem for families and friends separated by the conflict. The original lyrics went:

> I've sung this song, but I'll sing it again,
> Of the place that I lived on the wild windy plains,
> In the month called April, county called Gray,
> And here's what all of the people there say:
>
> CHORUS: "So long, it's been good to know yuh;
> So long, it's been good to know yuh;
> So long, it's been good to know yuh.
> This dusty old dust is a-gettin' my home,
> And I got to be driftin' along."

A dust storm hit, an' it hit like thunder;
It dusted us over, an' it covered us under;
Blocked out the traffic an' blocked out the sun,
Straight for home all the people did run . . . .

American farmers over several generations had inadvertently created a desert. They increased the amount of land under cultivation by cutting down trees and burning grasses. Cattle grazed grassland close to the ground. When rain did not come and winds did, there was nothing to hold the soil. It simply blew away. Look again at Rothstein's photograph of the Oklahoma dust storm. It was not a snapshot. The photographer carefully organized the picture's details, including the small boy holding his arm up to protect his eyes. Rothstein shot from a crouching position so that the image emphasized the depth of the dust. For all this, the photographer did not exaggerate the magnitude of the disaster. He wanted to show, in a single picture, the hopelessness of the situation. The new American desert also spelled disaster for many other farmers. Crops in Illinois, for example, were ruined not because of anything the local farmers there had done but because the prevailing winds blow from west to east.

The generations of farmers who contributed to creating the desert had acted rationally. So did farmers in and after World War I. Rising prices during the war led them to plant more. This is exactly what the logic of the marketplace dictated. And the logic of the marketplace was disproving itself. McNary-Haugen would have blocked the decline in price with its minimum below which commodity prices could not fall. It might or might not have stopped the ongoing and unintended process of desertification. What the Dust Bowl forced on everyone's attention was not the problem of overproduction but the necessity of protecting the environment from the unregulated operation of market forces. The New Deal would assume the long-delayed task of constructing a regulatory state that might find ways of protecting both people and the land from the operation of a ruthless business cycle while it preserved the market system.

Action in the First Hundred Days
Savings, innumerable decisions to put off purchases, according to orthodox economics, should have made borrowing easier and that should have given the economy a boost. But companies were reluctant to borrow in the face of declining demand. Even as businesses waited for new orders before expanding production, consumers delayed for the economy to improve before buying a new car or washing machine, and investors in turn held off waiting for everything to get better. None of those three sectors of the economy would make the first move. President Hoover tried to inspire confidence. If people would just take advantage of the bargain prices, all would be well.

But individuals, especially if they had children to feed, had to think of what was best for them, not what was good for the economy. The same attitude held true for officers of corporations who had to answer to their stockholders. Common sense said to wait.

As time passed and conditions deteriorated, conventional economic wisdom suddenly seemed worthless. A central theory of capitalism—that people pursuing their own economic interests in a free market would contribute to the wealth of everyone else—came into question. Farmers, bankers, manufacturers, consumers reacted in ways designed to help themselves. But the economy, disobedient to theory, worsened.

Meanwhile whole states and cities verged on bankruptcy. Many had responded to the downturn by creating public works jobs. But as real estate values plummeted, so did their tax bases and their bond ratings. How could they repay bondholders if their tax revenues continued to shrink? Hoover, who had received much credit for the prosperity of the 1920s, received the blame for all of the country's problems. Franklin Delano Roosevelt, the Democratic candidate for president in 1932, defeated Hoover in a landslide. He carried every region of the country except New England and every large state except Pennsylvania. FDR had a mandate for the "new deal" he had promised in Chicago in the summer of 1932 when he accepted the nomination. Its details remained vague throughout the campaign. Roosevelt won not because he articulated a clear and detailed set of programs. He won because he was not Herbert Hoover.

Within the daunting array of crises demanding immediate attention that faced Roosevelt when he took the oath of office, perhaps the most critical one was to convince people that, at last, government would take decisive action quickly. By March 4, 1933, Inauguration Day, about one-third of the labor force was out of work. The new president at once went on the attack. The First Hundred Days became legendary as the administration proposed, and Congress adopted, a staggering number of new programs.

In addition to closing the nation's banks and then reopening those that were sound, the New Deal created the Federal Deposit Insurance Corporation. This federal guarantee of individual savings up to $5,000 meant the depositor could know that a bank was safe by the FDIC sticker on its windows and doors. Even if the bank failed, the government would make good any investor's savings. The administration also swiftly addressed the farm crisis. The Agricultural Adjustment Act paid farmers *not* to plant crops. The idea was to break out of the logic of the market that had led farmers to expand production in a losing race with falling prices. Subsidies would reduce supplies and thereby shore up prices. That at a time of hunger the government was willing to reduce food production, and at a time of unemployment the government threatened the jobs of farm laborers, illustrated the contradictions that came with the mighty effort to restore the economy.

For the jobless, including youth who drifted from place to place seeking work, often hitching illegal rides on dangerous freight trains and living in hobo camps, FDR believed in labor, not in idleness fed by welfare as opponents claimed. Welfare programs such as the Federal Emergency Relief Act began in the winter of 1933 to feed the starving and clothe the poor, but the word "emergency" in the title proclaimed it was meant to be a temporary measure and it was. The administration's primary commitment in helping the unemployed and their families was to create public works programs. The Civilian Conservation Corps established camps where unemployed youth would work on public works projects, including restoring the land ruined by the Dust Bowl. Tens of thousands of young people, most of them males, found jobs in the CCC camps that provided food, shelter, and a small wage that the worker had to share with his family. It also provided meaningful work renewing the nation's land and resources. The Public Works Administration gave people jobs building roads, bridges, and other facilities. More controversial was a later program, the Works Progress Administration, which sponsored a Federal Theatre Project, undertook an oral history of slavery by interviewing survivors, created guides to all of the states, and supported other efforts in the arts and education.

Radical Temptations

As the New Deal got under way, Americans waited to see whether their government could effectively respond to their plight. Many had lost faith in orthodox economics. For an increasing number that meant rejecting capitalism as well. Some looked to the Soviet Union and either joined or flirted with joining the American Communist Party. Others were drawn to the example of fascist Italy and, as Hitler succeeded in restoring German prosperity, the Nazis. More difficult to classify were home-grown radicals, such as the Louisiana senator Huey Long, the "kingfish." Long promised that "every man" could be a "king" with a guaranteed annual salary financed by confiscatory taxes on the rich. He organized a campaign labeled "Share-Our-Wealth." A similar plan proposed by the elderly Dr. Francis Townsend of California would have given everyone over the age of sixty-five a pension of $200 a month, financed by a federal sales tax. Recipients would have to promise to spend each penny every month, further quickening the economy. Long was enormously popular, and had not an assassin silenced him in 1935, he might have influenced American history profoundly.

Historians routinely mention these far-reaching radical possibilities and note that several European countries adopted fascist governments in the 1930s. Why did Americans instead rally behind the New Deal?

The Roosevelt administration succeeded in heading off extremism of both left and right because it convinced the great majority that the government was on the side of the people. Part of its success lay in the array of new measures reaching deep into potential areas of trouble; states and local governments joined the national effort. Along with all that went a sense of energy, purpose, and connection with the public.

"Dear Mrs. Roosevelt"

In their own lives, the president and Mrs. Roosevelt succeeded in making ordinary Americans believe that they cared about people. For the president his so-called fireside chats became a prime way of speaking to a national audience and explaining how his proposals responded to their needs. For ER, as her intimate female friends called the First Lady, travel became a way of reaching out. She visited coal mines, towns half-deserted because of the Dust Bowl, sharecroppers' shacks in the Deep South, and Indian reservations. Everywhere she went, she spent time listening to people tell their stories, which she promised to bring to the president's attention. So firmly did people come to see Mrs. Roosevelt as their advocate that they poured their hearts out to her in letters; she received thousands a week, far more than she could read, much less answer personally. Children told her of their struggles in school or of not attending because they lacked shoes. Wives described their desperate efforts to scrape together a survival. Letter-writers shared their secrets, their fears, and their aspirations. Many assumed that the First Lady would intervene and fix their troubles. Aides drafted innumerable tactful replies explaining that Mrs. Roosevelt could not get husbands jobs on public works projects, could not arrange for a new bicycle or shoes. Many correspondents did not ask for favors. They wrote simply to explain just what their lives were like because they knew that Mrs. Roosevelt wanted to know.

This personal connection that millions felt to the First Lady had no precedent. Presidents' wives had begun to take more active public roles. Mrs. Hoover, for example, vigorously supported the Girl Scouts. But none became a visible presence in a husband's administration. None held regular news conferences. Mrs. Roosevelt did, inviting only female reporters since the White House press corps banned women from presidential press conferences.

Mrs. Roosevelt had the freedom to advocate positions her husband did not feel he could publicly endorse. In 1937 when the Daughters of the American Revolution, a group whose members claimed descent from veterans of that war, forbade the black opera singer Marian Anderson the use of Constitution Hall in Washington, DC, the First Lady promptly and publicly resigned, announcing that "I am in complete disagreement with the attitude taken in refusing Constitution Hall to a great artist." The DAR, she continued, had "an opportunity to lead in an enlightened way, and it seems to me that your organization has failed." She also helped arrange for Anderson's concert on Easter Sunday, 1937 at the Lincoln Memorial, an event attended by some 75,000.

The concert helped right a single wrong and publicize the countless wrongs segregation and discrimination inflicted on a daily basis. The New Deal, however, did comparatively little to promote civil rights, and then only under pressure. On June 25, 1941 President Roosevelt signed executive order 8802. It set up the Fair Employment Practices Committee (FEPC) that barred "discrimination in the employment of workers in defense industries or government because of race, creed, color, or national origin." A threatened march of 250,000 protestors on Washington had forced the administration's hand. The president sent his wife to negotiate with the organizers, and she strongly urged him to meet their demands. FDR went part of the way. The FEPC was a significant step. Millions of African Americans would finally receive the same wages as whites doing the same work. But it was also a half step at best. Workers outside the government and not employed in defense industries were not covered. The order did not end racial segregation on the job, even where it did apply. Most critical, in the eyes of march organizers, is that it did not integrate the armed forces. Yet millions of African Americans supported the New Deal and voted Democratic for the first time. They shared unequally in the relief benefits provided by the government. But they believed, correctly as events would show, that the party would champion their quest for equality. A major reason they thought so was Eleanor Roosevelt.

Reinventing the Republic: Regulations and Entitlements

Ordinary Americans, white as well as black, put their trust in the Roosevelt administration not only because they sensed a personal connection to the president and First Lady but also because they could see the government responding to their needs. The New Deal set up so many programs, almost all identified by their initials, that it is easy in the sea of letters to lose sight of the profound ways it changed the American republic. These changes were of three basic sorts: regulations, entitlements, and planning. All represented sharp departures from the traditional roles of the federal government. In asserting new powers, the administration had the support of Congress, at least initially. It did not have the backing of the Supreme Court. The new measures deviated so widely from the past that their constitutionality in time came under challenge before the Court. Much of the objection to New Deal initiatives would center on the interpretation of the Tenth Amendment, which reserves to the states or the people all powers not granted to the federal government in the Constitution. This came to be the most important struggle over reinventing the republic in the face of crisis.

Banking provides a clear example of the federal regulatory state the New Deal built. The FDIC did more than insure savings. It required savings and loan banks to concentrate on the home mortgage market. It stipulated the proportion of total deposits such banks had to keep on hand. And in doing so it reinvented the home mortgage. Mortgages would now run for much longer than five years, a typical stretch before FDIC. Instead of the borrower's simply paying interest each month and owing the entire principal at the end of the term, under the new loans the homebuyer paid amounts on the principal over the life of the loan, thereby establishing equity: that is, an actual and growing part-outright ownership of the home. Now, if the bank had to foreclose, the borrower would share in the proceeds of the sale. Some of these new rules protected the banks, some the depositor, some the borrower. They also provided safeguards for the government. It had now assumed the burden of insuring deposits. It had to regulate the banks to make sure that their policies made fiscal sense. In the early 1980s this would change. Democrats and Republicans alike embraced deregulation as a cure-all for the nation's ills. The federal government stopped regulating airlines, banks, and a number of other segments of the economy. In the case of the banks, a spectacular series of failures among savings and loan institutions resulted, the cost of which ran into the hundreds of billions. Since the FDIC continued to guarantee deposits, taxpayers picked up the bill.

A new Securities and Exchange Commission regulated stock trades, bond issues, and commodity markets. Corporations wishing to issue stock had to file detailed reports showing their assets and liabilities, and they had to update the information on a regular basis. The practice of buying on margin now required the potential investor to put up a much larger portion of the total purchase. The regulations created unprecedented amounts of paperwork that disgruntled employees and customers called red tape. You could scarcely cough, it seemed, without filling out a form. Yet much of the public conceded that the SEC was needed. Investment depends upon confidence no less than does banking. If a corporation misleads potential buyers of its stock, as did ENRON at the turn of the twenty-first century by improperly reporting earnings and disguising losses, it not only cheats the purchasers of its stock but spooks investors in general. The market thrives only when people think they can buy and sell in a carefully policed setting.

It would be tedious even to begin to list all of the new or enlarged agencies of the regulatory state that came of age during the New Deal. The same is true of the entitlement programs the Roosevelt administration set up, programs defining certain kinds of governmental assistance that Americans would have a right to receive. The Federal Emergency Relief Act rested on the premise that Americans have a legitimate claim upon the national government during hard times. Unlike the bonus that was limited to veterans of World War I, FERA payments went to anyone who met a set of criteria that defined need. If you were poor enough, the government owed you a check. By far the most important of the entitlement programs was the Social Security Act of 1935. This sweeping act established a pension system and with it the notion that sixty-five is the appropriate age to retire. It also set up payments for the disabled. If legally blind, for example, you had a right to assistance. And it created an unemployment compensation program. As in the pension plan for the elderly, both employees and employers contributed to a fund. These payments entitled the worker, if fired or laid off, to weekly checks drawn on the fund. Even AFDC, Aid to Families with Dependent Children, originates in this 1935 act. Frances Perkins, as secretary of labor and the first woman to hold a federal cabinet position, chaired the committee that created the Social Security Act. As the measure's chief architect she then helped shepherd it through Congress. Writing almost thirty years later in *The Roots of Social Security*, Perkins observed: "I've always said, and I still think we have to admit, that no matter how much fine reasoning there was about the old-age insurance system and the unemployment insurance prospects—no matter how many people were studying it, or how many committees had ideas on the subject, or how many college professors had written theses on the subject—and there were an awful lot of them—the real roots of the Social Security Act were in the great depression of 1929. Nothing else would have bumped the American people into a social security system except something so shocking, so terrifying, as that depression."

The notion that citizens have a right to assistance is fundamental to the polity the New Deal created. Arthur M. Schlesinger, Jr. quotes FDR as saying, "We put those payroll contributions there so as to give the contributors a legal, moral, and political right to collect their pensions and unemployment benefits. With those taxes in there, no damn politician can ever scrap my social security program."

Reinventing the Republic: Planning

Out of the Hundred Days came two measures that embodied the administration's commitment to planning, the Tennessee Valley Authority and the National Recovery Administration. TVA was a brilliant success, NRA a dismal failure.

In 1916 the federal government had acquired Muscle Shoals, land in Alabama on both sides of the Tennessee River. Over a stretch of thirty miles the river dropped 140 feet. The white water, or shoals, prevented navigation on the river. In response to World War I, the Wilson administration planned a dam on the site to generate electricity for a munitions plant. The war ended before construction could begin, and the plans were shelved. During the 1920s Congress occasionally took up the question of what to do with Muscle Shoals, pri-

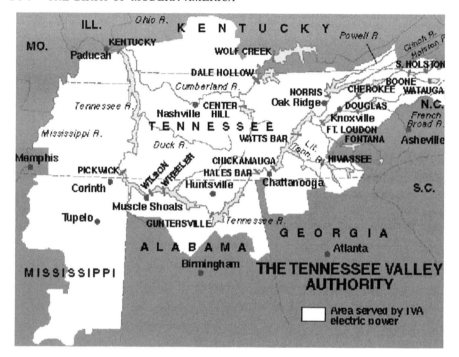

marily at the urging of Nebraska Senator George W. Norris, a Republican progressive who wanted to see the dam built as a way of bringing electrical power to the seven-state region through which the Tennessee flowed. It was among the poorest parts of the country, and power companies had made clear they had no interest in electrifying it. Norris' fellow Republicans defeated his bill. But the Roosevelt administration adopted it as its own. At its heart lay a sweeping assertion of federal power:

> The president shall from time to time . . . recommend to Congress such legislation as he deems proper to carry out the general purposes stated in said section, and for the especial purpose of bringing about in said Tennessee drainage basin and adjoining territory in conformity with said general purposes (1) the maximum amount of flood control; (2) the maximum development of said Tennessee River for navigation purposes; (3) the maximum generation of electric power consistent with flood control and navigation; (4) the proper use of marginal lands; (5) the proper method of reforestation of all lands in said drainage basin suitable for reforestation; and (6) the economic and social well-being of the people living in said river basin.

The TVA would do far more than construct a series of dams to control floods and generate power. It was commissioned to undertake sweeping conservation measures and, as its broadest commitment, promote the "economic and social well-being of the people" living in the region. This was an open-ended application of federal power.

Over the next two decades, the Tennessee Valley Authority transformed the region and the lives of its inhabitants. Electricity came to the backwoods. So did roads and jobs, first construction work and then work in the power plants and other federal facilities. The government, for example, built a large nuclear laboratory at Oak Ridge in Tennessee. A huge portion of the country that would otherwise have been left behind was ushered into the modern age (along with a high level of smokestack pollution). Yet the administration, concerned more for protecting the southern white wing of the Democratic Party than for racial justice, allowed race custom to dictate hiring practices in TVA projects. The momentous task for the northern Democratic Party of ending segregation in public places and guaranteeing voting rights for blacks would come in the 1950s and 1960s, a favor the Republicans of the region expediently seized upon to make themselves the majority party of the South.

The National Recovery Administration entailed an even more ambitious exercise in planning. In a fireside chat in which he described the First Hundred Days, FDR offered this explanation: "If all employers will act together to shorten hours and raise wages we can put people back to work. No employer will suffer, because the relative level of competitive cost will advance by the same amount for all. But if any considerable group should lag or shirk, this great opportunity will pass us by and we will go into another desperate winter. This must not happen."

The government would get all employers to act together by negotiating codes, industry by industry. Companies had no choice in accepting the terms. The codes were to stipulate wages, hours, and working conditions as well as control prices. Hiram Johnson, a retired general named to head the NRA, called together leading figures in each industry. They, along with NRA staff, hammered out the rules. Typically, industry leaders submitted versions of the codes, and the staff reviewed them. To protect the public interest, an important consideration because the process gave to the largest corporations the leading role in creating the codes, FDR appointed three advisory boards, one each for labor, industry, and social service.

As quickly as they were approved, the codes went into effect. Among them were provisions for raising wages and thereby turning workers into purchasers. With the new consumer demand, industry would increase production by hiring the unemployed. The plan, then, envisioned an economic stimulus within diverse sectors of society. For about a year General Johnson oversaw the establishment and implementation of the codes. The Blue Eagle, symbol of the NRA, appeared everywhere, including small private businesses proclaiming their adherence to the codes. Demand did rise somewhat and unemployment did decline. But wages remained static. The cheery claim of Roosevelt's campaign song that happy days were here again had not yet fulfilled itself.

Businesses, especially small enterprises, found the codes oppressive. A.L.A. Schechter Poultry Corporation and Schechter Live Poultry Market, both of Brooklyn, challenged the constitutionality of the Live Poultry Code in 1935. They raised several objections, among them that the companies were not engaged in interstate commerce and therefore not subject to federal regulation. Most alarming for the New Deal was their argument that the NRA violated the Tenth Amendment. Chief Justice Charles Evans Hughes and a majority of the Supreme Court agreed. Hughes wrote:

> Extraordinary conditions may call for extraordinary remedies. But the argument necessarily stops short of an attempt to justify action that lies outside the sphere of constitutional authority. Extraordinary conditions do not create or enlarge constitutional power. The Constitution established a national government with powers deemed to be adequate, as they have proved to be both in war and peace, but these powers of the national government are limited by the constitutional grants. Those who act under these grants are not at liberty to transcend the imposed limits because they believe that more or different power is necessary. Such assertions of extraconstitutional authority were anticipated and precluded by the explicit terms of the Tenth Amendment.

The Court also ruled that the NRA, in giving the executive such power to enact codes, unconstitutionally surrendered to the presidential branch of government legislative authority the Constitution gives only to Congress. The "discretion of the President in approving or prescribing codes, and thus enacting laws for the government of trade and industry throughout the country," the Court complained, "is virtually unfettered." Gutting the NRA, the ruling threatened other federal efforts in planning and regulation.

In 1936 the Court declared the Agricultural Adjustment Act unconstitutional, again citing the Tenth Amendment. The federal government "has only such [powers] as are expressly conferred upon it and such as are reasonably to be implied from those granted. In this respect, we differ radically from nations where all legislative power, without restriction or limitation, is vested in a parliament or other legislative body subject to no restrictions except the discretion of its members."

What would happen when the constitutionality of Social Security or the Tennessee Valley Authority came up for challenge?

Roosevelt did not care to find out. The 1936 election constituted a national referendum on the New Deal; it was also the largest land-slide in American history up to that time. FDR carried forty-six of the forty-eight states. Democrats dominated the House and Senate contests. The people had spoken, and the president had a plan to remove the Supreme Court as an obstacle to carrying out their mandate. In an uncommonly blunt fireside chat in March 1937, just three days after his second inauguration, he explained what he intended to do:

> [T]he only way to avoid a repetition of those dark days [of 1933] was to have a government with power to prevent and to cure the abuses and the inequalities which had thrown that system out of joint. . . . National laws are needed to complete that program. Individual or local or state effort alone cannot protect us in 1937 any better than ten years ago. . . . In the last four years the sound rule of giving statutes the benefit of all reasonable doubt has been cast aside. The Court has been acting not as a judicial body, but as a policymaking body. . . .
>
> We must have men worthy and equipped to carry out impartial justice. But, at the same time, we must have judges who will bring to the courts a present-day sense of the Constitution—judges who will retain in the courts the judicial functions of a court, and reject the legislative powers which the courts have today assumed. . . .
>
> What is my proposal? It is simply this: whenever a judge or justice of any federal court has reached the age of seventy and does not avail himself of the opportunity to retire on a pension, a new member shall be appointed by the president then in office, with the approval, as required by the Constitution, of the Senate of the United States.

Since six of the nine Supreme Court justices were over seventy, FDR's plan would enable him to nominate six new ones, turning 5-4 and 6-3 decisions against his New Deal into 10-5 or 9-6 decisions in favor. The scheme, critics charged, would cripple the independence of the Court and destroy the constitutional system of checks and balances. Not only reactionaries but libertarians of differing political persuasions feared that the president was grasping for dangerous and dictatorial powers. Yet there were many New Deal Democrats in both houses of Congress. Roosevelt, it appeared, had the votes. But he did not have the committee leaders, even the Senate majority leader.

The next move belonged to the Court. After Roosevelt's fireside chat, it heard a case challenging a Washington state minimum wage law. A few months earlier it had declared a similar New York statute unconstitutional. But Justice Owen Roberts switched sides, and the Court upheld the Washington measure on a 5-4 vote. By the same margins it upheld two vital New Deal programs, the National Labor Relations Act and Social Security. Roberts' votes became known as "the switch in time that saved nine." Since the Supreme Court was no longer blocking the administration's programs, Roosevelt's plan to pack federal courts languished.

Commentators at the time saw this as a major defeat for the president. It appeared that he had been unable to line up majorities in Congress behind his idea. Conservative opponents took heart. On the other side of the ledger, the Court had adopted the president's view of the Tenth Amendment. The "nine old men," as Roosevelt called them, no longer stood in the way of the new polity. The federal government would regulate, plan, and seek by means of entitlements such as Social Security to shift the distribution of wealth and power. FDR lost the court-packing battle but won the war over the role of government in daily life.

Tilting Toward Labor

Critical to that victory was the Court's decision to sustain the National Labor Relations Act of 1935 and the standard it created. An important provision within NRA had guaranteed the right of labor to organize and to bargain with employers. Once the NRA died, the new law, known as the Wagner Act after its sponsor Senator Robert Wagner of New York, restored that measure, reviving the main New Deal strategy for raising wages, shortening hours, and otherwise empowering labor. A National Labor Relations Board possessed the authority to supervise elections in which workers could decide whether they wanted a union. If a majority voted for a union, employers were required to recognize it as the sole bargaining agent for all of the workers. The legislation sought to encourage workers to organize in basic industries, like steel and transportation. If it succeeded, and usually it did, unionization would shift the balance of power in labor's direction, pushing up wages, cutting hours of work, improving conditions in the workplace, and giving employees a protector in the form of the union and the contract it negotiated.

The new Committee for Industrial Organization led the way. The CIO was a rebel group within the AFL under the leadership of John L. Lewis, president of the United Mine Workers. It aimed to press for the unionization of entire industries, their unskilled workers as well as skilled, in place of the organization by craft preferred by the AFL and to a large extent confining unions to skilled and relatively well-paid employees. Under the NRA it had already become active. The Wagner Act sustained its protections. Soon breaking away from the AFL entirely and adopting the name "Congress of Industrial Organizations," it kept the initials CIO, which had become familiar to workers. The CIO attracted many volunteers, some from the Communist Party, who fanned out across the country to persuade workers to join the new unions. Employers determined to exclude the unions. So a series of strikes broke out. In some the unions adopted a strategy, the sit-down, rarely used in earlier labor disputes. In past strikes, workers had walked out and set up picket lines to prevent others from taking their places. Corporations sometimes responded by hiring private thugs to fight the strikebreakers. Some state governors had even ordered the militia to prevent strikers from enforcing their picket lines. The sit-down changed the dynamics of strikes. A substantial portion of the union workers stayed in the plants, so no strikebreakers could start up the assembly lines. Employers hesitated to use force inside their factories, where costly equipment and inventory had to be protected. And strikers found it easier to keep up their morale out of the cold or the rain. They could play cards, tell tales, and encourage one another.

Among the most dramatic and historic of the sit-down strikes was that organized by the United Auto Workers, one of the new CIO unions, against the General Motors plants in Flint, Michigan. In Walter Reuther, the UAW and the industrial union movement in general possessed a powerful leader. The Flint operations produced all of the bodies for GM cars as well as the engines for its best-selling Chevolets. On December 30, 1936 the workers at Fisher #1 and Fisher #2 began the sit-down. For the next forty-four days the union and the corporation fought it out. GM shut down heat and electricity in the plants and tried to seal strikers off so that no food would reach them. Union comrades and family members broke through the cordon with food and other supplies. Next the corporation went to court, where a

Workers celebrate the new contract—Walter E. Reuther Library, Wayne State University

judge who owned several hundred thousand dollars of GM stock declared the strike illegal. On January 11, 1938, the Flint police tried to enforce the judge's order and drive out the strikers in Fisher #2, but retreated under a barrage of missiles consisting of any chunk of metal or ice the strikers could get hold of. This event has gone down in union history as the Battle of the Running Bulls, "bulls" being at the time slang for police. Meanwhile, workers in other GM plants in Flint also struck. The corporation used its spies to try to forestall any further sit-downs, but on February 1 workers from Chevrolet #6 captured Chevrolet #4 in the dead of night. They had seized the largest factory in Flint, and they forced the corporation to come to terms. Finally, on February 11, a one-page deal was struck. General Motors recognized the union as the sole bargaining agent in the plants that had struck and permitted the UAW access to all the others. Locals quickly formed as workers rushed to join the union. Wages went up. Working conditions improved. And the other automobile makers made similar arrangements.

One industry after another came under the umbrella of the CIO in the years immediately preceding World War II. The changes in the nation's class structure were profound. The distribution of wealth shifted in the direction of working families. Wages kept up with increases in productivity. Unions also won pensions for workers and health benefits along with shorter hours and longer vacations. After the Second World War blue-collar families enjoyed a level of prosperity and political strength that lasted until the 1970s. Factory workers earned enough to afford the American Standard of Living celebrated in the nation's folklore. Unions also grew politically powerful, becoming fiercely loyal to the New Deal and FDR, and the president openly acknowledged their importance to his political coalition. This too lasted for several decades after the war. President Harry S Truman's upset win over Governor Thomas E. Dewey of New York, for example, owed much to the efforts of the CIO.

The New Polity

The New Deal did not end the Great Depression. Only the preparation for World War II, and then the nation's entrance into the conflict, turned the federal government to the massive spending, with accompanying huge deficits, needed to restore prosperity. Roosevelt was too much the fiscal conservative to support such spending in peacetime. Yet the New Deal did reinvent the republic as sweepingly as Lincoln and the Republicans had done in the 1860s, in both cases as responses to modernization.

The Republicans abolished slavery, which they regarded as economically and socially backward as well as inherently immoral. They also created a national railroad system, established a national currency, underwrote the new state universities with land grants, and tried to turn the South into a version of the North, with good roads and public schools. And they redefined citizenship. Before the Civil War you were a citizen first of a particular state and secondly therefore of the United States. People routinely spoke of the United States in the plural: these United States are. . . . Once the Fourteenth Amendment became part of the nation's Constitution, you were first a citizen of the United States and then a citizen of whatever state you happened to reside in. No state (so the Constitution now declared though with little federal enforcement until the civil rights movement of the later twentieth century) could deny you basic rights of freedom and citizenship. People began to speak of the country in the singular: the United States is. . . .

The New Deal brought to fulfillment the second great phase in the modernization of the United States government to accommodate the forces of industrialization. Like the Republicans of the 1860s, it gave to the federal government powers and to citizens rights guaranteed by that government. And unlike civil rights for the freed slaves, which the federal government had embedded in the Constitution and then abandoned for over a half century, the entitlements assured by the New Deal remained secure under subsequent administrations—at least until that of George W. Bush. Bank deposits stayed safe, farm prices continued to be subsidized, workers' rights to organize were not grossly infringed upon. Planning, disastrous under the NRA and successful in the Tennessee Valley, became even more important during the Second World War when the mobilization of troops and materials required planning on a national scale. And what President Ronald Reagan in the 1980s would call the "safety net," the basic entitlements created by the Social Security Act, continued to grow after World War II. They thickened in 1970 when President Richard Nixon greatly expanded Social Security, adjusting pension payments to the cost of living and not to the amount the recipient had paid into the fund. Nixon also made the spouses of recipients eligible even if they had not contributed. This enormously increased the funds expended by the government. In effect, Social Security thereupon redistributed wealth, taking it from the Baby Boomer generation, which was just entering the labor market in 1970, and putting upon the Boomers the burden of paying for benefits. Barring any radical changes by the majority Republicans in the new century, that went far toward eliminating poverty among the elderly.

X

Legacies

[We] are, today, laying plans for the return to civilian life of our gallant men and women in the armed services. They must not be demobilized into an environment of inflation and unemployment, to a place on a bread line, or on a corner selling apples. We must, this time, have plans ready—instead of waiting to do a hasty, inefficient, and ill-considered job at the last moment.
— Franklin Delano Roosevelt, Fireside Chat, July 28, 1943

Nearly a year later, on June 22, 1944, FDR signed into law the Servicemen's Readjustment Act, popularly known as the G.I.Bill of Rights. The measure demonstrates how dramatically the Roosevelt administration had enlarged the role of the federal government. Like the 1924 Bonus Bill promising veterans of World War I a government check in 1945, it recognized the sacrifices made by the troops. But it did not guarantee a cash windfall that would take decades to collect. Instead it gave veterans immediate opportunities to better their lives.

One set of benefits subsidized their college education. Anyone who had served at least ninety days was eligible for one year of schooling. Every year of service beyond that was worth an additional year of full-time study, up to a maximum of four. The government provided $500 a year for tuition and a living allowance of $50 a month, more if the veteran had dependents. It was the veteran's choice as to what school to attend and what program of study to pursue. Millions flooded the nation's colleges and universities. Enrollment at Indiana University in Bloomington, for example, soared from 4,500 to 10,300 in a single year. In 1947, after most of the troops who had served in Europe, Africa, and the Pacific were demobilized, more than half a million Americans were attending college, up from 160,000 in the mid-thirties. Forty-nine percent of the undergraduates that year enrolled under the G.I.Bill. Millions of other veterans attended technical schools, taking courses in such fields as air conditioning repair and electronics.

Providing educational opportunities to former soldiers, sailors, marines, and members of the Coast Guard, many who would never

182

otherwise have had the chance, enabled them to enter white-collar professions or open small businesses. (Decades later, Congress was still discussing what compensation to offer the World War II veterans of the merchant marine, who did not wear uniforms but suffered the highest casualties of any branch of the service, higher than the marines.) And the nation's educational institutions benefited by receiving the tuition dollars. The G.I. Bill launched a building boom on campuses that lasted for the next two decades and more. And increasing the level of education for millions enriched the nation as a whole. Better-educated people not only earn more but build and fix, invent and discover more.

Putting veterans in school also sharply reduced the numbers seeking to reenter the job market after the defeat of Germany and Japan. The overly rapid demobilization following World War I had contributed to the sharp recession from 1920 to 1922, which President Roosevelt alluded to in his fireside chat. Another provision of the G.I. Bill guaranteed to veterans unable to find a job a full year of unemployment compensation. This spoke to the common fear that once wartime spending ended, depression might resume. Soldiers returning from World War II entered the labor market more slowly than their fathers had, leaving space to absorb them. And instead of looking for factory jobs or work in the mines, many sought positions in accounting, insurance adjustment, or electrical appliance repair, and found them. They succeeded because of a strong postwar economy and the relative scarcity of teenagers seeking work. Birthrates had dropped during the Great Depression.

Another important set of benefits dealt with loans, especially home mortgages. The government backed up to fifty percent of the value of the loans veterans took out to buy or build houses, purchase farms, or go into business for themselves. "It's a promise!" a General Electric ad announced. Such corporations had not produced for the domestic market during the war. They manufactured what the military needed. But they continued to advertise as a way of keeping their names before the public. This ad endorsed the G.I. Bill's housing provisions.

"Jim" was off to war; "[T]hat little house sketched there in the sand is a symbol of faith and hope and courage" and also a "promise of gloriously happy days to come . . . when Victory is won." A new house had been the stuff of dreams. Few were built during the Great Depression and virtually none during the war, when military construction required all of the available supplies and workers. Passage of the G.I. Bill gave the federal government's guarantee that the promise would be kept, the dream realized.

William Levitt showed how builders could keep pace with the enormous demand. The Levittowns in New York and Pennsylvania applied assembly line techniques to housing construction. In 1947 the company built 1200 houses on a former potato field on Long Island. One group of workers dug the foundations. As soon as they finished one, another group poured the concrete, and the next raised the scaffolding. Each team performed the same task over and over. The result was simple and affordable homes with small yards. Levitt also set up shopping areas for his towns and reserved space for churches, schools, and playgrounds. In 1950, according to *Time*, Levitt's company was constructing one out of every eight new houses in the country.

Hundreds of thousands, and then millions, of families moved out of urban tenements and into small ranch houses in the new suburbs. By moving out, they moved up. They enjoyed more space, pleasanter surroundings, and new appliances. Levitt again set the pattern by including in the purchase price washing machines and dryers, stoves and refrigerators, even television sets. Moving to Levittown or to one of the many comparable communities springing up meant you could finally share in that fabled American Standard of Living. So did the families of the plumbers, plasterers, and painters who built the new homes. As union members, save in parts of the South, they earned good wages to go with steady work.

The Wagner Act of 1935 had redistributed wealth by making industrial unionism possible. In the form of better pay and shorter hours, workers now shared profits that would have gone to shareholders. The G.I. Bill redistributed wealth just as much, perhaps more, but in a different fashion. Taxpayers underwrote a massive education

The Levittowner

PRICE: $10,990 $67 A MONTH

NO CASH REQUIRED FROM VETERANS

bill and subsidized a housing boom. The highly progressive income tax of the 1940s and 1950s forced the richest Americans to finance much of the cost. These two measures endorsed the idea that prosperity bubbled up from the majority rather than trickling down from the wealthiest, and made the federal government the champion of the "little guy," as the average citizen was called.

Postwar prosperity more than fulfilled the hopes of Americans who had struggled for sustenance during the Great Depression and then put up with wartime shortages and rationing, or the rigors of military service. Once companies like General Electric and General Motors retooled to turn out appliances and automobiles again, Americans embarked on a buying spree that would last for decades. They invested in outdoor grills, air conditioners, and other new or revamped products, and they bought into a dream of family life, and gender roles, they could see every night when they turned on their new television sets. The sit-com quickly became one of the staples of network programming. Many, like "Father Knows Best," glorified the nuclear family. Dad goes off to work in the office or factory every day but always finds the time to go to Junior's football games and Sis's recitals. Mom stays home. With the kids in school, she may make cookies for their after-school snack. Junior and Sis occasionally quarrel. But Mom or Dad gently shows them that they are both at fault. At the end of the half hour program everyone is smiling. Magazines endorsed the message with stories about how families enjoyed their leisure time together: "The family that plays together stays together." Churches chimed in: "The family that prays together stays together."

And families were getting larger. Couples who had postponed having children during the Depression or were separated during the war decided to wait no longer. The Baby Boom began even before the war ended and continued until about 1960, when the birthrate started to decline. Boomers grew up amid unprecedented prosperity. Many lived in the suburbs, attending schools built specifically for them. They played in newly laid out parks, enjoyed the facilities of recently constructed or expanded libraries for their school reports, and even worshipped in new churches. The most pampered generation in history, they became the most protected as well.

The G.I.Bill produced another profound change. No one in Congress objected to the provision that enabled veterans to enroll in Catholic schools (or any other school affiliated with a religious denomination). Anti-Catholicism, which had fueled such passions not long before, was on the wane. President John F. Kennedy's election in 1960 tolled its end. The Roosevelt administration deserves a share of the credit.

Roosevelt had given Catholics and Jews a number of important positions in the New Deal. These groups were core constituents of his coalition, and FDR did not forget his friends. Catholics and Jews also constituted much of the membership of the new industrial unions. Sidney Hillman, a Jewish immigrant and founder of the amalgamated clothing union, directed the CIO's Political Action Committee during the 1944 presidential campaign. A rumor had FDR telling important Democrats to "clear it with Sidney" before suggesting a vice presidential candidate. This unfounded story illustrates the visibility of Jews as powerbrokers in the administration.

They were also highly visible at least in the lower echelons of the military. The Roosevelt administration decided to use the army and other services to break down ethnic and religious hostilities. In previous conflicts, men from the same towns had served in the same units. Jews from New York's Lower East Side did not fight in World War I alongside Baptists from Georgia. In World War II, however, the military set about forming platoons and companies that included men from all over the country. Draftees from Brooklyn did their basic training in Mississippi, as the Jewish playwright Neil Simon has recalled in his comedy, *Biloxi Blues*. And servicemen from Biloxi might do theirs at Fort Dix in New Jersey. Units mixed Catholics, Protestants, and Jews; they mixed Irish, Swede, and Pole; they mixed unreconstructed rebels with Vermont Yankees. Religious and ethnic identities mingled, but blacks and whites stayed separate with rare exceptions until after 1948, when President Truman issued an executive order mandating that the military integrate its ranks, which began in earnest during the 1950s.

Films about the war presented soldiers with diverse backgrounds coming together as fighting units. The plots typically follow a platoon or company from basic training into battle and on to victory. Early scenes emphasize the difficulties men from different ethnic and religious groups have getting along. Slurs often give way to fists. Gradually the recruits learn to pull together and then to like one another. By the climactic battle scene they have become brothers. In a typical film a soldier sacrifices his life to save the buddy he originally despised.

Even earlier, a new ethnic hero had emerged in the movies. As far back as the 1920s and emphatically in the years after, movies celebrated the Catholic priest, rescuer of lost or misery-laden souls. In 1938 two of the biggest box office hits featured priests as central characters. In *Angels with Dirty Faces*, Pat O'Brien and James Cagney are boyhood pals who take opposite roads. Jerry becomes a priest, Rocky a criminal. Father Jerry works with the teenage boys in the parish to keep them from turning out to be "hoodlums like me," as Rocky says. In the end, Father Jerry prevails. The Dead End Kids go straight, just as the Motion Picture Production Code required. That year Cagney lost the Oscar for best actor to Spencer Tracy, another Irish Catholic, who won for his portrayal of Father Edward Flanagan, the founder of Boys' Town in Omaha, Nebraska. Flanagan, like the fictional Father

Jerry, worked with adolescents who had gotten in trouble with the law. The most successful of all the heroic priest films is *Going My Way*, the biggest hit of 1944. It stars Bing Crosby as Father Chuck O'Malley. He too rescues teenage boys from temptation. He also straightens out the parish finances and arranges for its elderly pastor to visit his native country: Ireland, of course. Like Tracy, Crosby won the Oscar for best actor, and the movie won the award for best picture. That next year Crosby again played Father O'Malley in *The Bells of St. Mary's*. It was another box office success.

Anti-Catholics had traditionally imagined priests as manipulating their flocks to follow Rome's orders. Priests in the movies are portrayed as ordinary guys with a touch of the

saint in them. Father O'Malley likes to fish and go to baseball games. Father Jerry can reach the Dead End Kids because he grew up in the same neighborhood and got into the same kinds of trouble they do. The movie priest possesses a good sense of humor and a willingness to poke fun at himself. His heroism comes from his selfless dedication to people in trouble.

So movies late in the Depression decade anticipate the fading of anti-Catholicism after World War II, when ethnic rivalries gave way to a spirit of victory won in common. Anti-Semitism, in contrast, had gained force in the years before the war, in part because of the efforts of a real Catholic priest, Father Charles Coughlin. In 1926 he began broadcasting sermons over a Detroit radio station. Initially, the programs aimed at children. The priest would typically tell a Bible story and paint a moral for his audience. Then as the Great Depression worsened, he began to talk about economic and political issues. By 1932 his audience numbered in the tens of millions, and the "radio priest" received 80,000 letters a week, many containing donations. In some heavily Catholic neighborhoods, residents would recall that they could take a walk on Sunday afternoons and not miss a word of Father Coughlin's program. Every radio was tuned in to his station, and his deep and musical voice glided through every open window.

At first the radio priest supported FDR and the New Deal. But the president never gave Father Coughlin the kind of voice in policy making that he felt he deserved. So he became a harsh critic and, in the election of 1936, formed the Social Justice Union, which ran William Lemke for president. Roosevelt's landslide victory temporarily put the radio priest off the air. Once back on the radio, his message included ever-larger doses of anti-Semitism. The Social Justice program had always rested upon a fierce anti-Communism, and Coughlin presented himself as the alternative to the "red serpent." Heartless bankers drove workers into the arms of the Bolsheviks, Father Coughlin charged. The priest emphasized names like Kuhn-Loeb when he condemned bankers. He explained Nazi policies against the Jews as a natural reaction to the danger that the Communists would take over Germany. Jews, he said, had been behind the Russian Revolution. It took intervention by the Catholic hierarchy, and in time threats of a federal investigation into Coughlin's probable connections with Nazi agents, to push him to the margins of society. Given all that he had done, the radio priest got off lightly. He was forced to close *Social Justice* and accept a public rebuke from the archbishop. But he did not have to face a trial. His prominence and influence with millions of Catholics protected him. The government decided that prosecuting him might alienate followers and impede the war effort. Father Coughlin stayed on at his parish in Royal Oak, Michigan and continued to operate the huge shrine he had built there. He also got to keep the profits from *Social Justice*, the payments from the German government, and whatever funds he had siphoned off from the donations over the years. The Treasury Department had planned to audit his tax returns, but Treasury Secretary Henry Morgenthau decided that some of the public might see an investigation as a Jewish effort to take revenge.

The Nazi attempt to annihilate Jews, gypsies, homosexuals, and anyone else they considered physically or mentally defective discredited eugenics as well as Father Coughlin and destroyed the intellectual bases of racism. The American soldiers who liberated concentration camps at the end of the war saw where anti-Semitism could lead. Newsreel footage of the same scenes played in movie theaters around the country. Prior to the Second World War, a student of anthropology would read in the textbook about biologically-programmed characteristics that supposedly explained the differing levels of development of various peoples. After the war, the new textbooks taught that racial characteristics do not explain human behavior. Instead, the student now learned, human beings are fundamentally alike. During Hitler's regime proponents of eugenics, like Harry Laughlin of the Cold Spring Harbor laboratory, had received honorary degrees from German universities. Nazis credited American scientists with demonstrating the necessity for racial purity. No one wanted to boast of those honors, once it became clear what the pursuit of supposed racial purity meant in practice.

Church membership remained high in the postwar years, but the "acids of modernity" continued to eat away at traditional religious and moral ideas. A new popular morality, with its roots in the interwar era and just before, continued to shape the way more and more Americans evaluated ethical choices. Other than in a very general set of moral principles, it was based not upon the Judeo-Christian tradition but upon the secular values of the market and the republican political heritage. Both capitalism and republicanism emphasized the right of the individual to act freely. There were limits, but these were based upon the rights of others rather than upon the intrinsic good or evil of any action. One popular formulation held: My right to swing my arm is limited by the proximity of your nose. Current battles over morality go back to Sadie Frome's determination to "have some pleasure," on the one hand, and Billy Sunday's crusade against dancing on the other. They remain among the many reminders that we live in the world that emerged during the interwar decades.

Socially at least, we are citizens of the state the 1920s and the New Deal made. But despite the successes of the New Deal and the quarter century of prosperity that followed World War II, Americans continue to wrestle with the same economic dilemma that bedeviled the 1920s and 1930s: Consumer demand can continue to rise only if wages keep pace with productivity, but business executives and shareholders want to hold down wages to maximize profits. From the New Deal through President Richard Nixon's first term, wages rose steadily and the share of the total national income held by the bottom sixty percent of families increased. President Ronald Reagan adopted tax policies designed to put somewhat more wealth in the hands of the top twenty percent, the largest share going to the top one percent. The Clinton administration reversed that, but President George W. Bush returned with unrestrained joy to Reagan's tax and fiscal policies, and markedly changing income distribution in the United States to favor the very rich.

Consumer spending varies with the vagaries of the economy, but the consumption ethos articulated in the 1920s prevails. Many compete to see who has the biggest SUV, the priciest watch, the biggest house, the greenest lawn. We also persist in avidly consuming mass-produced fantasies, some now dubbed, without a hint of irony, "reality" television. The Internet and DVDs make every sort of sexual fantasy available to anyone with the money to spend.

Most important is that we continue some though not all of the culture wars of the twenties and thirties. Anti-Catholicism and anti-Semitism have largely disappeared. Conservative Catholics and fundamentalist Protestants now cooperate in joint campaigns against abortion and gay marriage. Fundamentalists militantly support Israel, believing that the return of the Jews to their homeland is prelude to the Second Coming.

We have also lowered racial barriers, but are far from eliminating them. We continue to war over who is a real American and a true patriot. These divisions are to a large extent geographic. The South and the Mountain West hold far more conservative views than the Northeast and the Pacific Coast. And differences are religious. White evangelicals are markedly to the right of Jews, liberal Protestants, and probably most Catholics. Many blacks are social conservatives on issues like gay marriage but strong advocates of governmental programs to help the disadvantaged. Other beliefs go with gender. Unmarried women express more liberal views than men. I write this in the winter of 2005, after a presidential contest that has vastly heightened all of these divisions. It is necessary, and difficult, to remember that they are normal. They flow directly, if not altogether honorably, out of our history.